The Technique Of
BREEDING
BETTER
DOGS

Dr Dieter Fleig

RINGPRESS

THE TECHNIQUE OF BREEDING BETTER DOGS

RINGPRESS

English Language Edition First Published 1996 by
Ringpress Books Ltd,
P.O. Box 8, Lydney, Gloucestershire GL15 6YD.

© 1996 DR DIETER FLEIG AND RINGPRESS BOOKS

Originally published in Germany 1992 by Kynos Verlag

Discounts available for bulk orders
Contact the Special Sales Manager at
the above address. Telephone 01594 563800

ISBN 1 86054 055 4

Printed and bound in Singapore
by Kyodo Printing Co

CONTENTS

Foreword

One point must be made clear right at the beginning!

"Anyone who undertakes to write a book on dog breeding must, of necessity, assemble his material from the research and expertise of many specialists. No one should ever presume to believe themselves capable of providing their readers with a full picture solely from one's own experience. I am therefore both willing and happy to admit that a considerable part of this book documents the knowledge of others, to whom I should like to express my gratitude for allowing me to make use of their knowledge, research, and experience. It is reasonable to suppose that this book documents in many ways the standard of knowledge on dog breeding arrived at today."

This is a quotation, a remarkable observation, made by the author of *The Technique of Breeding Better Dogs*. With this book, Dr Dieter Fleig has fulfilled a special task, the task of creating an all-embracing document on the practical work of breeding dogs. This book encompasses almost all the relevant present-day canine and scientific literature as well as the author's own personal and practical experience and knowledge gained from discussion with experts in the field, all of which have been incorporated into this work in the most readable style. There is no doubt at all that breeders of dogs and experts on the subject will be able to appreciate this book! It would be correct to describe it as a 'must' and thus as a standard canine reference work.

The Technique of Breeding Better Dogs is clearly arranged in nine chapters. It contains a bibliography, as well as many outstanding photographs and sketches and a number of statistics in the form of tables, graphs, guidelines, and recommendations. It is easy to find one's way around in the book, and with the aid of the index, the required information is quickly pinpointed. Here is an example: your bitch is pregnant and you want to know the size and shape of the whelping box you are going to need. Turn to the chapter on Whelping and you will be given an answer in clear words and well-arranged figures, supplemented by a sketch of a suitable whelping box that anyone with a little skill can easily construct. You will also find tips for building a puppy room or even a whole range of kennels and much more besides. You can read about the fluctuation of temperature prior to parturition, the course of a normal birth, and whelping problems that may arise.

The author includes in Chapter One: The Breeder a quotation from that great canine expert Dr Hauck, who wrote as early as 1930: "The most important function of the breeder is to maintain the vitality of a breed, followed by its physical appearance and performance and, if possible, to alter and improve upon them! It goes without saying that the necessary knowledge must be acquired before breeding is commenced." And he goes on to say: "Responsibility is the keyword defining the term dog breeder. The breeder who is not aware of the responsibility he or she bears to find good homes for each and every puppy produced should give up any breeding ambitions, or else confine them to creatures that are less dependent on their environment, on individuals, or on families."

As a geneticist and one who has been involved in canine matters for more than forty years, I have nothing to add to this. The remarks are all too true and they are warranted. I should like to congratulate the author, Dr Dieter Fleig, on this book. No other book can compete with it today!

W. SCHLEGER.
Director of the Veterinarian Institute for Genetics, University of Vienna, Austria.

Introduction

It is almost forty-four years ago to the day since I first became involved in breeding dogs. I was a little tired and had put my feet up on the couch. My German Shepherd bitch, Senta, was sharing my repose. I must, I suppose, have dropped off, when suddenly I felt something warm and wet on my legs, and Senta began energetically to lick Alf, her firstborn. There I stood – or rather lay – at the beginning of my career as a dog breeder. My mother saw things quite differently! The couch was in need of a good deal of cleaning, and in any case, mother did not think much of my "dog fad."

I had planned everything so well – or so I thought! My bitch, Senta, was too tall by over an inch (three centimetres), so to even this up I had mated her to a lovely, small, black dog that was almost an inch (two centimetres) too small! The puppies were sure to be exactly the right size, weren't they? I must admit I was not destined to become a very successful German Shepherd breeder in those days.

The years that followed were full of new experiences. We have bred our way through the alphabet twice (in Germany, the breeder must name all the puppies in the first litter with A like Alf, the next litter with B like Berta, and so forth), and for more than thirty years, we have always owned good stud dogs. It has been a long road, full of mistakes and full of learning, and seven breeds of dog have accompanied me on my way. An all-important period was, without doubt, the ten eventful and successful years as head of the breed commission consolidating the Bull Terrier breed in Germany, as well as eleven years of issuing our own newspaper on the breed. In this way, one naturally becomes the adviser of many breeders and dog lovers.

Despite my own lack of knowledge when I started breeding dogs, I have, in the past thirty years, been astonished at the terrifying ignorance of almost all dog owners when they begin to breed. Even after ten years of breeding experience, many breeders still show an astounding lack of knowledge. The sad thing about this is that many puppies, and brood bitches, have to pay for this ignorance with their lives or with their health.

The Technique of Breeding Better Dogs is a book title that needs a little explanation. However, there are some dog lovers who may well object when the word 'technique' is used in the context of mating and birth. For many hundreds of years, the mere mention of the process of reproduction in both man and animal was avoided. To talk of it was taboo – it simply was not 'done' to speak of it! These things took place in the dark beneath the bed covers, and in the case of our dogs, in the cellar or garage. Since these are purely natural, preordained procedures, mankind did not consider that he needed to know much about them.

Heiko Gebhardt, in his book *You Poor Dog*, has dealt with the incredible nonsense breeders perpetrate every single day when mating their dogs. He could have written a second book with the same title! My own ignorance and lack of knowledge when I first began to breed dogs was the incentive that resulted in me writing this book.

Fortunately, in the past thirty years or so, man has adopted a very much saner attitude to his own sex life. Today, sexual techniques are openly spoken about in human relationships. The sweeping away of many taboos has helped the human world a great deal. Hopefully, this book will succeed in showing the dog lover how mating, birth, and puppy rearing can be carried out in the natural way, without human intervention. The owners of stud dogs may learn that, in many ways, their dogs know better than they do what has to be done. If I manage to succeed in convincing the owners of bitches to breed only animals that are healthy and of sound disposition, and to exclude bitches lacking in instinct from their breeding programmes, I feel this book will serve its most important purpose.

The information contained in this book may make it easier for many breeders to do without veterinary assistance at matings, births, and during the rearing of puppies. If difficulties do arise and the veterinarian has to be called in, the breeder may not feel quite so helpless, being better able to understand the directions given, and also instrumental in seeing that things go right. The knowledge you have acquired can, in these situations, be worth its weight in gold.

In choosing the title *The Technique of Breeding Better Dogs*, my intention was to emphasise that, in this book, the breeder must not expect any advice beyond that given on the subjects of mating, birth, and the rearing of puppies. The complexities of which dog should be chosen for which bitch is a completely different matter. The science of genetics has expanded enormously in the past forty years, and knowledge that is essential for every serious dog breeder has been accumulated. This knowledge is assembled in other books such as Walter Schleger and Irene Stur's *Dog Breeding in Theory and Practice. A Genetic Guideline for Successful Dog Breeding*, and Leon F. Whitney's *How to Breed Dogs* (Howell Book House).

It should be noted that it is not enough just to read the one book! These two books supplement one another, and together they afford the breeder a good foundation for successful dog breeding. Without wanting to appear pretentious, I feel bound to say that the techniques described in my book on dog breeding are as indispensable as the knowledge of the laws of genetics.

I am especially indebted to the Veterinary Universities of Vienna and Utrecht, Professor Dr K. Arbeiter, Professor Hendrickse, Dr E. Koeppel, and Dr Holzmann. The aid that they unstintingly gave has enabled me to illustrate this book abundantly on the subjects of mating and birth. I am deeply indebted to them for advice and knowledge in the field of veterinary science.

I attach great importance to this book. In writing it, I have been driven by the hope that my words may, in the end, lead the dog breeder to adopt a more natural attitude.

DIETER FLEIG.

Chapter One

THE BREEDER

WHAT CONSTITUTES A DOG BREEDER?

Eberhard Trumler, the well-known expert on animal behaviour, puts things very clearly: "In general, anyone who takes his bitch to a dog to be mated may call himself a breeder. But just as a distinction must be made between the person who goes out with a gun and one who holds a game licence, so must we distinguish between this kind of breeder and the holder of an official permit to breed dogs. (In Germany, every breed club has established requirements that each dog must meet to be accepted in the studbook. A breeder must obtain club approval for each mating in order for the puppies to be registered.)

Dr Hauck, the grand old man of the Austrian canine world, states categorically: "The most important function of the breeder is to maintain the vitality of a breed, followed by its physical appearance and performance and, if possible, to alter and improve upon them! It goes without saying that the necessary knowledge must be acquired before breeding is commenced."

It is important to state here, at the beginning of this chapter, that far too many dogs are being bred. If we take a look at the numbers of registrations within the various dog clubs, the random puppy production among all those for whom club regulations are too strict, and the unchecked increase in the dog population due to negligence on the part of owners, and then compare it with the steadily growing anti-dog lobby and environmental restrictions, the question inevitably arises: where are all these puppies to find good homes among responsible people? A visit to a shelter overcrowded with unwanted dogs (particularly in the holiday season), and constant reports in the press concerning abandoned dogs, will show the bitter fate to which our easy-come easy-go society condemns this avoidable over-population.

Responsibility is the key word in defining the term dog breeder. Breeders who are not aware of their responsibility to find good homes for each and every puppy produced should give up their breeding ambitions, or else confine them to creatures that are less dependent on individuals, or on families. It is staggering to see with what irresponsibility certain matings are carried out – no better than risky experiments in order to produce a top dog. Breeding one show winner in a litter (which may bring in a good deal of money) is no justification for producing dogs that, owing to their unstable temperaments and susceptible constitutions, should never be sold to anyone at all. Often, it is the irresponsible breeder who ends up paying for his mistakes. The real victims, however, are the dogs themselves.

The main prerequisite of the good breeder is the extent of responsibility he or she bears for every single dog bred in their kennels. This responsibility does not end with the sale of the dog but continues throughout its life. Every dog, without exception, should always be able to find a home with its breeder in case of need. The true breeder feels bound to care for the dogs he or she breeds much as parents feel bound to support their children. In all the years I have been breeding dogs, I have always done my best to find out in advance what kind of life the puppies were going to have with their new owners. However, it is not always easy to judge people at face value. This has, on various occasions, led to me taking dogs back and finding different homes for them. We also frequently receive calls for help concerning dogs in need, and it is deplorable to see the way the majority of breeders react when requested to rescue dogs of their own breeding.

There are, today, a number of sales contracts available. In most cases, the breeder secures the breeding rights (the right to use stud dogs on his own bitches), almost always to the purchasers' disadvantage. The most important clause is usually completely overlooked, namely the clause that permits the breeder to buy back the puppy if it has fallen into the wrong hands. Too late, the breeder discovers the shortcomings of these sales contracts when he learns that his puppy is being kept in sub-standard conditions or is becoming aggressive towards both man and animal, and he is unable to do anything at all about it.

I applaud the breeders who fight for the well-being of their puppies, and who cover themselves legally, so that they can assert their influence. I would happily buy from such a breeder, for they prove to me, the purchaser, that their dogs mean a great deal to them.

BREEDING FALLACIES

A further field of responsibility is the careful selection of breeding stock. This selection is by no means any easy matter, and I shall go into it in more detail in the relevant chapters. Adequate room in the house must be available (more about this in the chapter on kennels), and I shall have a lot to say about the correct rearing of puppies.

The aim of the true breeder is a constant striving for perfection, and this must be a deep-seated ambition. It would be better for those who do not see it this way – those who regard breeding as a sort of leisure occupation, a mere hobby – to spend their time in a different way.

And here I come to another important point: a problem which is part of human nature, and is most probably the cause of the glut of puppies flooding the market. We are inclined to transfer our own feelings to the world of the dog. There is hardly a dog owner who believes that his dog should not be allowed to propagate itself. If I tell a dog owner that it would be better not to use his dog at stud, his reaction could hardly be more negative than if I cast aspersions on his own powers of reproduction. I am usually treated to a detailed account of how interested the dog is in the opposite sex, how he loves mounting bitches, and how often he breaks out to get at any bitch in season in the neighbourhood. These, I am told, are obvious signs. This may be true, but it is just as true to state that the dog will not suffer the slightest physical or psychological injury if he is prevented from mating. The fact is that once a dog is actually allowed to mate a bitch, he will not become easier to manage; he will usually become a good deal more difficult.

Among horse breeders – and here we are talking of real breeding – a very small number of stallions, top-class animals, are required for planned breeding management. Ninety-five per cent of all male foals are gelded, which makes things easier for their owners! In the case of the dog, there is no cogent reason to do this, unless it is to disabuse the owner of the mad idea that it is necessary for his dog to contribute constantly to the growing dog population. I know owners of mediocre stud dogs who, thanks to their own misguided expectations, have managed to damage a whole breed. No distance is too far for them. They travel to the owners of the bitches, and no bitch is of too poor a quality – the dog needs it, so they say. This attitude has nothing whatever to do with breeding. A good portion of common sense, some objectivity, and, if necessary, the psychiatrist's couch could do a lot to put things straight here.

Parallel to this way of thinking are the owners of bitches who believe that their bitch should be allowed to have puppies at least once in her lifetime. Think of all that fulfilment which she would otherwise miss! Added to this, the vet advises that it will help to avoid damage to her health, malignant tumours, and so forth. All I can say is: change your vet. Don't waste your money on him or her! Scientific research over the past eighty years has proved without any doubt that cancer of the uterus, pyometra, mammary tumours, and so forth, occur no more frequently in virgin bitches than in those that have had litters.

What about all that maternal fulfilment that your bitch is being deprived of? Read this book through to the end and you will soon see that the family dog, much-loved and rather spoiled by everyone, has a much better life than many a brood bitch.

But the children – they do so want some puppies! Even if, at this moment, you are beginning to regret having bought this book (you actually wanted to breed didn't you?), that is the very last reason to justify bringing puppies into the world! If necessary, buy your children a guinea pig. If properly treated, it makes an ideal family pet and can even be pushed up and down in a doll's pram. But a child's natural wish to pet an animal and to see it grow, is a totally wrong motive for breeding dogs!

Dog breeding – indeed, the breeding of all animals – is a serious matter and should be carried out free of all human sentimentality. It calls for a great love and understanding of animals and, not infrequently, involves a great deal of work and considerable financial sacrifice. These facts should always be kept in mind. Even if my words may put off some potential breeders, these people will not lose out. They will understand more about breeding by reading this book, they will be spared disappointment, and their dogs will lead much happier lives!

THE PIONEERS

The majority of our dog breeds owe their existence to the talents of a very few breeders. The welfare of a breed stands or falls with the wholehearted involvement of the leading breeders, their inexhaustible energy and imagination. They also need some financial assets in order to develop their own particular line within a breed. Going through the literature of the past century, it becomes clear that, in almost every breed, the new, forward-looking ideas on the part of the competent breed organisations have seldom or never borne fruit. People cling to old ideas and mistrust the new; envy and ill-will toward the successful run like a red thread throughout history. It would be quite true to say that the advanced ideas of any breeder met, at first, with the fiercest resistance, often to the point of exclusion from the breed club. Yet, later developments frequently showed that these outsiders came to be regarded as pioneers of their particular breed. I should like to illustrate this point by two examples.

Raymond Oppenheimer was one of the first breeders to recognise that the pure-white strain of the Bull Terrier was bound, in the long-term, to harm the breed severely. He was convinced that it would not only be detrimental to health, but also lead to a considerable loss of quality. Yet, it was only by exerting all his influence as a well-known breeder, even threatening to leave the breed club and go it alone, that he was able to get his ideas accepted. The ban against mating coloured Bull Terriers with white Bull Terriers was repealed by a very slight majority. The further development of the breed has confirmed these natural genetic laws. The dogs thus bred did not turn out to be piebald, but they gained both in soundness and quality from outcrossing with coloured dogs. No breeder today would ever dream of breeding a pure-white strain, as it is common knowledge that he would be damaging both himself and the breed.

Raymond Oppenheimer gave dog breeders yet another lesson. In his kennels, he had a stud dog called Bar Sinister, who was by far the best dog at that time. However, this dog had one single fault – a major fault in the eyes of the experts – he was a monorchid. Dogs with only one testicle may not be entered at shows, and in Germany they are not allowed to be bred. With complete disregard for all objections, Raymond Oppenheimer used this dog at stud, and he went on to become the most influential and successful Bull Terrier stud of all time. Those breeders who avoided Bar Sinister because of his missing testicle, fell far behind in the following years and lost touch with the considerable improvement in quality. It is interesting to note that many made an attempt to catch up again by using two full brothers of this dog, an attempt which singularly failed. They had an even greater number of monorchid dogs in their litters than in those sired by Bar Sinister. They had failed, it seems, to appreciate the genetics of dog breeding.

THE INFLUENCE OF LARGE KENNELS

The bigger breeder has a considerable advantage over the smaller breeder. He can build up a stock of brood bitches and retain high-quality puppies from his litters. In this way, his brood bitches form a firm foundation for his kennels. A critical look at the progeny class at any dog show will go to prove that dogs from certain kennels present a uniform appearance; they are as alike as two peas in a pod. In carefully planned lines, this similarity goes far beyond the uniform breed type. The good breeder is able to present a uniform kennel type through many generations. In order to build up a well-planned strain of this kind along genetic lines, a considerable number of closely related dogs are required. Any book on genetics will explain just why this is so.

It is a well-established fact that the larger, well-run kennels exert the most influence on the steady progress of a breed. A single leading kennel has frequently influenced an entire breed. In the larger kennel, there are greater opportunities, but also incalculable risks, for a breed. If, either unwittingly due to negligence or from mercenary motives, an error is made in one of the big kennels and breeding stock afflicted with hereditary diseases or poor temperament is systematically used for breeding, a whole breed may deteriorate in a very short time.

Another example comes to mind here. There was a Bull Terrier stud dog whose outward appearance left nothing to be desired. His conformation was a breeder's dream, but this dog had a very poor temperament. Conclusions of this kind are sometimes hastily made, and it is necessary to make careful distinction between hereditary nervousness and environmental influences. In this particular case, it was not difficult to see that the dog was passing on his own weakness. At the leading trophy show of the year, ten of the country's best bitches were invited to compete for the most sought-after trophy in the Bull Terrier breeding world. Among these top bitches were five of this dog's daughters – confirmation of the fact that he was passing on his own excellent exterior. The sad thing was that, even without the show catalogue, these five daughters were easy to pick out as they stood trembling in the ring with tucked-in tails. The second, but very unpleasant proof of, the hereditary strength of the nervous sire.

Through these bitches – thanks to their beauty – the genetic inheritance of this nervous dog was carried on. Even though the breeder withdrew the dog from stud work on account of his disposition, matters took their fateful course. Ten years later, grave defects in character continue to appear within the breed. The dog in question now lies far back in the fourth or fifth generation but, thanks to inbreeding, he appears four, six or even more times in the pedigrees. Every geneticist knows that the hereditary traits for fearfulness and extreme aggression lie closely bound together. A considerable number of the dog's offspring had to pay with their lives for the breeder's lack of judgement in campaigning such a stud dog. They had to be put to sleep because of their extreme aggressiveness.

One further remark about the influence of the larger kennels on a breed. Thanks to the great number of good breeding stock available, the large kennel is able to exert a lasting impression on the development of the breed, but I should not like to be a dog in one of these kennels. Owing to the large number of dogs involved, the breeder cannot, as a rule, spend much time on individuals. The dog/owner relationship is, to put it mildly, much less close than it would be in a family with a fully-integrated, single dog. Under these circumstances, the kennelled dog can never fully develop its potential as a companion for humans, and the breeder can never know whether the dog possesses all those qualities that will allow optimum integration into the human environment. There is always the possibility that dogs bred in large kennels will be more successful show dogs than family companions.

HOBBY BREEDERS

I am now going to take up the cudgels for the numerous, small, hobby breeders. Despite the indisputable influence of the larger kennel, the small kennel is the backbone of a sound breed. I am firmly convinced that our family dogs can never fully develop their qualities, those characteristics of such importance to us, except in close companionship with their human partners. It is, in fact, only in the family that proof is seen of whether the dog possesses all the qualities desirable in the breed. In small kennels with three or four dogs (better still with even fewer), breeding stock can be found that gives daily proof of sound temperaments.

In the world of the show ring, so much stress is laid on anatomical features that the mental qualities of our dogs have come to be neglected. The fact is that by far the greater part of the psychological defects in a dog cannot be assessed by the show judge. Clearly, the wrong breeding targets are being set, as long as prizes in the show ring are held to be more important than the true character of the dog. Every breeder should constantly bear in mind that he or she is breeding dogs for people, and for life in our present-day world, not for the show judge!

The hobby breeders have an invaluable role to play. In general, their dogs are well kept, that is to say as family dogs and companions, and it is to these breeders that the whole of this book is ultimately dedicated.

THE NEED FOR HONESTY

It is unfortunately, human nature to prefer to talk about success rather than failure. It is also a natural trait to take a somewhat malicious pleasure in the failures and disappointments of rivals, believing that your own reputation gains by comparison. In dog breeding – and certainly not only there – this all too human quality has had very harmful effects. All breeding is subject to setbacks. In some breeding lines, the increasing incidence of hereditary defects requires urgent action, yet, in many cases, these hereditary defects are carefully hushed up. The breeder fears the setback, the malice of their rivals, and the poor reputation that his or her dogs would incur, if such reverses became known.

Let me give another example. For many years, Staffordshire Bull Terriers in Germany continued to have very small litters. For me, the breed counsellor, it seemed strange that in the breed's home country, England, litters were, on average, considerably larger. The explanation for this enigma came, in the end, from a new breeder. Over the telephone, she told me that in her litter of six, there were three puppies with a cleft palate – thus doomed to die from birth.

When this lady told other breeders that she had informed the breed counsellor of the deformity, she was severely reprimanded. When giving notice to the club, such puppies were either not mentioned or else reported dead at birth. In no case should hereditary defects of this kind be reported, since she was told this could damage the reputation of the breed. I could easily give a further ten examples of how deformities were purposely hushed up. Breeders, who are well aware that there are deaf puppies in a litter, will do all they can to prevent the breed warden who checks the litter from noticing. The puppies are then sold to gullible purchasers. See nothing, hear nothing, say nothing! That is the motto of those playing this evil game at the expense of our dogs.

There are dog clubs, too, whose statutes claim that their aims are to advance the breed. Despite this, they have for years accepted the fact that in some breeds fifty per cent of all puppies born come into the world via caesarean section. In many of these dog clubs, people have become so used to this state of affairs that they no longer inquire about the actual birth procedure when checking the litter. Eberhard Trumler condemns all those breeders who accept repeated caesarean section births for their cruelty to animals.

To put it concisely: breeders who cover up hereditary defects occurring in litters are acting as gravediggers to a breed. Breed clubs that continue to disregard hereditary deficiencies, such as lack of maternal instinct in the brood bitch or mating instinct in the stud dog, should be excluded from the privileges of the responsible kennel club.

Every geneticist stresses the fact that hereditary defects can be eradicated by well-planned breeding. But this can only be done if breeders are prepared to make sacrifices. One basic rule must be absolute honesty. Defects that are recognised may be dealt with; deliberately concealed defects are like a cancerous growth in dog breeding. Breeders who conceal defects, either from egotistic motives or from a false sense of loyalty (maybe to the owner of the stud dog), ought to be barred from breeding.

I know, from experience, just how much it hurts when a much-loved brood bitch has to be taken out of the breeding programme. However, in the interests of the soundness of the breed, there is no alternative. In all fairness to the breed, the necessary action must be taken. Any stud dog, even if he is a most successful show dog, should be withdrawn from stud if he has produced serious defects or weakness in temperament when mated to several bitches. A responsible stud dog owner will do this on his or her own initiative.

BREEDING FOR PROFIT

"No woman can earn more money than I do with my puppies!" These words, spoken by a rather silly woman I once met, still echo in my ears. What she was doing had nothing whatever to do with breeding. Her bitch was, unsurprisingly, failing to cope with a litter of ten week-old puppies without human aid. This 'breeder' had attempted to solve the problem by putting the puppies on a bitch with four-week-old puppies. "It saves all that trouble with the bottle," I was told. Naturally the bigger puppies had pushed the smaller ones aside, and these ten pups were in a terrible state. Until I told her, this mercenary woman did not even know that the milk of a bitch with four-week-old puppies was unsuitable for puppies that were only a week old. After spending a number of years as a breed warden, I could easily write a book on so-called breeders!

· This book will, however, be dealing with dog breeding and not with "Dogs for Profit", and so I must contradict the maxims of this woman right from the start. As a general rule, the serious breeder will be investing money in this hobby and not making a profit. Good breeding stock costs a lot to buy, and is not cheap to keep. The stud dog that is suitable for a particular bitch seldom lives right next door, and, often enough, a long journey is involved in taking the bitch to the chosen dog. Veterinary services are not cheap, and neither is good dog food. In order to campaign a stud dog or make a top brood bitch known, journeys to many shows have to be undertaken. Summing up, it will usually be seen that at best the breeders cover their costs. The time factor involved is purely hobby!

Yes, of course, I have heard of huge sums of money being paid for top dogs, and of puppies fetching unbelievable prices. Equally, there are any number of pictures on the market, and once in a while a Rembrandt is sold for a great deal of money. These are special cases. A lot of speculation goes on in life, and lottery wins are rare. That is one side of the coin, and on the other side, there are the valuable breeds of dogs that have deteriorated because high puppy prices attracted the wrong sort of breeder.

I cannot deny that a number of people have earned money from breeding dogs. The general rule, however, is that the breeder has to make considerable sacrifices for his hobby – and that is an excellent thing for dog breeding!

MAKING SACRIFICES

We have been breeding a rather complicated breed for more than twenty-five years. Bull Terriers are usually difficult mothers. For the first twelve days, the litter must be under constant supervision. Some bitches lie on the puppies and smother them, others become aggressive toward their young – a very tiresome heritage from the days of the fighting dogs. Few beginners can imagine the time and patience involved in rearing these puppies. Constant vigilance is essential, so that when the person on watch wants a break for even a few minutes, he or she must first get a partner to come and take over. During this time, a hard camp bed in the kennels takes the place of a comfortable bed. Unfortunately, many newcomers to the breed did not at first believe these precautions to be necessary. Dead puppies proved the point.

We have often reared large litters by hand. On one occasion a bitch was hit and badly hurt by a reckless driver. Another bitch had a lovely litter of ten and needed a lot of help with the puppies. Yet another had very poor milk production and was not a good mother, so she had to be helped. Any breeder who has reared a litter with the bottle from the start will know just how much work is involved. The puppies have to be fed, and there is a short break of around half an hour before feeding is due to begin again. Only the person who is prepared to bear a personal burden of this kind, without complaining, should get involved with breeding. Indeed, the true breeder goes to work with pleasure, and, despite great fatigue, experiences great satisfaction when caring for the tiny puppies. An aversion to mopping up urine and removing faeces, or a lack of understanding of hygiene would be a severe handicap to a would-be dog breeder.

And here I should like to say a word of praise in recognition of all those people who, in spite of the hardships, find fulfilment in breeding dogs. These are quite special people, many of whom never become accustomed to handing over the puppies they have so lovingly reared to a new owner.

Breeding dogs the right way brings a great deal of pleasure, a very important factor in the breeder's life. And how much pleasure is there to be gained from seeing these puppies again later in life? Some owners even become a little jealous when they see that their dog has suddenly become the breeder's dog again when they meet up. Only those who know how the handling and attention given in puppyhood affects the mental health of the adult dog are able to understand their dog's reaction.

I must admit that seeing these healthy well-balanced dogs, clearly leading a happy life, has always been a rich reward for all our efforts. This is so much more important than breeding a homebred show winner or a Champion!

Chapter Two

KENNELS AND RUNS

DEFINING KENNELS

Kennels – a word that most dog lovers regard, at first, with distrust. A kennel is synonymous with being shut up, with separating the dog from the human. But, in this, we are mistakenly transferring human feelings to our dogs. The kennel can – according to how it is used – be either a prison for our dogs or a much-loved, free area and a comfortable living space, as we shall see.

Every enthusiastic breeder registers their own 'kennel name', and is proud of the fact that the dogs bred by them bear this kennel name. This also applies even if the puppies have never seen the inside of a kennel but have been reared in a room in the breeder's own house. In this chapter, the term 'kennel' will be used in the sense of the space or area we require for the breeding of dogs. Understandably, the amount of space required differs considerably according to the size and temperament of the dogs being bred. Toy breeds do not require much more than a corner of their owner's living area. Large breeds such as St Bernards, Great Danes, and many of the Sighthound breeds require a great deal of freedom and would feel incarcerated when limited to an apartment or house.

There are, however, 'breeders' who see things quite differently. In a four-room apartment on the fifth floor of a vast tower block, a litter of six- or seven-week-old puppies were running around the whole apartment. These lively, damp and sticky puppies had left their marks on the wooden floor and carpets. The whole apartment was permeated by the smell, and I was told that the urine had seeped through to the apartment below, causing furious complaints. The puppies were of a medium-sized breed and the kennels belonged to a respected committee member of the breed club! Unsurprisingly, anti-dog feeling was rife in the whole tower block – nor did the inhabitants relish the loud terrier voices in the early hours!

What I am attempting to emphasise with this example is that however enthusiastic a breeder may be, he must take into careful account the amount of room required for raising a litter of puppies. Young dogs need light, warmth, and space. The puppies described above were, of course, very well acquainted with people, but I have no doubt that their new owners would have had problems house-training them.

THE 'IDEAL' FACILITIES

Let us deal with a well-arranged kennel in which the breeding of dogs may be run pleasantly, successfully, and easily for both dogs and their owners. I will start by considering the very best possible facilities.

The ideal place for breeding dogs is a large room, either inside or attached to the home. Windows placed high in the walls should afford adequate daylight. The room should be centrally heated and should also be fitted with hot and cold water. This arrangement is really ideal. The floor, made of either asphalt or wood, should be covered with a layer of washable insulating material. The sealed surface should not be too slippery, or it will not give sufficient hold for the puppies when they become mobile.

According to the number of dogs in the kennel, this room can be partitioned to make roomy individual boxes, a workroom, and a storeroom. Again, the size of the boxes depends on the breed to be housed. For a medium-sized breed, the optimum size is around six square metres (65 square feet) per box. The partitions, made either of wood or metal, should be about 180 centimetres (6 feet) high and constructed so that the dogs can neither see one another, nor sniff at one another.

Ideally, each of these boxes should have a trap-door leading to a separate run. We have always found a metal trap-door most satisfactory, though the dogs have to get used to the door swinging back into place rather sharply. All other types of door, made of either rubber, plastic, wood, or other materials, soon fell victim to the teeth of the kennel inhabitants. A sliding bolt for shutting the door is a further necessity. For over ten years, we have had three dogs – a stud dog and two brood bitches – in kennels of this type, and we have never had any problems of any kind.

KENNEL RUNS

Now for the runs, and here I intend to differentiate a little between large and small runs. If adequate space is available, a two-metre-high fence made of heavy-gauge chain-link is to be recommended. A trench at least 15 centimetres (6 inches) should be dug, into the ground, and the bottom of the fence should be buried, facing inward in the trench, so that any dog trying to dig its way out will come up against the wire. In our experience, wire with fine mesh to keep rabbits out is most effective for this particular purpose. Higher up, the wire need not be of such a fine mesh.

If the fencing has lost some of its height being dug in, a strip of chain link at the top will raise it again. The posts should be sunk about 30 centimetres (12 inches) into the ground and should stand 220 centimetres (seven feet) above ground. Runs constructed in this way provide optimum security. They look a good deal better if the fence is screened from the outside by a hedge of conifers or shrubs. If the area available for the run is small, ready-made fencing is to be recommended. The units, which should be 175 x 125 centimetres (6 feet x 4 feet), are easily

Complete kennel building for assembling out of doors with a six square metre run. Height of building approx. 6ft (2 metres). Height of sections, 175 centimetres.

Outside run, partly-paved, partly-grass slope for puppies.

Park paling fencing, approx. 6 ft (2 metres in height).

erected and they are very durable. A steel post for every second unit affords the required stability. Attention should be paid to the lower parts of the units: the wire mesh should be sufficiently fine so the dogs cannot get their teeth into it. The wide-meshed wire matting so frequently found in advertisements is totally unsuitable. Dogs can get their teeth into it, and smaller breeds can even get their heads through the mesh – a situation that can prove really dangerous. A further disadvantage is that this type of fencing does not keep the dogs apart.

Nothing can beat the steel frame with the welded wire lattice. The finished sections are galvanised and will last from fifteen to twenty years. The initial investment is worthwhile, as they need no maintenance or repairs. In this unit construction system, closed walls are, as a rule, also available. The welded wire lattice is replaced by a galvanised metal sheet. This provides an excellent partition between dogs and, at the same time, serves as a screen towards neighbouring properties. It also affords the dogs in the run protection against wind and weather.

Depending on the breed, part of the run should be covered over. This is relatively easy to construct, particularly if you employ some local labour. A steel frame, roofed over with one of the modern materials, is suitable. It should slope slightly to afford run-off. However, the ready-made units made by specialist firms are, in all probability, cheaper and of better quality.

Make sure that the door handles are dog-proof. Dogs can be very clever at opening doors. Firms usually specialise in door handles that dogs cannot activate.

As regards the surface of the runs, there are a number of points to be considered here. Soft ground in a much-used run rapidly turns to mud in wet weather. Small grassed areas will not

Easily assembled kennel sections with steel posts.

Safety positions for door handles.

Spring door handles.

survive where urine and faeces are a daily occurrence. Dogs' nails require stone flooring, or they do not become worn down enough. Stone flooring is easily cleaned, as it can be washed down with a hose, but it is totally unsuitable for dogs to lie on (see diseases of the kidneys). It is therefore important to find a compromise. About two-thirds of the run may be laid out with either concrete or stone slabs. In this area, it is advisable to have a slightly raised wooden platform for the dogs to lie on. Dogs like lying on a raised surface, and they infinitely prefer lying on wood to stone. The remaining third of the run can be grassed, which makes an ideal place for the dogs to urinate and leave their faeces. If the removal of faeces is attended to daily, it is usually possible – according to the size of the dogs and the area – to retain a good layer of turf.

Many people recommend a gravel bed for runs, or a mixture of sand and gravel. I do not consider this a good idea since the small gravel stones are not an ideal surface for promoting the tight paws required by many Breed Standards.

When planning the outside area, it is vital to consider the influence of wind, rain, and sunshine. Protection against too much sunshine, wind, and rain is absolutely necessary. Apart from the roof construction and side-wall sections mentioned earlier, sailcloth has also proved itself to be a very useful protection on the side of a run that is exposed to the weather. When planning a run, incorporate existing natural protection, such as trees, shrubs, walls, and so forth. This applies especially to those cases in which the dog room is not a part of the actual house and the kennels and dwelling are separate units. The open run, with a simple dog kennel as a protection against the weather, must be rejected out of hand for the keeping of dogs, and it is equally unsuitable for any attempt at breeding. When dogs are housed in such a way, the owner has no reasonable control over his dogs and would not be available to deal with an emergency should one arise.

OUTSIDE KENNELLING

If the kennels are located away from the house, I must warn owners against making do with one of the pint-sized sheds, around 170 centimetres (five feet eight inches) high and 150 centimetres (five feet) wide, in which a human can scarcely crawl. The whelping kennel and the night-time kennel are separated from the large covered run, but working in a dwarf's house of this kind is quite intolerable. In order to be able to deal with your dogs efficiently as a breeder, the building should be at least 200 centimetres (six feet eight inches) high right round or, better still, 205 centimetres at the front and 200 centimetres at the rear to afford good run-off, and it should be equipped with properly installed gutters. The base of a building of this kind should not exceed 125 by 250 centimetres (four feet two inches x eight feet four inches). In this area, a comfortable night-time kennel and a covered daytime kennel can easily be accommodated, the two connected by a trap-door. Do not forget, light is essential in a room of this kind. This may be fitted either in the door or in the roof. An optimum here is also an electrical installation for both lighting and warmth in the form of radiant heating.

Not only may the adult dog be housed in this way, but also the brood bitch, together with her puppies (from the age of about three weeks), will be comfortable in this building. The puppies have to be reared in the home for the first three weeks of their lives.

Most kennel buildings on the market are made of wood. Wood is a natural, sound material but, unfortunately, it does require a great deal of maintenance. The cleaning of floors and walls is problematic, and urine is sure to soak into the floor. In more recent years, manufacturers have designed kennel buildings and small garden houses made of substances which are much easier to keep clean. Equipped with removable floor sections and walls of insulating material, these structures easily compensate for the higher purchase price by their durability and their labour-saving design.

Puppy run with door section and weather protecting wall.

Rearing puppies in buildings that are separated from the home by any distance is totally unacceptable. I am thinking here of the breeder who rears puppies on his 'allotment', as, I believe, is still the case in some areas. It is quite impossible to leave growing puppies alone for days or even hours, in a situation of this kind. The dangers to the puppies either from their own mother, from the weather, or from other dogs are far too great. But the greatest danger of all is that puppies reared in this way are not being adequately prepared for their future lives, for they have too little contact with human beings and the surrounding world.

The breeder must be fully aware that rearing puppies takes up a lot of time. Breeding is a full-time job, and the responsible breeder would not attempt to breed unless he (or a member of his family) can afford the time. Dogs should never be bred unless adequate space is available, and sufficient time can be given to caring for the mother and her litter. I have come across breeders who are away at work all day; they feed the brood bitch and puppies before they leave and on their return. Then, when the puppies are eight weeks old, they sell the pups (who have had minimal contact with people) for a hefty sum to unsuspecting buyers. A puppy buyer should never buy from such a breeder!

WHELPING QUARTERS
Up to now we have been dealing with a functional, labour-saving kennel arrangement, and not with the actual whelping quarters. The section intended for the brood bitch and her family should be arranged so that the dam can, at times, get away from her puppies. A detailed plan for the whelping box itself will be given in the chapter on preparations for the birth. Once the puppies are around three weeks old, their dam will need a second bed beside the whelping box, where her puppies cannot follow her. A practical solution here is a raised platform, which dogs generally prefer. The roof of the whelping box may well be adapted for this purpose.

Practical fencing sections have long proved themselves useful for the puppies' run, a kind of play-pen for the growing litter. This pen is, as a rule, made up of four fencing sections, each two metres (six feet eight inches) in length, so that the puppies have four square metres of space at their disposal. Fencing of this kind is also available with a puppy door that opens at a height of 30 centimetres (twelve inches). The dam can easily jump in or out over this half-door, but her puppies cannot follow her out. A pen of this kind is also most useful in outside runs. Puppies can be lodged in a sheltered corner of the garden, thus ensuring that the well-tended garden is not ruined, and the puppies cannot disappear into inaccessible corners. These fencing sections are light and transportable, and easy to erect. When the play-pen is no longer required in the garden, it can be stored in a very small space. This fencing, once used by a breeder, soon becomes an indispensable part of his or her equipment.

ADAPTING YOUR HOME

We come now to the breeders of small breeds who, partly for the dog's sake and partly due to shortage of room, raise puppies in their own home. As a rule, a room is set aside for this purpose. Of course, in this case there is no trap-door into the outside world, and no way into a run, such as has been described earlier in planning a kennel. Yet, a room can be adapted so as to meet all the requirements of a kennel.

Fencing sections are recommended for the 'home' kennel. As an additional safeguard, it should perhaps be mentioned that the wire mesh of the lattice fence should be so fine that the puppies cannot get their teeth through it. This problem could also be solved by fixing a metal plate to the fence frame. Puppies cannot climb over this, nor can they see their neighbours. There is, however, one big disadvantage – the puppies cannot see out at all. The correct solution is side metal plates between neighbours, and a lattice fence for the front. The bitch can have her sleeping quarters in the pen and, when the time comes, she can move into the whelping box. Everything that I have written about the larger kennels and runs applies to the indoor mini-kennels and runs. For medium-sized dogs, an overall area two-by-two metres (i.e. four square metres, or 40 square feet) would be suitable, for small and Toy breeds the space required is a little less, though the area should not be greatly reduced in size. The floor covering for indoor runs of this kind should be of the impregnated linoleum type. This is very easy to keep clean. It is, I feel sure, unnecessary to stress the fact that youngsters and adult dogs must be taken out of doors at regular intervals, and allowed to run in natural surroundings where they can relieve themselves. When rearing puppies in the home, it is absolutely essential to remove urine and faeces as quickly as possible.

I have seen indoor kennel arrangements of this kind housing up to twenty Toy dogs in comfort. Separate divisions for adult dogs, for youngsters, and for puppies facilitates organisation. In most cases, the room has central heating and hot and cold water, and, generally, there is a camp bed handy for the breeder. Many top-quality dogs have been bred in kennels of this kind, but it goes without saying that a good deal more effort is required here than in kennels with an outside run.

Just one more word about rearing small breeds of dog, but an important one! I should like to warn all breeders to avoid molly-coddling their dogs. In order to grow into sound, healthy dogs, they need to be hardened off from an early age and become accustomed to all kinds of weather. Neither the small nor the Toy breed should be so delicate that they are constant visitors to the vet. Most dog owners are unaware of how beneficial sunshine, wind, rain, and snow are for a dog's health – and this applies just as much to the small dog!

I have no hesitation in recommending a home kennel arrangement to the beginner, who, as a rule, starts off with just the one brood bitch. It does not require a large initial investment, and, if need be, the spare room can be used for the one-litter-a-year breeder. In my own experience, most breeders start off with only one bitch. This indoor kennel arrangement is quite adequate, except, of course, for large breeds. Never set up whelping and puppy quarters in the kitchen – that is, unless they are very clearly partitioned off! This could lead to a great deal of work and a considerable lack of hygiene.

THE DOG-MAN RELATIONSHIP

Finally, in this chapter on kennels, I should like to point out some general principles for housing dogs. Dogs in their natural state are pack animals. One of the worst forms of cruelty to animals is to keep a dog alone in a kennel, even if it is taken out for a walk or for work for half-an-hour, twice a day. A dog needs constant social contact. It can never attain a state of well-being if it is cut off from contact with people, dogs, other animals, and a world full of interesting experiences.

It is quite a different matter if several dogs are housed together. These then form a pack among themselves with their own hierarchy. Given spacious kennelling and runs, good food and care, these dogs clearly feel well and happy. The only difference is that they are not household dogs but kennel dogs. Their social behaviour is directed towards the other dogs and not towards humans. The fact that these dogs feel well and happy as kennel dogs gives us no indication whether they or their progeny would be capable of fitting harmoniously into a 'mixed man-dog pack'.

Experts on animal behaviour agree that an optimum dog-man relationship can only be achieved if the puppy is given as much opportunity for bodily contact with human beings as possible during the decisive stages of its development. (More about this in the chapter on rearing puppies.) It has been made abundantly clear that in the dog's future life, the more intense this early contact is, the better its relationship will be with humans. For this reason alone, each individual dog in the pack should be brought out several times a day on its own so that the owner can give it undivided attention. Only in this way can the bond between the dog and its owner be strengthened.

In practice, the ideal solution is to allow the dogs to range freely and play with one another in the kennels and runs at those times when we are unable to attend to them ourselves – for some of us have to go out to work. In this way, the runs become the dogs' own free, living space in which they can move around, play, chase one another, or sleep, just as they please. Perhaps it would be better to put it this way: at such times when we are unable to be with our dogs, the kennel with the run affords the second-best solution. I must add a warning. Only dogs who are not quarrelsome can be allowed to live together without human supervision.

However, this must not be allowed to turn into an easy way out! If you are at home and have enough time, the dog should never be shut out and excluded from human company, and you should devote at least half-an-hour every single day to each individual dog in your care.

Chapter Three

THE BROOD BITCH

It is quite impossible to over-emphasise the importance of the brood bitch in dog breeding. The brood bitch is the foundation of all good kennels; a careful selection of top-quality bitches is the key to all successful breeding.

It is really sad to see the mediocre bitch being taken to show after show in the hope of finding a judge who will be unseeing or lenient enough to give the qualification necessary to obtain the continental breed club's permission to mate her. Once she has attained the qualification she can at last be bred from! Remarks such as: "She is not quite good enough for a show bitch, but if we use a good dog on her she will make an excellent brood bitch!" are not infrequently heard. Outside the Continent, there is no qualification needed in order to use a bitch for breeding – and so the risk of using poor-quality stock is even greater.

Let us consider for a moment the breeding of thoroughbreds – an industry which involves huge sums of money. A great deal of emphasis is laid on the dam's breeding. Bruce Low, the well-known English breeder, transferred this breeder's wisdom from the world of the horse to that of the dog. He assessed the quality of his stock according to the female line. The knowledge of genetics available to all of us today does not confirm this particular theory, yet it would be complete nonsense to suppose that the bitch does not need to possess the same excellent qualities as the dog. Breeding regulations that do not set the same high standard for both the brood bitch and the stud dog merely serve to document the lack of knowledge on the part of those in the dog clubs who lay down these regulations.

Eric F. Daglish underlines this fact in his very well-written book, *Dog Breeding Based on Genetics*. He writes: "The fact cannot be emphasised sufficiently that a kennel breeding with mediocre bitches is at a very great disadvantage." I should like to go still further and put this more strongly. Breeding with mediocre bitches is not breeding, but merely puppy production. Good brood bitches are expensive, poor brood bitches are not cheap and, in the end, may prove even more expensive! You will have difficulty selling their puppies, and if you do find buyers for them, you will, in all probability, damage your own reputation as a breeder by selling such puppies. Without top-class bitches, your breeding ambitions are doomed to failure from the very start.

EVALUATING A BROOD BITCH
What then makes up a good brood bitch? In the first place, her pedigree. I cannot and will not write a book on genetics, but let me say just this: the quality a bitch passes on is less a matter of the visible, of her outward appearance, her phenotype, but much more one of her ancestry, her so-called genotype or genetic shadow. (I shall be going into this subject in greater depth in the chapter on the stud dog.)

The pedigree is of vital importance in assessing the worth of a brood bitch. If you are new to the breed, then you will be well-advised to rely on the integrity and knowledge of an expert. An experienced breeder should know not merely one or two of the dogs listed in the bitch's pedigree but, if possible, all of them, and he should know their good qualities and their faults as well. Only in this way is it at all possible to foresee, with any certainty, what the bitch may pass on to her progeny.

When purchasing a brood bitch, do not rely too much on your own intuition or on a few show results, but rather on well-founded expert advice. It is a common trait that those who have been breeding dogs for a couple of years or so are often very free with their advice. A little more experience, above all proof of considerable success, would be a somewhat better recommendation.

Success in the show ring is, of course, important. Unfortunately, the method of selecting breeding stock via the show ring has often proved a very one-sided affair, frequently leading breeders to lay too much emphasis on individual points. The judge may like the dog for its particular type of head, he or she may grade it up or down because it has all the premolars or because one or some are missing, or he may favour a special tail carriage or a certain type of coat colouring. But even if the judge's assessment of the dog's anatomy is perfectly correct, it is one-sided, and therefore it would be unsafe to accept it as an evaluation of worth for breeding purposes.

Nothing will ever convince me that it is not the breeder's responsibility to produce dogs that are healthy, intelligent, have ability to work, and are beautiful. I have chosen the order of the words consciously and with a purpose: *health, intelligence, working ability, and beauty*. The show ring turns this word order right round and judges the dog merely according to its beauty. Yet, even this judgement is problematic since the interpretation of 'beauty' is based on man-made Breed Standards.

The German government passed an animal protection bill that became law on January 1st 1987. This law prohibits the breeding of animals that would be liable to suffer. There are a number of Breed Standards, still valid today, which responsible veterinarians and dog experts have been campaigning to change for years, since these Breed Standards lay down anatomical features that are diametrically opposed to the ideal of a healthy dog. For years, committees formed by members of the dog-breeding associations have been working on the question of which points can be cut out from certain Standards and which others can be considerably altered or modified – they have been working on how to avoid breeding 'cripples'. Perhaps these facts will serve to underline the reason for the priorities I have set out above. If dogs are to be bred for people, then these are the priorities that must be adhered to.

The following quotation is taken from the results of Eberhard Trumler's research: "The greatest performance a living creature is capable of is the bearing of young and the bringing of them into the world without difficulty and in good health." I should like to add to this, and I feel sure Eberhard Trumler would agree with me: to rear them naturally and without complications. In its further chapters, this book will show just what this actually means, and it will also show how frequently there is a wide gap between these aims and reality.

Have you ever found points such as these laid down in a Breed Standard? The Standard concerns itself with coat colour, coat texture, tail carriage, structure of the mouth, and, fortunately, also with temperament. But what about the most important requirement for a bitch: that she should have a pelvis suited to giving birth?

In 1962, the scientist M.J. Freak wrote: "In the past, a bitch unable to give birth was condemned to death, and, with her, her progeny – a hard but effective method of natural selection. Present day advances in veterinary science, the Caesarean section, may well have led to the breeding of skeletal types unsuited to the process of normal birth. The veterinary profession bears a great deal of responsibility for making both breeders and veterinarians aware of the fact that the ability to bear young is one of the most vital functions, and for incorporating this ability as one of the main selection points."

A voice crying in the wilderness called out this warning in 1962. The German veterinarian and researcher Professor Dr Wilhelm Wegner took the warning up in his *Kleine Kynologie* in 1975. But go to one of the modern animal clinics and inquire whether any improvement has been made! Are you still of the opinion that titles won at shows are the correct measure for the worth of a brood bitch?

M.J. Freak demonstrates the mercilessness of nature's own methods of selection. Bitches unable to bear their young are cut out, together with those young, from the reproductive cycle. This natural mode of selection cannot possibly be replaced by the principles laid down today at shows or by the points set out in our Breed Standards.

My advice to you is: never buy a brood bitch if her mother has had to undergo a Caesarean section. Look carefully into the past and try to discover whether there have been whelping difficulties in the dam's line. The sire's line should be gone into equally carefully, since stud dogs can also pass on whelping problems. In this particular case, I am thinking of weakness of birth contractions, a problem that occurs more and more frequently in our brood bitches. (I shall have more to say about this in the chapter on whelping.)

There is a theory, frequently voiced by so-called breeders, which seems impossible to eradicate. The belief is that if a bitch is lacking in confidence, is nervous or shy, she should be mated and her condition will improve! In fact, this is totally unfounded. There is unlikely to be any change in the bitch's temperament, and she will, with the greatest certainty, pass her uncertain temperament on to her offspring, thus damaging the breed. She will not only pass on her poor temperament via her genetic make-up, but she will also pass it on through her own behaviour. During the impressionable weeks of early development, the dam's nervousness will form part of the puppies' environment. It will convey itself to the puppies, and they will copy it. Never, therefore, breed from any bitch that has not got a completely sound temperament! Before buying your brood bitch, make quite sure you know what her temperament is like, and also that of her ancestors.

FINDING BREEDING STOCK

How do you go about finding a good brood bitch on which to found your kennel? I am a strict opponent of the selling of adult dogs. This feeling is based primarily on the knowledge that the uprooting of an adult dog, its removal from an environment in which it feels at home, will have a very severe effect on its life. Dogs are members of the family, and, except in dire emergency, they should be treated as such. After all, you do not cast off your own children.

For a number of reasons, I have been compelled to wait to import young breeding stock from England until such time as the permanent teeth have come through. In the UK, the attitude to mouths – the number and position of the teeth – is comparatively liberal, whereas in Germany this attitude is very restrictive. Dogs that have incorrectly placed teeth or missing premolars are, for the most part, excluded from the German breeding scene, notwithstanding all the other excellent qualities they may possess.

In my experience, top-quality, young dogs with good pedigrees are seldom to be found. The breeder who has picked out and reared these puppies for himself would handicap his own kennels if he allowed top-quality youngsters to go. Admittedly, money can play a part, but this is not always the case.

I recall finding a most beautiful eight-month-old bitch, from a leading kennel, who was up for sale. Three very experienced breeders helped me pick this young bitch. We were all delighted with her, and she appeared to be especially promising for breeding. Unfortunately, she had been kennelled all her life, and she had not had very much contact with people. In her kennel, she appeared to be a wide-awake, lively youngster, but after we had brought her home, her physical development came to a stop and she never reached the maturity normal to the breed. She also suffered lifelong psychological injury. She never actually recovered from the shock of this transplantation, despite – or perhaps due to – the fact that she was fully integrated into the family.

Another dog, a most promising twelve-month-old youngster with an excellent pedigree and beautiful conformation, had, on first inspection, a correct, complete scissor bite. This particular dog's lower jaw continued to grow after the age of twelve months, and one month later he had developed a pronounced undershot mouth – a thing that very rarely occurs! Despite his many other good qualities, this dog had no chance at all in the German breeding world.

Then, we had a piece of really good luck. There was a two-year-old bitch, which I had admired at several shows in England and very much wanted to bring back to Germany with me. Due to divorce, her owner was forced, for financial reasons, to part with her. We brought her over to Germany, and she became one of the most successful brood bitches we have ever owned. Perhaps I should emphasise just once more how lucky we were to get her! All too often, when you are buying an adult dog, it does not come up to your expectations. This may be a genuine case of a dog failing to achieve its potential, or it may be that you were led astray by sales talk on the part of the original owner. You may once in a while be lucky, but the risk and the financial outlay are many times as high as the cost of a good puppy from a top-quality litter.

"More haste, less speed" is a very old saying, and there is none more appropriate to your position if you want to buy a good brood bitch as a puppy. Study pedigrees, inspect litters, and do not give way to the temptation to take one of those charming little puppies home with you on your first visit to a kennel. Your breeder's common sense should prove more steadfast than your emotions! Dog breeding requires a cool head, clear planning and, frequently, good advice given by an expert,

In every breed there are a number of top-quality brood bitches. You should take a good look at each of these. Try to discern first of all whether their phenotype – the bitch's outward appearance and temperament– and her genotype conform with one another. In this respect, both negative and positive variations are possible. Her genotype is to be seen from her pedigree, her siblings, and especially from her progeny, if she has any. Take advice from an expert, but do not forget the order of priorities listed earlier on: *health, intelligence, ability to work, and beauty*. Never allow yourself to be misled by Champion titles or show wins. The order of merit set out above lays down the proper priorities. Carefully check breeders, check the stud dog proposed for the bitch according to the above list of priorities, and check the rearing conditions in the kennels.

Nothing is perfect on earth, neither in dogs nor in people. If, however, you follow the method set out above, you will, in all probability, find one or two matings from which really good puppies may be expected. If you want to make quite sure that, two years from now, you will have at least one good brood bitch in your kennel, it is advisable to buy two puppies from two different, well-chosen litters. By doing this, I have been able to buy good brood bitches as puppies on several occasions. This method has yet another inestimable advantage: the puppy grows up in its own family, in its own world. This is of tremendous importance for the full development of its physical and psychological characteristics. Dogs that come into the family as puppies usually grow into very pleasant companions.

Yes, patience is needed, a great deal of patience, and a certain amount of expertise. Apart from this, you should have the courage to accept the correct priorities in dog breeding. Unfortunately, within dog-breeding organisations, this can sometimes prove to be an uphill struggle. Anyone who has spent around twenty years as an official in one of these clubs knows just how often the same old subjects are thrashed out over and over again. However, let us hope that the breed clubs are still willing to learn.

WHEN TO BREED?

You bought your brood bitch as a puppy. She has grown well, she comes up to your expectations, and she is mature enough to be mated. Additionally, in Germany, the bitch must pass the selection requirements of the breed club. However, it is important to bear in mind that permission to mate the bitch is not a recommendation. The breed club has given permission for the bitch to be bred from, nothing more. It has already been agreed that the breeder who wishes to be successful must set a very high standard indeed for his brood bitch. It has also been agreed that, apart from the requirements for a show dog, the most important factors are: *health, intelligence, ability to work, and beauty*, since the good breeder breeds dogs mainly for the family life of the owners, and not just for dog shows.

Physical maturity (the first season) and the age suitable for reproduction are by no means one and the same – neither is this so in the case of the human being. For this reason, the responsible breeder of small and medium-sized dogs will not breed his bitch until her second season, at the earliest at fourteen months. Larger breeds, which need more time to reach maturity, should, depending on the development of the bitch, not be mated until they are from eighteen to twenty-four months old.

This age stipulation is, in the first place, for the protection of the bitch. It has been scientifically proved that when a bitch is in whelp, her further physical development is either delayed or comes to a complete stop. The puppies draw everything they need for their own development from their dam's body. Pregnancy rules out any further maturation on the part of the bitch.

A domestic dog comes into season twice a year. This is a result of domestication; the wild dog only comes into season once a year. In my opinion, it is, therefore, completely wrong to breed a bitch in consecutive seasons. Anyone who has seen a five-year-old bitch that has already reared six litters will see that the price of this kind of exploitation is wear and tear of nerve and body, and premature ageing. Apart from the economic point of view, I can find no argument to justify a bitch being exploited in this fashion, and I could never agree, provided she has her season regularly every six months, to her being mated more often than every second season. If she has an irregular cycle, the basic principle should be to ensure that there is a gap of at least ten months between litters.

Mating a bitch for the first time after she has reached the age of four is a hazardous business, for she could have considerable difficulty in giving birth, as is the case with women over forty. Sad to say, I have known cases in which a stud dog owner has had no hesitation in letting a dog mate a seven-year-old bitch that had never been mated before. These 'breeders' were clearly more interested in gaining a stud fee than in caring for the health of a bitch.

From the age of eight, a good brood bitch has most surely earned a peaceful retirement. She may, by that time, have reared six healthy litters. There is no reasonable excuse for mating an eight-year-old bitch again. She has already contributed her share to the progress of the kennel. There is always the argument that the bitch is in very good health and showing no signs of old age. This is a very important aim in any breed of dog, but it should not be put to the test by getting yet another litter out of a bitch who is over eight years of age! It should always be remembered that the pregnancy, the birth, and the rearing of the puppies make tremendous demands, both physical and psychological, on the bitch. After a certain age, she should not be required to bear such a burden.

Spared in this way, a bitch may well live for an additional, well-earned couple of years. As for dogs, this is quite a different matter that I shall go into in the chapter on stud dogs.

CARE OF THE BROOD BITCH

If there are a considerable number of dogs and the bitch has to be kept mostly in the kennels, the breeder must find the time to be with her as much as possible. The bitch needs to have complete confidence in her owner during the entire process of mating, whelping, and rearing her puppies. This can only be achieved if she is allowed to be in close physical contact with the breeder as much as possible. She should be taken out for a walk for at least an hour every day. Plenty of exercise and a spacious run are prerequisites for a healthy brood bitch. She should be kept in good condition, even a little bit thin, but never allowed to get fat and short of breath. The better her condition, the fewer the problems to be expected..

Provide good nourishing food, such as raw meat, cereals, vegetables and fruit, yoghurt, cottage cheese, and eggs – a varied diet will help to keep the bitch fit. Never give her too much food. At the end of five minutes her food bowl should be licked quite clean, otherwise she has been given too much. Our own bitches never get as much as they would actually like. They all love their food, and all of them are astonishingly greedy!

Yes, you can also feed all-in-one foods. The experts in the food industry have brought the production of well-balanced foodstuffs to such a fine art that deficiency diseases cannot occur. Such is the definition laid down by the competent food-production regulations. Our dogs, however, delight in a little variation, so they get something different each day. This varied diet, naturally, also includes quite a lot of the commercial products. One meal a day is the right way to feed a dog, and it is best to give this before its period of rest begins. We feed our dogs before going to bed and have found this to be the best possible time.

MAKING THE DECISION

By now some readers may well begin to doubt, after reading this chapter, that the bitch they already own fulfils all the qualifications necessary for a good brood bitch. On this point, you should employ all your critical faculties. The really good breeder is one who looks his or her own dogs over with as critical an eye as they look over those of their competitors. Should there be any doubt at all, then allow your bitch to live the pleasant life of a much-loved family member, and give up all ideas of breeding from her. Even if she has been successful in the show ring and also happens to be an excellent representative of the breed, if she does not fulfil the requirements for health, intelligence, and ability to work, you will be doing the right thing, benefiting the breed, if you give up the plan of breeding from her.

I know exactly what you feel like! For ten years I stood in the ring as a judge, and I know all those human sensibilities. The dog owner is especially sensitive when it comes to appraising his own dog. But sentiment is not a sound basis for a successful kennel, and it does not help to improve a breed, so at this point, I must simply appeal to your common sense.

Remember at all times: the success of a breeder is based on the quality of his brood bitches. Kennels with mediocre bitches are doomed to failure and – another most important point – far too many dogs are being bred! Be critical, responsible, and very particular when selecting your brood bitch.

Chapter Four

THE STUD DOG

For centuries, it was believed that in the breeding of animals the sire played the sole, decisive role in the quality of the progeny. The male carries the semen, and it was thought that this contained the embryo and that the female was merely the soil on which the young developed and, thereafter, the source of milk to feed the offspring. Geneticists, beginning with the Augustinian abbot Gregor Johann Mendel (1822-1884) have been contradicting this erroneous belief for more than a century. There are no serious, scientific differences of opinion about the fact that both male and female are equally responsible for the quality of their young. It is not the parent's sex that is responsible for the extent of the influence exerted, but the prepotency of his or her hereditary qualities. This again depends to a great extent on the degree of inbreeding in the animal in question. Animals stemming from intense inbreeding, from sibling matings, are considerably more prepotent than those less closely bred. Well, I have once more digressed into the geneticists' field. You will find further details on this subject in the books on genetics in dog breeding.

THE STUD DOG'S INFLUENCE

Let us return to our stud dog. There is one single, but very forceful, argument according to which the influence of the dog in dog breeding is considerably greater than that of the bitch. One single dog can, depending on the breed population, produce between 50 and 150 litters per year. In extreme cases, a single dog might sire up to 1,000 puppies. In comparison, a bitch could hardly bear 20 puppies. This is the sole, but surely very considerable, difference.

In many breeds there are stud dogs that, owing to their qualities and the extensive use made of them, have set their unmistakable stamp upon the breed. Eric F. Daglish writes: "Most experienced breeders are aware of the fact that now and again a dog comes to the fore which is so prepotent that, quite independent of the bitches he mates, he passes on his own outward appearance to his progeny."

This statement is perfectly correct, but there are two problems. The first is that this prepotency can also work in a negative respect, since a single dog can, roughly speaking, throw back a whole breed several generations. And again, this statement may well be used as an excuse to mate poor-quality bitches to such a superstar. The geneticist should inform these breeders that the shortcomings of their bitches will not necessarily appear in the first generation, but more certainly in the second and following generations.

BREEDING AGE

As we have seen, the stud dog has, at times, a decisive influence on the progress of a breed. This brings us to a further consideration. As has been seen, show wins tell us something about a dog's anatomy, and about his beauty seen in relation to the Breed Standard, but they tell us nothing about his health, intelligence, or ability to work. The much-admired multi-Champion may well have a catastrophic effect on a breed. The dog who mates numerous bitches because of his show successes might well have a limited intelligence, or some other shortcomings in temperament.

This means that we should be far more careful in selecting our stud dogs. The stud dog should possess a high degree of excellence in all respects; he should be healthy, intelligent, and show ability to work, if undesirable developments are to be avoided in a breed. The best recommendation for the individual dog is his own progeny. Here, we once more come up against a barrier of human prejudice. Puppies begot by young dogs mating too early in life suffer from cranioschisis – failure of the skull sutures to close. This is an old wives' tale – and yet, there are still a number of rules and regulations in Continental dog clubs that do not permit dogs to mate until they are fifteen, sometimes even eighteen, months old.

Let us take another look at the UK. A promising young dog is often given a chance to mate a bitch as early as possible, perhaps at six or maybe at nine months. It is an utter superstition that a dog's sperm is infertile the first time he mates. The very fact that this promising young dog has been allowed to reproduce himself at such an early age makes it possible to assess his hereditary qualities by the time he is eighteen months old. His own progeny are his best recommendation.

I do not intend to advocate the excessive use of a young dog before he has completed his physical development – depending on the breed this could be between twelve and twenty-four months. If, however, the young dog is biologically capable of reproduction, his physical development is unlikely to suffer any form of damage if he is allowed to mate one or two bitches per month. Clearly, the use of a very young – or a very old – dog constitutes a certain amount of risk for the breeder, as the bitch may not conceive. This is a risk the breeder simply has to take. The young dog is in no way harmed in his development by an occasional mating, quite the contrary, he gains most valuable experience.

It is a proven fact that a very close bond between the dog and his owner sometimes leads to a complete lack of interest in his own kind. I shall return to this point later on. The experienced breeder allows a dog to mate a bitch for the first time at the age of around nine months in order for the dog to learn what is required. Another glance toward England: if possible, the very promising young dog is not mated to any bitch, but rather to his own dam, his sister, or, if necessary, his half-sister. Inbreeding is the surest way to bring to light the qualities and shortcomings of a strain. Why this is so is a thing that geneticists can best explain. The young dog who has proved his worth in this intensely inbred litter will make an interesting mate for many bitches.

ESTABLISHING GENOTYPE

In the previous chapter on the brood bitch, I said that I would be going into the question of phenotype and genotype in more detail in this chapter. There is no doubt at all that the intensely inbred test litter described above is by far the most direct method of establishing the genotype – the genetic qualities of an animal. And again, the law of heredity tells us the genotype is, to a very large degree, dependent on the animal's ancestry. Every individual has its genetic shadow.

This genetic shadow is, in fact, written down in black and white, since every pure-bred dog has a pedigree, in many cases covering five generations. The more intensively the breeder studies the breed strains of the past thirty years, and the greater number of individuals he actually knows (not merely from seeing a photograph), the more information is it possible to gather from a pedigree of this kind. However, let us harbour no illusions; on a three-generation pedigree, there are fourteen individual ancestors, by four generations the number has risen to thirty, and in five generations to a total of sixty-two! Does any one of us know as many as sixty-two individual dogs in a pedigree –

or even half as many? This is where the problem lies. Apart from the names of the ancestors, the pedigree contains the dogs' registration numbers, now and again a Champion title and perhaps a Working Certificate or two, and, in exceptional cases, the coat colour or type of coat. Is this enough for us to be able to discern clearly the genetic shadow behind our stud dog? For many years interested breeders have been calling for a photographic pedigree for our dogs. This would take the form of a five-generation picture gallery. If this could be achieved, it would be of tremendous advantage to the genuine breeder. Is there any reason why this should not be possible.

In any number of breeds, it would be perfectly feasible to set up a picture gallery furnished with the hip X-ray plates of the ancestors over five generations. Are these X-ray plates adequate documentation for assessing the quality of the ancestors? Is there nothing of greater importance? It is not my intention to belittle the radiographic examinations carried out on practically every dog in some breeds. They are indispensable in the battle to combat a grave hereditary disease and are, for that reason, to be recommended highly. What I do not understand is why only the dog's hips are documented, and not the entire dog! A picture-gallery pedigree would be a great advance, but I have to admit most dog owners are quite satisfied with the pedigree in its present form – they add up the Champion titles and Working Certificates of their dogs' ancestors and are perfectly happy. But the breeder? Surely he or she would prefer to have a good deal more information.

BUILDING A PICTURE
Around 1948, a very interesting first step in this direction was taken. The intention was not merely to establish the appearance, temperament, and performance of the individual dogs, but to enter this in the dog's pedigree. In this way, anyone studying the pedigree would have a complete picture of all the dogs in it, and not just a mass of registration numbers. The first step was taken by the German Shepherd Dog Breed Club in Merseburg, in what was then the German Democratic Republic. This method later received widespread recognition in the whole of Eastern Germany. There is a very well-written book covering this subject *Hund und Umwelt* (*The Dog and His Environment*) by Dr F.K. Dorn. Interested German-speaking readers will find a great many worthwhile suggestions in this book.

Here are just a few of them. The system was divided into four categories: A = Type, B = Appearance, C = Conformation, D = Temperament. Awarding scores of between 0 and 9, an attempt was made to arrive at a thorough analysis of these four points. A kind of scoring system was established containing four numbers, each unit expressing the values from A-D. It was not easy to express the findings under the four headings in ten digits. This scoring system is perhaps best explained by an example:

Under the heading D = Temperament:
0 means "nervous, timid"
3 means "aloof, cautious, not self-assured"
8 means "unafraid, self-assured, not aggressive"

Under the heading A = Type:
1 means "too little substance"
8 means "too heavy and clumsy"

Under the heading B = Appearance:
0 means "lack of pigmentation"
5 means "excellent appearance, outline, and harmony"

Let us suppose the digits 2485 are printed after the dog's name in his pedigree. This would mean: "Light type, typical of the breed, lacking shoulder angulation, hard courageous, self-assured, good-tempered, pronounced defending drive."

The aims of the Merseburg scoring system were to make good breeding stock easy to recognise. Every pedigree was to contain a key, every dog on the pedigree a clear description, by means of four digits, of his appearance, temperament, and characteristics. As far as I know, the system never functioned satisfactorily due both to weaknesses in the system itself and to human fallibility in operating it. All the same, I believe it is high time for us to devise a way of imparting more information through the pedigrees of our dogs. Dr Dorn tells us: "If all dogs in a pedigree are scored for these characteristics, we should have a clear picture of the hereditary qualities of the whole 'bloodline' of a dog."

There is no room in this book to discuss the tremendous advantages that modern computer techniques, geared to a well-devised scoring scheme, might have for the world of dog breeding. This is a matter for the geneticists. For our purposes, all we need to know is that it is vital for us to assemble detailed information on the ancestors of our breeding stock – information which, unfortunately, cannot be ascertained from the entries in the stud books. At present, there are only two ways open to us. Firstly, the closely inbred test litter described above and, secondly, the knowledge a few people have about a number of our dogs' ancestors.

As long as titles – awarded according to phenotype and beauty – are given more weight than the evaluation of those qualities of real importance to dog breeding, such as health, intelligence, and working ability, it is unlikely that the dog that actually has most to contribute to the breed will stand at the forefront among stud dogs.

In addition to the intensive research into our dog's ancestry, a study of his siblings and, above all, of his progeny will be of further assistance. When checking them through, it is not the show wins that are of importance but, once again, health, intelligence, and working ability. This is a point that I cannot stress too strongly. In the interests of our dogs, and in the interests of those who buy puppies, we must cease to allow ourselves to be misled into overrating those ideals of beauty set out in a Breed Standard.

Let us broaden our horizons by taking a look at the breeding of horses, and numerous examples may also be drawn on from livestock breeding in agriculture. In all these fields, a sire is not regarded as a valuable stud animal until his progeny have demonstrated his genetic qualities. Progeny competitions are still rather rare, even at our dog shows today. Their importance for evaluating the hereditary qualities of a stud dog have hardly been recognised. Let it be understood, in livestock breeding it is not the beauty of this progeny that is placed in the foreground, but its performance.

In the UK, competitions are run every year in many breeds to find the best stud dogs and brood bitches. The sole criterion, in this case, is the quality of the progeny. It is quite clear, from whichever angle we look at it, this system is badly in need of improvement, since the only thing that counts is the progeny's show results. It is, of course, perfectly acceptable if we are breeding dogs exclusively for the show ring, but completely wrong if we are breeding them as family dogs, which most will become.

AGE LIMITS

A few words may be added here on the question of how long a dog should be used at stud. Most puppy buyers would like to have a four-footed companion that will accompany them for many years. We breed dogs for people, and one of our aims is, therefore, to breed for a good long life.

Today there are some breeds of dog whose expectation of life is a mere four-to-six years, rarely ten years or more. Dogs suffer increasingly from a variety of diseases simply because the health factor has been badly neglected. All this calls urgently for a change of policy.

If we want to breed dogs with a good, long life expectancy, then we must select for the quality of a bright and vigorous old age. This vigour can nowhere be better demonstrated than in the fertility and vitality of a dog up to a great age – that is to say until he is ten or even twelve years old.

In an experimental situation at the Society for Domestic Animal Research, a twelve-year-old Saluki dog was the leader and progenitor of a mixed pack, and this dog and his family lived out of doors all their lives, For this dog to retain his leadership, he had to be fit, healthy and capable of mating. Vigour and vitality are shown by older dogs in their ability to mate, and in their fertility. A long expectation of life is one of the most important aims in breeding dogs, and vigour in an older dog shows us that this aim has been achieved.

Obviously, I am not suggesting that an old dog of ten years or more should be allowed to mate between twenty and fifty bitches per annum. Clearly, the amount he should be asked to do should lie somewhere between the older dog's natural sexual drive, and the use he can still be to the kennel. I do not believe there is any value in imposing breeding age regulations on stud dogs. However, the owners of bitches must be aware that there is always the risk with the older dog that he will, one day, become infertile.

A STUD TEAM

On the Continent, stud dogs are for the most part privately owned. They belong to people who have dogs as a hobby, and this is a very good thing. In a number of breeds in other countries, a leading kennel with its top-flight stud dogs can exert a tremendous influence on a breed. In Raymond Oppenheimer's Ormandy Bull Terrier kennel, there were always from four to six first-class, quality, adult dogs standing at stud. Putting their trust entirely in his judgement, breeders took their bitches to him to be mated. Raymond Oppenheimer was recognised internationally as the leading expert in the Bull Terrier breed. He always knew which of his dogs was best-suited to any bitch brought to him, and his team was so well put together that the most important, well-tried bloodlines were represented by one or more of his stud dogs. Thus, there was nearly always just the right dog in the kennel for every bitch.

Raymond Oppenheimer was the outstanding expert in the breed. His stud dogs, his knowledge of breeding, and the trust the owners of bitches put in him, all served to exert a tremendous influence on Bull Terrier breeding. It is, therefore, not in the least surprising that year after year top-flight dogs from his kennels were awarded the trophy for the Stud Dog of the Year, an award that goes to the dog with the most outstanding progeny. Nor is it surprising that at least one-third, at times up to 50 per cent, of all important matings in the breed took place at his kennels.

As has already been seen, a breed can be considerably influenced not only by kennels of top-quality bitches, but also by a team of stud dogs either homebred or brought from other breeders. The example I have given above serves to document the marked influence top-quality dogs can have on a breed. Yet, I never felt happy on my visits to these kennels. I was compelled to acknowledge everything that had been achieved and to admire the excellent dogs and their beautifully-cared-for surroundings. But the life of top dogs of this kind was most monotonous for they were, after all, mere tools for breeding show winners. Four to six Champions and another four young dogs, each in solitary kennel confinement! Cared for perfectly, of course, kept in excellent boxes, taken out for walks once a day, and provided with large runs; but inevitably, they had far too little social contact.

SELECTING A STUD DOG

How do you go about obtaining a stud dog? This is a difficult question. In all probability, you will find yourself at first in much the same position as the man who wanted to own a stallion in an industry where roughly 95 per cent of all male animals are gelded. In horse breeding, the selection process is very rigorous, which is all to the good!

Basically, choosing a young dog for stud purposes is very much the same as the method described in the previous chapter for choosing a good brood bitch. Top-quality parents, a first-class pedigree, if possible, a puppy from a mating already tried once before, the best possible rearing conditions and that extra little bit of good luck! However, all this does not mean that your dog is going to be a great stud dog. There is so very much in a dog-man relationship, so much give and take on both sides, and the foremost question should never be whether your canine companion is to become a top class stud dog.

If, however, you have been lucky enough to find a really good specimen, you will also be taking on a responsibility to the breed. Give your dog every possible chance to develop: rear him carefully, feed him correctly, give him plenty of exercise every day, let him run free, and let him play under safe conditions. Do not merely bring him along for his show qualities. Help him to develop his intelligence, and give him a chance to develop his abilities. Beautiful but dumb – that is not quite enough, neither in the woman nor the dog! And by the way, it is a mere superstition – or rather, a lazy way out – when it is said that a superb anatomy and working ability preclude one another. The best example to disprove this is to be seen in the thoroughbred horse throughout the world. There are a great number of beautiful dogs that also stand out for their health, intelligence, and working ability. It would be false modesty – or sheer incompetence – if a breeder decided to limit himself to just one aim.

MAINTAINING STANDARDS

You may already be a successful breeder, with a kennel of top-quality bitches. If this is the case, do not buy a stud dog! I have seen this mistake made time and time again. Breeders cannot resist the temptation to use their own stud dog on their own bitches. In fact, it is often the breeder's own stud dog that stands in the way of the kennel's success, for a bitch should always be mated to the dog that is best-suited to her in every possible respect. I know, of course, that it is very tempting to keep a stud dog; it saves a great deal of travelling, and cuts out the risk of arriving on the wrong day. And to add to this, when dogs and bitches all live together, they frequently develop a great deal of affection – even love – for one another. Is it right? Should we, for the purpose of breeding, prevent our dogs from making their own choices?

For over twenty years, we have kept our brood bitches together with a stud dog. And very soon a rumour was running rife that our dog was not capable of mating since we always took our bitches to other stud dogs!

I recall one breeder who had an inferior bitch and a very good dog. He turned down my advice not to breed with the bitch, saying: "I shall mate her to my dog and see what comes of it." That was his decision. I could easily have told him what would come of it – mediocre and inferior puppies! He overrated the quality of his dog, and his love of both animals had made him blind to the bitch's defects. This attitude constitutes a grave danger for a good dog. Due to lack of knowledge – at times for financial gain – the dog is allowed to mate inferior bitches. How is it possible, later on, to prove that the poor-quality puppies stemming from him are not the result of his own poor, hereditary qualities? We know for certain that the genotype of a stud dog or brood bitch can only be judged by the quality of his or her progeny. Negligence in permitting a good stud dog to mate inferior bitches has ruined a number of reputations.

Even worse is the excuse that the inferior bitch would have been mated anyway, if not by your own dog then by one of your rival's dogs. If it is not possible to exclude the bitch from breeding, then it is surely better to mate her to our dog? For whom is it better – for the stud dog owner's purse? That is undeniable. For the dog? A distinction must be made here between his enjoyment of the sexual activity, and his good reputation, which will easily be damaged by poor-quality offspring. One inferior bitch with her inferior puppies can easily mean that five other bitches are not brought to be mated to that particular stud dog. Then where is the financial gain?

What about the breed as a whole? Neither the inferior dog nor the inferior bitch should be used for breeding. Every stud dog owner should reject the poor excuse that if his dog is not used, the rival's dog will be. And every owner should consider his dog too good to mate an inferior bitch. This attitude would go a long way to improving a breed. If you are fortunate enough to own a good stud dog, enjoy your good luck. There is a great deal of pleasure to be had from being able to see and admire his progeny at shows and working tests. Dog breeding requires stud dogs. A breed does not have to have an unlimited choice of sires, but those that are made available should be of the highest quality. Every stud dog owner bears the responsibility for seeing that his dog is used with discretion.

If you want to use your dog at stud, a further prerequisite is a good knowledge of mating behaviour. The following chapter deals with the mating of our domestic dog and should prove a valuable source of information.

Chapter Five

THE MATING

We humans have a tendency to judge everything that goes on around us by our own standards, our actions, our feelings, our anatomical and physical make-up. Man regards himself, all too easily, as the standard by which everything is to be measured. The root of many misunderstandings is the humanisation of our dogs. This happens time and time again, even though the human intellect, which enables us to differentiate, is perfectly capable of seeing and understanding distinct differences. This conflict does not arise with animals, as they have not been equipped with sufficient intelligence to project themselves, imaginatively, into the world of human emotions.

In many spheres, the mating behaviour of our dogs is very different from that in humans. Without an exact understanding of the anatomy, the physical development and psychological behaviour of our dogs, breeders and owners of stud dogs will repeatedly make serious mistakes when mating their dogs, and this leads, in the final analysis, to unsuccessful matings and unsuccessful breeding. The so-called forced mating comes to be regarded as normal, although it is nothing less than a form of cruelty to animals, and, as often as not, it does not prove successful since certain factors vital to the favourable outcome of a mating have been disregarded.

I, therefore, recommend that every dog lover studies this whole chapter on the mating behaviour of our domestic dogs, even though its contents - by the nature of the subject – may not make for very easy reading. A knowledge of the dog's anatomy, its natural mating behaviour, and an awareness of the difficulties that might arise, go a long way towards the successful and healthy breeding of dogs.

ANATOMY OF THE BITCH AND HER OESTROUS CYCLE

In the chapter on the stud dog, it has already been mentioned that, in the very early days, the function of the female was thought to be one of merely providing the medium on which the embryos were fostered, and, later on, supplying the milk to nourish the offspring. It was denied that father and mother, via their genes, had an equal share in the shaping of their common offspring.

Today, now that this heresy has been laid aside, things have gone almost to the other extreme. Immersed in the planning of hereditary characters and the laws of heredity, this "medium for nourishing" the puppies, the bitch's body, and her spirit are completely forgotten. The knowledge of how body and spirit work together in the mating behaviour of our dogs is a thing the dog lover is left to discover unaided. We are going to begin here with a description of the bitch's anatomy and her oestrous cycle.

Included in this book are many line drawings and graphs. These are not merely intended as

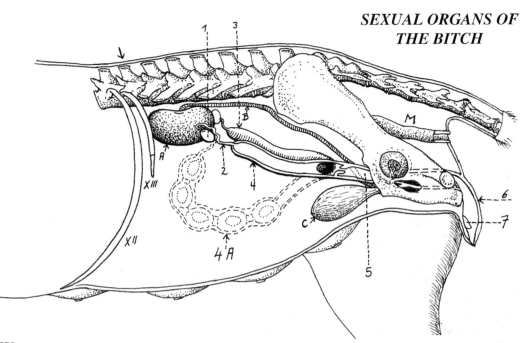

SEXUAL ORGANS OF
THE BITCH

KEY: *The abdomen is viewed from the left side showing the two last thoracic vertebrae (Arrow = 13th thoracic vertebra,) the six lumbar vertebrae, the sacrum, the first five coccygeal vertebrae, the ribs (XII and XIII), and the side view of the pelvis.*
A = left kidney, B = ureter, C = urinary bladder (the bladder's outlet into the vagina is to be seen in the oval opening in the pelvis), M = rectum with anus.
1 = ovary, 2 = fallopian tube, 3 = right uterine horn with ovary and fallopian tube, 4 = longitudinal section of the left uterine horn with outlet of right horn followed by the cervix, 5 = vagina, 6 = right lip of vulvar cleft and 7 = the outer end of the clitoris.
4A = the altered position of the left uterine horn (uterus) in the fourth week of pregnancy, showing five foetesus.

illustrations for this book; I sincerely hope that every breeder will take the trouble to study them carefully. They show anatomical details and document hormonal processes that are essential to our understanding of our dog's mating behaviour. To begin with, we will examine the bitch's sexual organs.

It would not be inappropriate to compare, at this point, the sexual organs of the woman with those of the bitch. Although all mammals have, in general, a great deal in common, there are some very distinct differences. The uterus of the bitch, for example, does not consist of one body but of a pair of long tube-like arms. These are the uterine horns, in which the embryos develop. It is a remarkably long way from the vagina to the ovaries. The sperm has to cover this distance in order to reach and fertilise the ovum. The copulation process in the dog is adapted to this situation. This will all be gone into in detail when discussing the mating process.

Medical terminology stems largely from Latin. In order to avoid misunderstandings, the following names of the sexual organs of the bitch are given in both Latin and English:

NOMENCLATURE: SEXUAL ORGANS OF THE BITCH

Labien	Lips of the vulva
Introitus vaginae	Vaginal orifice, vulva
Vestibulum	Vestibule
Hymen	Maidenhead, hymen
Vagina	Vagina
Cervix uteri	Neck of the womb
Uterus	Womb, uterus
Salpinx	Fallopian tube
Ovarium	Ovary
Mamma	Mammary gland.

The oestrous cycle of the domestic dog differs from that of the wild dog. The wolf and the jackal only come into season once every twelve months, and that is in the early part of the year, so that their puppies are born in the spring. Scientists are of the unanimous opinion that the household dog's two heats a year are the result of domestication. Many people probably do not know that, in the case of wolves and jackals, the sexual activity of the male is also confined to this one season; he is not capable of mating at any other time. In comparison, our domestic dog is on the look-out all the year round for a bitch in season, and he constantly gives evidence of this by marking his territory.

Let us return to our bitch. Her heat, which occurs twice a year, is part of a four-phase oestrous cycle:

I Interestrous (or anestrous) period: approx. 90 days
II Proestrus: 10 days
III Oestrus: 12 days
IV Involution (Metestrus): 60 days

At this point I should like to add an important observation. I always hesitate to quote exact figures for these individual phases; they could be so easily misunderstood and would lead to incorrect conclusions. The above figures are intended as a rough and ready guide based on a considerable variation in range from breed to breed, and even from bitch to bitch in any one breed! Mathematical calculations are, in many ways, simply not applicable to animals, and this is especially the case with regard to the sexual behaviour of our dogs. Thinking in figures should be treated with great reserve; its place should be taken by close observations of our dogs' behaviour.

Admittedly, this does make things very much more difficult! How much easier it would be to be able to plan the 'honeymoon' well in advance, to be able to fix a date with the stud dog owner, to take a few days off work to fit a schedule. Females, however, do not function like machines – not even our female domestic dogs!

The bitch's oestrous cycle is regulated by the pituitary gland. Naaktgeboren considers, probably quite rightly, that there is a close connection between environmental influences and the production of pituitary homone, secreted by the pituitary gland. This applies to differences in temperature, amount of daylight, precipitation, and many other factors that have still to be analysed but which influence these periodic fluctuations, delaying or accelerating the individual phases. Many dog owners have noticed that after long, cold winters their bitches are slow to come into season. Others have observed that if a number of bitches are kept together, they all come in heat either at the same time or shortly after one another – a clear example of an environmental influence in dog breeding.

THE PROESTRUS

Some days before the beginning of the proestrus phase, and shortly before the first drops of blood are to be seen, the bitch's vulva begins to swell, thus announcing the approaching heat. Bleeding denotes the onset of the heat itself. Far too many dog owners overlook the very first day because bitches, as a rule, lick themselves scrupulously clean. However, it is of vital importance, when planning the probable day of mating, to ascertain the exact beginning of the heat, and it has, therefore, proved useful to place a couple of white cloths on the bitch's bed. This usually helps to clarify the matter.

Another sign that the bitch's heat is either about to begin, or has already begun, is frequent urination. The bitch no longer discharges the contents of her bladder in one action, but squats repeatedly and carefully releases a few drops at a time, sometimes even raising one hind leg as she does so. She is marking the ground for the dog. In this way, she does, in fact, attract a number of dogs that may even attempt to mate her. She is, however, in this proestrus phase, and is not ready to be mated. She will either snap at her admirer, sit down, or lie on her back. The experienced dog knows the situation, and he will take little notice of the bitch until she has actually entered the oestrus.

Bleeding in the proestrus phase starts off by being dark-red in colour and gradually becomes paler. The vulva and vagina are very much swollen, considerably enlarged, and taut. The outward changes in the in-season bitch are clearly visible.

THE OESTRUS

It is of very great importance for the breeder to be able to ascertain the onset of ovulation, the oestrus itself, and thus the correct day for mating his bitch. The main period of sexual activity always coincides with the release of the eggs from the ovaries (ovarium), and their movement into the fallopian tubes (salpinges). A mating at this point is most favourable for fertilisation, since the dog's sperm meets the released eggs on their way through the fallopian tubes.

If it is possible to keep a dog and a bitch together throughout the entire period, it is almost 100 per cent certain, due to the inner changes in the bitch and the influence these have on the natural behaviour of both dog and bitch, that the two will mate at the right moment and, in all probability,

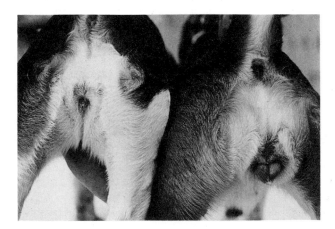

Two bitches: Left normal state, right bitch on heat.

Photo: Hendriksen.

more than once. The day and hour at which this happens is the right moment. Frequently, the opinion is expressed that the mongrel wandering around the streets is much more 'vigorous' than the pure-bred dog, requires no assistance at all when mating, and is, therefore, not degenerate. It must be said here that by far the greater majority of our pure-bred dogs possess great vitality and strong instincts, but it is often the human being who takes it upon himself to determine the right day for mating. However, humans do not have the organs of sense that enable dogs to give and receive natural signals pinpointing when the moment for mating has arrived.

I shall, therefore, start by repeating what has been said in nearly every book specialising on this subject, i.e. that the right day for mating lies between the tenth and thirteenth day after bleeding commences. This is probably quite correct for the majority of dogs – majority in the sense of more than fifty per cent. If you are the owner of a Bull Terrier, for example, I should have to revise this and advise you not to take your bitch to the dog until around the fifteenth day. This recommendation is based on more than twenty-five years of experience with this breed, having owned many successful stud dogs, and on achieving a success rate of more than eighty per cent on all matings during this period.

This is an example of the variation from normal of an entire dog breed, and some individuals may range even further. Our dogs have successfully mated bitches on the eighth day, and in another case, on the twenty-third day, after bleeding commenced. There are reports of bitches having been mated on the fifth and on the twenty-seventh day and having produced litters.

One outward sign of the approach of the correct day for mating is that the bleeding nearly ceases, the discharge becomes pale, almost colourless, and the vulva and vagina, which have been taut and swollen up to this time, becomes softer and smaller. Then there is an old breeder's trick: rub the end of the bitch's back near the root of her tail, or stroke gently around her vulva. If the bitch is approaching the peak of her oestrus, she will hold her tail to one side. This is a very characteristic movement, and is certainly a very good sign. However, this sign alone is not enough! Many bitches react in this way as early as the seventh or eighth day, and sometimes even after the eighteenth day. What is of vital importance is that when her vulva is stroked the bitch is clearly seen to raise her pelvic region. She presents her vulva and thus meets the thrust of the dog's penis. This movement of the vulva only takes place at the peak of the heat, the oestrus.

In order to discover whether the bitch is ready or not, breeders are frequently recommended to make use of a test dog, taking care that nothing happens. My advice is to take very good care indeed, since, if the dog is at all experienced, something really might happen!

There is yet one more aspect to be considered. From a safe distance, perhaps from behind a fence, a bitch may show every sign of wanting to attract the dog. We have had bitches that actually presented their rear ends to the neighbouring dog beyond the fence. Should the dog, however, come into close physical contact with the bitch, should he attempt to mount her, to clasp her body with his forelegs, unless the heat has really reached its peak, the bitch will snap at him or else sit down firmly. There is a very great difference between showing off one's attractions and allowing an admirer close approach.

Just one more important point. We have known many bitches, I believe it would be correct to estimate their number at around ten per cent, that have shown willingness to mate over a period of eight to twelve days. In this case, even though the bitch is willing to mate, ovulation is, naturally, not taking place during this entire period.

As has already been explained, the oestrous cycle of the bitch is regulated by hormones, the various phases being brought about by a secretion of the hormones oestrogen and progesterone. Perhaps this is the right moment to make it clear that menstruation in the human has a totally different function than that of bleeding in the bitch. Menstruation takes place in the woman fourteen days after ovulation, whereas bleeding in the bitch commences from ten to twelve days prior to ovulation. Menstrual bleeding in the human and bleeding in the dog serve two completely different functions. This is a point that should be clearly understood.

SCIENTIFIC TESTS

We are trying to establish the right day for mating. Obviously it is a very good idea for the owner of the bitch to consult the veterinarian – that is, if no test dog happens to be available. The veterinarian will take a vaginal smear and, after examining this, will advise the bitch's owner when to set out on a possibly lengthy journey. To be honest, as the owner of stud dogs, I can tell a tale or two regarding this method! As a result of one smear having been taken, dozens of bitches have arrived at our house on the wrong day. Those veterinarians were not masters of their trade, and drew false conclusions from the examination of one single smear.

It is possibly a good idea to have a little basic knowledge of how such a smear is taken and evaluated. A long-handled swab is inserted deep into the vulva. Care must naturally be taken not to injure the bitch. The secretion, thus obtained, is smeared on a glass slide. After allowing this to dry, the smear is stabilised and placed under the microscope for examination. The microscope enlarges approximately 250 times.

It has already been said that the progress of the cycle is regulated by hormones. The variation in the composition of the smears reflects the progress made in the bitch's oestrous cycle and, in this way, indicates the correct day for mating. The following description is taken, for the most part, from an article written by Eugene Witiak.

At the commencement of the bleeding (proestrus), red blood corpuscles and epithelial cells dominate. Only a few white blood corpuscles are present. The non-nucleated cells, characteristic of this period, are round and dark-red in colour. In the further course of the proestrus, the cells undergo changes; they increase considerably in size, become flat and polygonal, and the cell nucleus becomes visible. Halfway through the proestrus, very many cell nuclei have become apparent or are in the process of change. Considerably fewer red blood corpuscles are present.

Examination has shown that the onset of ovulation coincides with the virtual disappearance of cells containing a nucleus and of red blood corpuscles. The following is a rule of thumb for the earliest time for mating:

1. The number of cells containing a nucleus must amount to at least 75 per cent.
2. Absence of white blood corpuscles.
3. Low number of red blood corpuscles.

The reappearance of white blood corpuscles indicates that ovulation took place from twenty-four to thirty-six hours previously. The oestrus, the peak of the heat, generally comes to an end thirty-six to forty-eight hours subsequent to the first appearance of white blood corpuscles in the vaginal smear. The involution period is characterised by a rapid increase in the number of white blood corpuscles, the disappearance of the visible cell nuclei, and the return of cells containing no nucleus. The method for ascertaining ovulation is calculated upon the number of cells containing a nucleus in relation to those without a nucleus. That is the moment when mating must take place.

Science assumes that, in principle, it is possible for a bitch to conceive if she is mated, at most, three days before, and two and a half days after, ovulation. For my part, I am inclined to accept this with some reservation, since the duration in which the male sperm remains fertile is not in dispute. One thing is certain: the closer the mating is to the time of the ovulation, the more probable it is that there will be a considerable number of puppies, and the mating will be more

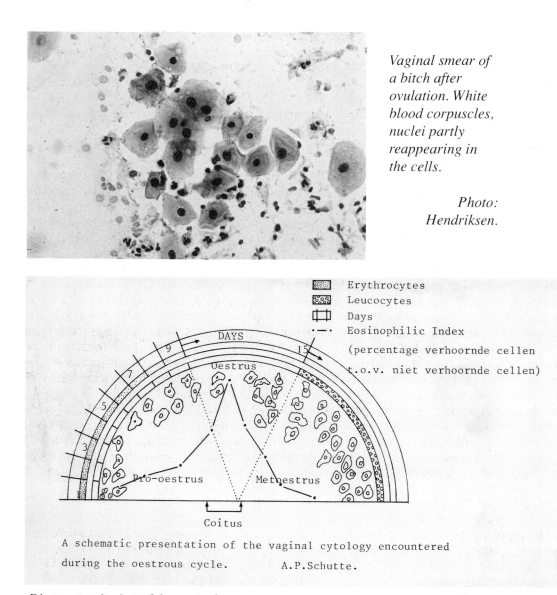

Vaginal smear of a bitch after ovulation. White blood corpuscles, nuclei partly reappearing in the cells.

Photo: Hendriksen.

Erythrocytes
Leucocytes
Days
Eosinophilic Index
(percentage verhoornde cellen
t.o.v. niet verhoornde cellen)

DAYS

Oestrus

Pro-oestrus   Metoestrus

Coitus

A schematic presentation of the vaginal cytology encountered
during the oestrous cycle.   A.P.Schutte.

Diagrammatic view of the vaginal smears taken during the oestrous cycle. Courtesy: A.P. Schutte. The different types of cell are shown here as they appear at the various stages of the heat.

natural – this I consider to be the most essential factor, the dog's behaviour. If we take another look at the rapid development shown by these smear readings, it becomes clear that the more we are able to learn about the internal processes in the bitch via a number of vaginal smears, the easier it is to ascertain the right day for mating. However, once again, I should like to recommend caution when calculating in days! Professor Dr Hendrikse, who practised for many years at the Institute for Artificial Insemination at the University of Utrecht, writes that the proestrus phase may range from five to fifteen days and may, in individual cases, last even longer. This shows clearly that the vaginal smear method can only successfully be applied if smears are taken at intervals of not more than forty-eight hours, beginning with the sixth day after bleeding commences. Daily smear examinations are urgently recommended for the ovulation phase itself.

We have now arrived at the cause of so much frustration on the part of stud dog owners. One single smear is a mere snapshot; it tells us little or nothing about the past or future progress of the cycle. The final stage alone, the point when it is already too late, is clearly disclosed by the presence of myriads of white blood corpuscles. However, we are not so much interested in the final stage as in the peak!

Modern clinics have made considerable advances in determining the ovulation phase. Tests have been developed to ascertain the amount of progesterone in the blood. (Progesterone is a steroid hormone secreted by the ovaries.) Using this method, a blood sample is taken three times a week. When the amount of progesterone rises above a certain level, mating must take place within the next twenty-four to forty-eight hours. This system has proved considerably more reliable than vaginal smears, but it is also much more expensive and far more complicated. A special laboratory, equipped with very costly apparatus, is required for testing the blood samples. It then takes six hours, with the aid of the appliances, to obtain a progesterone count. The procedure is certainly of great interest but, as a rule, hardly likely to be feasible for a breeder.

I hope that, by now, readers have come to the conclusion that there is more involved in ascertaining the right day for mating than simply counting to ten or twelve. Let me just once more emphasise the fact that the instincts of our dogs are a great deal more reliable than all the appliances invented by man. All breeders would be well advised, despite the opportunities for having vaginal smear tests taken by veterinarians, not to forget the old established test dog method.

The focus of all that has been said, up to now, is that in dog breeding there are biological processes at play upon which the human being has no influence at all. There is only one thing the breeder can do, and that is to summon up patience, patience, and, once again, patience! Living creatures are not machines, and this again makes dog breeding rich in surprises. Patience, knowledge, and time to be successful, these are the things the breeder must have at his disposal.

ANATOMY OF THE DOG

Let us begin at once with a description of the dog's sexual organs. The dog's testicles are contained in the scrotal sac, suspended between his thighs. Closely attached to each testicle is an epididymis, which is connected to the testicle by numerous fine ducts. The sperm matures and is stored in the epididymis. When ejaculation takes place, the matured sperm is propelled out of the epididymis through the spermatic duct into the urethra, at the point where it passes through the pelvis. The secretion from the prostate gland is discharged into it here. Since the spermatic duct and the duct leading from the prostate gland are separately connected to the urethra, it is here that the two ejaculate fluids combine. The erection of the penis is brought about by changes in blood pressure in the corpora cavernosa: additional blood is pressed into the cavities, the penis arteries expand, and the return flow of blood is, at the same time, reduced.

The partially erect penis is now inserted into the bitch's vagina. Full erection, involving the engorgement of the bulbus, is then achieved by rapid pelvic thrusting and friction. In this, the first phase, only pre-ejaculate is ejected. Maximum erection does not take place until the two dogs have tied – that is, the copulatory lock has been achieved. At this point, the male is no longer able to withdraw. The erection of the penis is regulated neuro-vegetatively (i.e. it is controlled by the

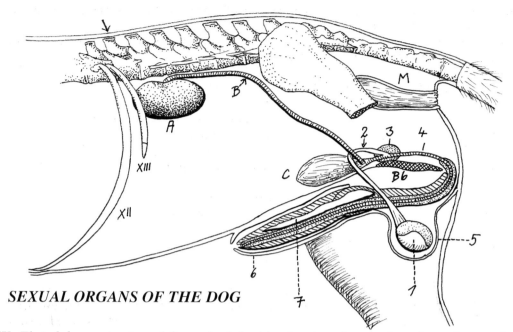

SEXUAL ORGANS OF THE DOG

KEY: *The abdomen is viewed from the left side showing the two last thoracic vertebrae (Arrow = 13th thoracic vertebra), the six lumbar vertebrae (spinous processes are now shown), sacrum, the first coccygeal vertebrae, the ribs (XII and XIII). Part of the pelvis has been removed. The pelvic floor is shown in longitudinal section (Bb).*
A = left kidney, B = urethra, C = urinary bladder, M = rectum (longitudinal section).
1 = left testicle with attached epididymis, 2 = spermatic cord, 3 = prostate (shown in section to afford a view of the outlet of the spermatic cord into the urethra), 5 = scrotum, 6 = prepuce, 7 = penile bone.
The urethra is enclosed in the inner cavernosum penis from the edge of the pelvic floor to its orifice (spotted); the penis is enclosed in the outer cavernosum penis. When the bulbus glandis, situated at the root of the penis, swells, the rear cavernosum penis extends back to the pelvic floor.   *Source: E. Trumler.*

vegetative nervous system). Engorgement of the bulbus is brought about by the slowing down or throttling of the return flow of venous blood. The two dogs cannot separate or release themselves until detumescence of the penis occurs. The subsidence of the dog's penis in the later course of mating makes it possible for the two to separate, so that this process must be considered an inherent part of the dog's reflex mating behaviour.

In portraying the bitch, it has already been stated that, owing to her anatomical structure, the sperm is obliged to cover a very long distance. The tie of the two dogs during mating is most certainly a bridge built by nature herself. The copulatory lock inevitably prevents the flow back of the ejaculate and, thus, the early loss of sperm. More will be said on the subject of the tie when we come to the mating process itself. All that needs to be mentioned here is the time that elapses before detumescence occurs, which may be anything from five to forty minutes. Extremes are two to three minutes, and sixty minutes or more.

Once again for better understanding of the technical terminology, here is a list of the names of the male dog's sexual organs in Latin and English.

NOMENCLATURE: SEXUAL ORGANS OF THE DOG

Penis	Organ of urination and copulation
Praeputium	Foreskin, prepuce
Glans penis	Bulb of penis
Bulbus glandis	Bulbous part of penis
Os penis	Penile bone
Corpora cavernosa	Erectile body
Scrotum	Scrotal sac, scrotum, purse
Testes	Testicles
Prostata	Prostate
Ductus deferens	Spermatic duct.

The spermatozoa and their function were discovered as early as the 17th Century by A. Leeuwenhoeck. They are remarkable for their singularly long tails and snaking movement, and their discoverer named them spermatozoa, little animals, since he actually believed them to be animals. Due to their snake-like movement, the sperm are able to propel themselves in the direction of the bitch's ovaries where they meet – always supposing the time is right – with mature ova.

THE STAGES OF EJACULATION

Let us now consider what the dog ejaculates, and when. The dog having mounted the bitch directs his penis into her vagina with strong thrusting movements and, at the same time, ejaculates a small amount of clear fluid. This is known as the pre-ejaculate. It is watery, clear in colour, and contains no sperm. The quantity ranges between a very few drops and some millilitres. This fluid is a secretion discharged by the prostate gland. When the dog has completed his intromission, he stops thrusting, and the main secretion, containing an abundance of sperm, is ejaculated. At the same time, the bulbus is engorged and the tie begins.

This second ejaculate is a milky fluid of high viscosity. The whiter and more viscous the secretion, the greater the number of sperm it contains. The amount of secretion ejaculated varies (according to the size of the dog) between 0.5 and 2.5 millilitres. If the second ejaculate is transparent instead of being milky, it is a sign that it contains too few germ cells.

In the further course of the tie, yet a third ejaculate takes place, (postsecretion) and this contains no germ cells. The post-secretion is a clear fluid secreted by the prostate gland, and it can amount in volume to as much as fifteen millilitres. This third ejaculation serves to flush the second emission into the bitch. The volume of the second ejaculation is too small for it to be able to travel of its own accord as far as the decisive organs of the bitch. The greater volume of the third ejaculation, flowing as it does through the entire tie, serves to carry the sperm from the vagina into the uterine horns and as far as the ovaries, where fertilisation takes place.

I am describing this process in detail for a special reason. Having discussed the matter with many breeders, I was surprised to discover that only about every tenth one had wasted a single thought on the process, and few knew anything at all in detail. From this lack of knowledge arises such mistaken ideas as, for instance, the belief that without a tie nothing can happen. To make the matter quite clear, the second ejaculation takes place before the heavy engorgement of the bulbus. Should the dogs move apart after the male has entered the bitch entirely and has ceased thrusting, it is quite certain that the second ejaculation has taken place even though there has been no tie. If the dogs tear apart at this moment, the flushing action of the third ejaculation is missing, and the sperm inside the bitch now have to make their own long journey unaided.

We have had successful matings in our kennels, even though dog and bitch separated after only thirty seconds. From one such mating, ten healthy puppies were born. The owner of another bitch went on to another dog a few hours after a mating of this kind – he wanted to make sure – and in the end the bitch had puppies from two different sires in one litter.

ANALYSIS OF SPERM

An interesting study, a series of tests, on the ejaculate of dogs has been carried out by J. Hendrikse and H.W. Antonissee at the Faculty of Veterinary Medicine at the University of Utrecht. At the Institute for Artificial Insemination, a total of 2,025 ejaculates were tested, and it is well worthwhile taking a closer look at the test results. I am grateful to Professor J. Hendrikse for permission to publish his statistics here.

The aim of the tests was to study the quality of the sperm. This is determined by individual motility, the presence of morphological abnormalities among the sperm, and the number of germ cells (in 100 millions).

What is understood by the quality of the sperm? A decisive factor is healthy sperm with great

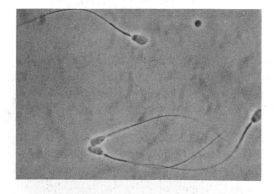

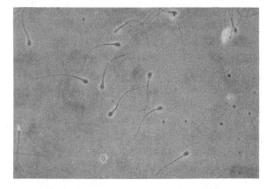

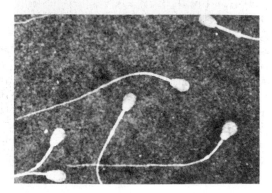

PHYSIOLOGICALLY HEALTHY EJACULATE

Note the long, motile tails. (The differences in size apparent in the three illustrations is the result of variations in microscopic enlargement.)

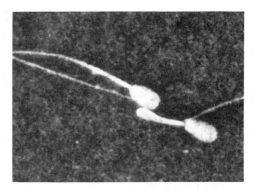

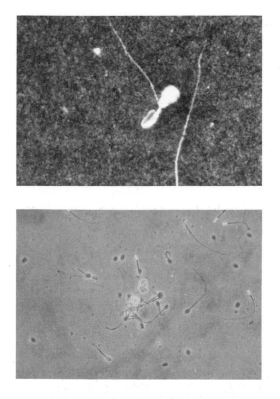

MORPHOLOGICAL ANOMALIES

TOP LEFT: Rolled up tails.

ABOVE: One healthy and one rolled up tail.

LEFT: Specimen slightly enlarged.

motility (capable of motion). The shape of healthy sperm can be clearly identified and also the long motile tails. The differences in size, apparent in the photograph included, are the result of variations in microscopic enlargement. Abnormal sperm present a very different picture. An ejaculate of this kind frequently contains sperm with rolled up tails, and stunted sperm. If we consider that the motility of the sperm is contingent primarily on its long-tailed form, it is not difficult to imagine that a stunted tail, or any other deformity, must to a very great extent hamper fertilisation. In the Utrecht study, ejaculates showing morphological abnormalities of more than 40 per cent were not included in the test results and statistics.

As a matter of course, the total amount of sperm is of great importance. Again, at Utrecht, all ejaculates showing too low a sperm count were excluded from the test material, these were ejaculates with fewer than 100 million sperm per millilitre. These figures serve to illustrate very clearly the tremendous surplus with which nature is at work – especially if we consider that only six to fifteen of the most active sperm ever reach an ovum! There is a definite correlation between the size of the dog and the total amount of sperm. More about this further on.

Not only is the shape of the individual sperm of decisive importance but also its motility. This aspect too was tested, evaluated, and counted under the microscope. Ejaculates whose motility values were below the set standard + +, and in which the content of motile germ cells was below 50 per cent, were not included in the results and statistics. The greater the motility in the following tables and the higher the content of fully motile sperm, the better the values.

The Utrecht study dealt first of all with the influence of the age of the dog on the quality of the sperm. Table 1 shows very clear results:

TABLE 1: INFLUENCE OF THE DOG'S AGE

Age of Dog	No. of Ejaculates Tested	Individual Motility ++ – ++++	Morphological Abnormalities %	No. of Sperm x 10
			%	
1-2	597	3.18	72.00	13.45	672.4
3-4	604	3.19	71.99	13.58	713.9
5-6	405	3.16	71.17	14.72	673.8
7-8	293	3.08	70.14	14.28	560.6
9-after	125	3.09	69.12	16.85	423.2
Total	**2024**	**3.15**	**71.38**	**14.17**	**653.5**

Up to the age of six years, no particular changes were established. Yet the fact should not be overlooked that in the five- to six-year-old dogs, a greater number of morphological abnormalities were determined. In the seven- to eight-year-old dogs, a considerable reduction in the number of sperm is clearly to be seen, and in the dog of nine years and over, the values fall still further. This does not mean that a dog of this age cannot father healthy puppies, yet the risks are greater in an older dog. An interesting factor is the influence of size upon the ejaculate. This is clearly indicated in Table 2:

TABLE 2: INFLUENCE OF THE DOG'S SIZE

Size of Dog	No. of Ejaculates Tested	Individual Motility ++ – ++++	Morphological Abnormalities %	No. of Sperm x 10
			%	
very large	831	3.14	70.60	15.03	898.4
large	409	3.14	71.42	14.12	645.9
medium	381	3.19	72.20	13.47	464.7
small	404	3.19	72.19	12.61	312.6
Total	**2025**	**3.15**	**71.38**	**14.07**	**592.8**

This table clearly shows variations in the number of produced sperm in relation to the size of the dog. Owing to the greater volume of the larger dog's ejaculate, the sperm count is naturally higher. The motility of the sperm is, however, more pronounced in the smaller breeds, and at the same time, morphological abnormalities are considerably fewer. These facts may well be interpreted as nature's way of compensating for the smaller quantity.

Now and again, it is argued that frequent use of a dog at stud has a negative effect on his fertility and diminishes the quality of his sperm. In the Utrecht study, this aspect was also investigated. The volume and sperm quality of ejaculates taken from matings repeated at from one to two days were tested. No noteworthy differences in quality were established.

In the following breed table (Table 3), ten very large breeds, six large breeds, six medium-sized, and six small breeds were tested. The average age of the test dogs is referred to in the table:

*The aim of
every breeder
is to produce
top-quality
puppies of
sound
temperament.*

*Photo: Carol
Ann Johnson.*

ABOVE: A Labrador Retriever bitch nurses her puppies. Consideration must be given to providing clean and hygienic facilities for whelping and rearing the litter.

BELOW: A good brood bitch will instinctively know how to care for her puppies.
Photos: Carol Ann Johnson.

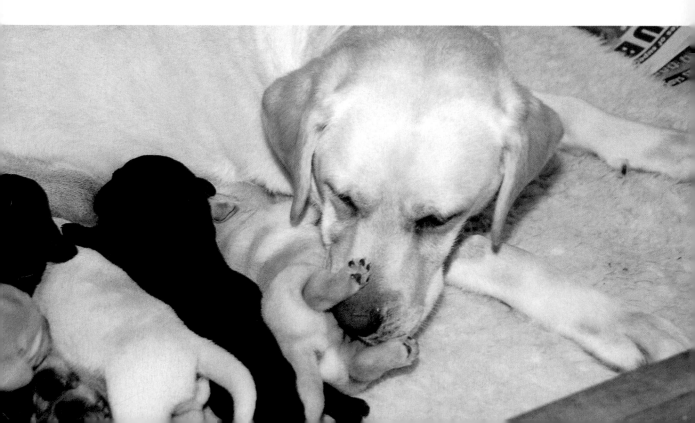

ABOVE: A nice, evenly-matched litter feeding from their mother.

BELOW: If the litter is large, or there is a problem with the bitch's milk-supply, the puppies will have to be given supplementary feeds.

Photos: Carol Ann Johnson.

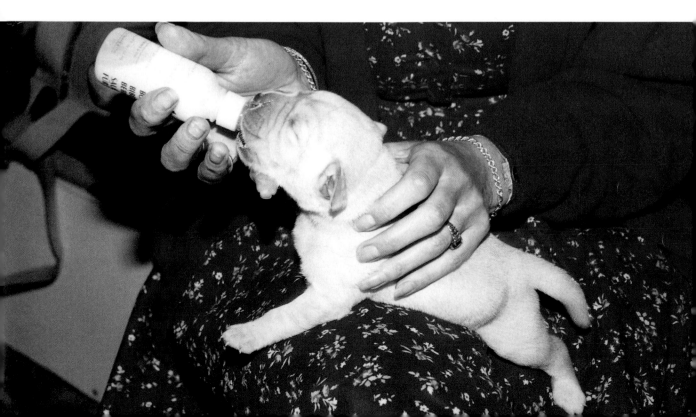

ABOVE: These newborn Golden Retriever puppies are blind and their ears are closed.

BELOW: For the first two weeks, the mother will care for all the puppies' needs, feeding them and cleaning them.

Photos: Steve Nash.

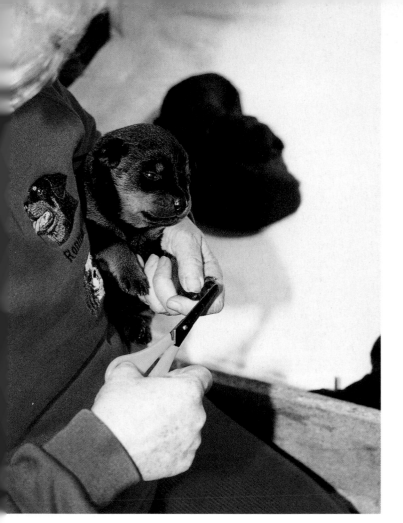

LEFT: It is important to trim puppies' nails regularly or they will scratch the dam when they are feeding, causing her severe discomfort. This Rottweiler puppy is seventeen days old. His eyes and ears have opened.

BELOW: The first worming treatment. A syringe is used to administer a liquid wormer.
Photos: Steve Nash.

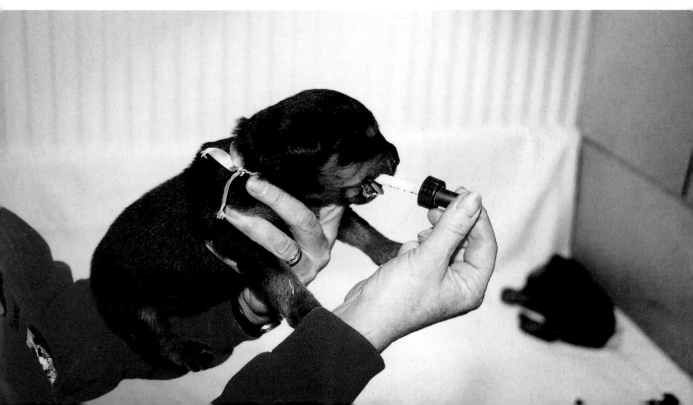

ABOVE: As the puppies become more mobile, the bitch may stand up when they are suckling.

BELOW: Weaning is now underway. Puppies benefit from being fed from a communal dish.   *Photo: Steve Nash.*

ABOVE: Some mothers are more tolerant than others. This Golden Retriever bitch still allows her puppies to suckle, even though they are also feeding independently.

BELOW: There are some benefits for the mother, such as cleaning up the puppies after they have just eaten a meal!

A Shetland Sheepdog puppy ready to explore the outside world. Fresh air and space to play in are essential elements of good rearing.

Photos: Carol Ann Johnson

TABLE 3: RESULTS IN INDIVIDUAL BREEDS

Breed	No. of Ejaculates Tested	Age of Dog	Individual Motility ++ − ++++	%	Morphological Abnormalities %	No. of Sperm X 10
Afghan Hound	79	3.9	3.1	69.4	15.2	595.4
Bouvier des Flandres	84	3.6	3.2	70.4	16.2	867.8
Greyhound	146	4.3	3.2	72.6	12.3	734.8
Belgian Sheepdog	45	5.0	3.1	71.6	11.2	757.3
German Shepherd Dog	65	4.4	3.2	73.1	13.6	976.2
Irish Setter	25	5.0	3.2	70.2	19.3	789.0
Irish Wolfhound	28	2.2	3.0	66.3	19.8	1170.6
Leonberger	27	3.4	3.3	71.7	16.2	1829.3
Newfoundland	158	4.8	3.1	70.8	13.1	773.0
Rottweiler	81	4.2	3.2	72.3	15.6	964.8
Old English Sheepdog	25	2.6	3.4	74.4	17.2	620.9
Collie	45	2.8	3.3	72.4	14.7	734.8
Germ. S'haired Pointer	27	6.0	3.1	70.4	16.7	416.6
Golden Retriever	129	5.0	3.1	70.8	14.5	732.6
Labrador Retriever	43	5.1	3.1	71.1	14.7	630.3
Samoyed	29	6.0	3.1	70.7	14.0	650.4
Bassett Hound	75	3.2	3.1	71.4	16.6	580.6
Bulldog	37	3.8	3.2	70.3	15.6	770.6
French Bulldog	35	2.5	3.3	74.9	9.2	304.5
Bull Terrier	52	3.5	3.1	70.0	14.5	545.3
Dachshund	69	4.0	3.2	72.9	14.9	359.6
Whippet	31	5.9	3.1	71.1	11.1	316.4
Pekingese	56	2.6	3.2	73.3	12.4	212.5
Shih Tzu	36	3.0	3.2	72.3	14.1	231.1
Boston Terrier	125	6.8	3.3	74.0	10.5	330.7
Cairn Terrier	38	4.5	3.1	70.0	12.8	269.2

The above table serves to confirm earlier statements. In large breeds of dog, the sperm volume is greater than in small breeds. Parallel to this, in large breeds there is a higher percentage of morphological abnormalities.

There is one more factor that should be mentioned here, since it is of particular interest when we come to the section on artificial insemination. The number of ejaculates tested is clearly connected with the work of the Institute for Artificial Insemination of the University of Utrecht. I shall, therefore, be returning to these findings in due course. The important point here is the number of ejaculates tested for individual breeds. These figures indicate that certain breeds have had to make use of the services of the Institute to a considerable degree. The statistics given refer to the year 1984.

MATING

In this chapter, I should like to show how breeder and stud dog owner can work together to create the best possible mating conditions for their dogs. But before I begin, I will describe the way the majority of matings normally proceed at the present time.

A SUPERVISED MATING

One of the most important factors in awakening the mating instinct of the two dogs is their initial meeting. In kennels run by the so-called professionals, little time is spent beating about the bush; the whole affair is just a routine matter both for the stud dog owner and the owner of the bitch. When the bitch arrives, often after a long trip, the owner is asked to take her for a short walk so that she can relieve herself. The dog, too, is taken out for the same purpose.

The dogs' collars are then carefully tightened, and both dogs are put on the lead. If the owner of the bitch is considered reliable and capable of controlling the bitch, he or she is permitted to assist. If not, assistance will be given by a more experienced handler.

In the most favourable case, the bitch is allowed to greet the dog at the end of her lead. Once the dogs have touched noses, the handlers immediately get down to business. The bitch's owner is told to stand in front of her, to hold her firmly by the collar, and not to allow her to move away either forwards or sideways. The stud dog owner now brings the dog up behind the bitch. The dog is allowed to sniff briefly at her and lick her a little. He then mounts, clasps the bitch with his forelegs, and begins to work forward. If he does not find the vulva right away – this can happen frequently with beginners – the dog's owner gets down beneath the dogs and supports the bitch so that she cannot sit down. The owner then manipulates the vulva in such a manner that the dog's forward thrusting is brought into the right position.

Experienced dogs are used to being helped and continue to drive forward. The dog's owner now clasps both animals from behind, and – according to the size of the dogs – interlaces the hands beneath the bitch's stomach, and presses the insides of the knees against the dog's thighs. This hold is so skilful that the pair have no choice at all but to remain clamped together.

Even so, the situation requires careful checking. An over-active dog will continue to thrust in his excitement, even though he has not found the target. Now and again, the friction caused by rubbing against the bitch's thighs leads to an ejaculation, and the entire emission drips gently to the ground. Experienced dog owners, therefore, feel carefully to check that everything is in order, and that the penis has penetrated deep into the vagina.

We already know that when the dog ceases to thrust, the second ejaculation takes place, accompanied by heavy engorgement of the bulbus. The pressure, thus exerted, is initially unpleasant for the bitch, and she may try to evade it and tear herself away. The bitch's owner must take great care to calm her down and hold her fast. In my experience, in about 20 per cent of all matings, the dogs do succeed in wrenching themselves apart. This is the stage in which the bulbus is becoming heavily swollen. If the technique employed by the handler prevents the dogs from coming apart during the first two to three minutes, the state already previously described takes effect. The vaginal muscles contract so firmly round the penile bulbus glandis that withdrawal is made impossible until such time as the vaginal muscles relax, and that usually takes some little time (i.e. anything between ten and forty minutes).

Once they are tied in the copulatory lock, the dogs should be kept calm and should, at all costs, be prevented from trying to drag apart. Due to the contraction of the vaginal muscles and the engorgement of the bulbus, the pressure on the penis becomes so great that the dog tries to get down off the bitch. First the forelegs are dropped down to one side, and then one hind leg is lifted over the bitch's back and placed upon the ground. In the end, the two dogs come to rest back to back, tail beside tail, at an angle of approximately 180 degrees. Skilful handling will help the dog to get into this new position, lifting his hind leg over the bitch's back and turning him with the greatest of care. To accomplish the movement without undue pulling and tearing, the stud dog owner manually directs the positioning.

This tail-to-tail position is the typical, natural mating position of the canine species. Even after the move has been completed, it is still advisable to hold both dog and bitch by their collars and to calm them so that they continue to stand steadily. We know that during the tie the third voluminous ejaculation takes place, the flushing of the second ejaculation into the bitch. It is interesting to observe how the dogs work their tongues while standing in this position, and along the bitch's body wave-like ripples pass, leaving the impression that she is literally milking the dog with her vaginal muscles. In the first few minutes of the tie it is quite possible that the bitch will try to evade the internal pressure by sinking down, allowing her hind legs to collapse. The two handlers should act at once to prevent her, since the dog might otherwise be torn or injured.

Earlier on, I mentioned that there is a critical stage at the beginning of the tie when the vaginal muscles and the bulbus are not yet completely locked. Most breeders and stud dog owners regard this stage with considerable trepidation, since it is almost universally believed that conception is only possible if there is a good, long tie. Thus, in order to make doubly sure, it is common practice among stud dog owners to hold the dogs firmly clamped together until the tie comes to an end.

On one memorable occasion in mid-winter, we took a bitch to be mated. Owing to the icy weather, the mating took place in the front room on some old carpets. My bitch weighed around thirty kilograms (66 lbs.), the dog as much as thirty-five kilograms (77lbs.). The dog's owner held him closely embraced, my wife steadied our bitch by her collar, and I lay beneath the bitch, who had taken it into head to sit down! However, the most amusing part was the bitch's behaviour. The effort of holding the dog brought sweat dripping from the stud dog owner's face, and approximately sixty kilograms of dog rested its weight on me – meanwhile the bitch enjoyed a lively TV show throughout the entire forty minutes. The movement of her ears and the expression on her face showed how attentively she followed the activity on the TV screen!

At another mating, we were assisted by my driver who took over the part of the stud dog owner. The comment he made later is worth recording: "If matters were equally complicated in the human being, I would take myself off to a monastery!"

The supervised mating as I have described it, is common practice throughout the world today. Describing these practices, these methods and skills, and explaining them is the ultimate object of this book.

Toward the end of the mating ceremony, the check on the return flow of venous blood is slackened, bringing in its wake detumescence of the bulbus and the release of the two dogs. The approach of this moment is clearly marked by the dogs' behaviour. They become restless and make renewed efforts to pull apart. It is advisable to continue calming them. The parting comes quite suddenly, marked frequently by a kind of gasp expelled by the dog.

When the dogs finally separate, a jet of fluid usually gushes out of the bitch's vagina and pours on to the ground. The less informed breeder regards this with dismay, visualising some of his hoped-for puppies now lying dead in the grass. The careful reader, however, is well aware that this fluid is merely a part of the third ejaculate and contains, therefore, hardly any sperm.

AFTER THE MATING

The next step is a frequent cause of dispute among experts and breeders. Some recommend allowing the bitch to run free. Often, she is clearly suffering from the long period of forced inactivity, and if she is allowed to run free, she is likely to go racing wildly around in her reaction to the released tension. In the horse world, it is common practice to set the mare free after mating, allowing her to gallop around to her heart's content. In the case of the dog, all the experts are unanimous in saying that the bitch must, under no circumstances, be allowed to urinate after being mated. The reader who has studied the bitch's anatomy, depicted in detail in the previous chapter, is aware that the contents of the bladder are discharged via the vagina. Urination would carry away sperm which would otherwise make its way onwards through the bitch's sexual organs. Urination is, therefore, forbidden!

Some breeders, bearing in mind the fact that the purpose of the third ejaculate is to transport the sperm upward toward the bitch's ovaries, seize their bitch the moment the two dogs separate. The bitch is turned on her back, taken on the owner's lap, and, with her tail end positioned higher than her front, she is held in position for five to ten minutes. The breeder soothes the bitch and strokes her stomach, hoping in this way to influence the movement of the sperm in the direction of the ovaries. Afterwards, the bitch is put straight back into the car or into her box, care being taken to see that she does not urinate, and there she is left to sleep for a while.

I consider a period of rest and the prevention of urination sensible precautions, but the procedure described above of holding the bitch upside down after a normal tie appears to me somewhat exaggerated. Just consider nature's lavish waste, the millions of sperm set free. Only a very few of them are able to – only a very few of them need to – reach their target. The amount that has flowed into the bitch during the ten to twenty minute tie is surely enough.

It is a good idea to allow the bitch to rest, although one or two matings have cost me several pairs of chewed shoes, torn car upholstery, and ruined clothing. We had put our rather wound-up bitch straight back into the car, and she appeared to need to work off her exciting experience in this way. Now we have a solid pen in the back of the car, with plenty of old rags in readiness; there the bitch can dig and tear to her heart's content, and nothing of value need be sacrificed.

We humans are always in a hurry! A quick chat after the mating is over, and away we go home, probably on a journey of a hundred miles or more. Please do not do this. Allow your bitch to sleep undisturbed for an hour or two after mating. She needs this. Do not forget what is happening inside the bitch when the two dogs separate. The journey in the direction of the ovaries, this race between sperm, has not yet run its course. The conditions for a continuation of this movement are most favourable in a bitch at rest.

One very experienced breeder, who had owned a great many bitches, convinced me that the constant slight bumping of a car – even on a smooth road – has a very adverse effect upon the bitch. This breeder was also breed adviser to a number of dog clubs and had, in a series of tests, been able to ascertain that bitches compelled to travel by car immediately after mating much more frequently failed to conceive. I was neither able, nor willing, to try this out on my own bitches, but this theory certainly seems to make sense.

We must now return to the stud dog, who we have neglected while dealing with the bitch! Unfortunately, this is just what the majority of breeders actually do. After copulation, the dog has a certain amount of difficulty in drawing his penis back into its sheath. Due to the engorgement of the bulbus, the penis is considerably enlarged. The shorter the tie, the greater the difficulty. After the tie, it is the stud dog owner's business to attend to his dog. To start with, he should tell him what a splendid chap he is and how very well he has done his job. It is to be hoped that both the owners have repeatedly said this to their dogs throughout the entire mating procedure. The dogs should be given the assurance that what they are doing is right, that they are pleasing their owners – this is of decisive importance for future matings.

The stud dog is now doing his best to retract his penis, and a movement characteristic of this stage is walking slowly backwards, step by step. He frequently sits down and tries to facilitate the retraction by repeatedly licking his sexual organs. Calming him down, praising him, rubbing him gently on the back, especially along the croup above the root of his tail, and stroking firmly along his flanks from front to rear will help in this process. Afterwards, when everything is back in place, the dog should be allowed to rest and sleep for an hour or two.

A NATURAL MATING

To be quite honest, I am actually not at all happy about all these handling skills that I have just been describing. Admittedly, they are common practice. This is exactly what takes place in the great majority of matings. But is all this really necessary? There should be a way in which dogs can meet, play together, and mate quite naturally without all this human assistance.

Let us return to the moment when our two dogs first meet. It would be ideal if – even before the bitch comes into season – the two could be brought together and, in making normal social contact, could come to like one another. This would be the most favourable situation, but unfortunately in most cases, it is just wishful thinking.

When a bitch that is already in season comes to us to be mated, we like to give her and the dog an opportunity to get used to one another. So we put the dog in one run and the bitch in the adjoining run. The two are now able to make contact in the presence of their owners. Both are off the leash, but wearing collars. The wire-mesh inhibits any undesirable clash, and the dogs are able to make nose-to-nose contact and become accustomed to one another. The bitch relieves herself in her run, leaving a scent mark for the dog. On the leash, and in the company of their owners, many bitches can behave quite ferociously, but in this way – one dog on each side of a fence – the tension is gradually relaxed.

When the time is ripe, the two begin to demonstrate liking and show an increased interest in one another. At this point, they frequently begin to stimulate one another. The dog, of sound temperament and sure of himself on his home ground, becomes increasingly interested. The bitch, too, shows by her behaviour that she does not dislike him. On occasion, she even presents herself to him rear-end on, and with her tail held to one side.

We breed Bull Terriers, a breed whose social behaviour has been disturbed by the unfortunate fighting dog legacy. They will, as a rule, not suffer any other dog to approach their territory. For the last twenty-five years, we have owned stud dogs, and with the aid of the simple method for establishing first contact, we have been able to achieve an excellent success rate on all matings after a free preliminary courtship.

Much here depends on the way the bitch's owner handles the situation. If the bitch is at all aggressive toward the dog, he must make it clear to her that her suitor is a splendid fellow and her aggressive behaviour is totally misplaced! Problem bitches are usually those that are kept solely as pets, those that are too shy, or unused to strangers. They need to be encouraged, to be given the feeling that this is a rather nice dog with which she may play. If, on the other hand, the owner is a little heavy-handed with his bitch and she is too intensely under his thumb, then it is a good thing to find another assistant.

Should it prove impossible to overcome the tendency to aggression, it is most probably not the right day, and a new date should be fixed. If it is still impossible to overcome the bitch's aggression, either by checking it or postponing the date, then the mating must be cancelled. In our kennels no bitch wearing a muzzle, or with her muzzle taped, has ever been mated.

Let us now return to our two dogs who have had a good opportunity to get acquainted through the wire-mesh fence. This period of making contact should last for at least ten minutes and can, if needed, easily be extended to an hour or two. When the dogs' behaviour begins to indicate that they are becoming interested in one another, or that the bitch is at least no longer afraid of the dog, the door between the two runs is opened and the dog allowed to go in to the bitch. Frequently, I open this door under strong protest from the bitch's owner, who is busy telling me just how difficult the last mating was, and that his bitch is sure to be either aggressive or else frightened. I am allowed to open this door "on my own responsibility", and up to the present, everything has always gone off well. The very fact that the dogs are off the leash, plus the peaceful surroundings, and the time allowed for the bitch to get used to the new situation, help both animals to relax.

Anyone who has had the good fortune to be present at a mating arising out of natural affection is only too glad to forget the more-or-less tolerated mating described earlier on. Attentively, the dog inspects the scent mark left by the bitch; she, for her part sniffs at his ears and neck and also his penis. It is particularly noticeable that in this scenario it is not only the dog that does the courting. If the bitch has been brought to the dog on the right day, she also does her level best to stimulate the dog. It is perfectly normal, a part of the game, for the bitch who is sexually excited and active to mount the dog, especially if he is spending too much time in following up her scent marks.

Obviously, the dogs will not always follow this pattern of behaviour. As has already been repeatedly stated, dogs are not machines! Now and again, a growl or even a playful snap may be heard. It may even be that the bitch presents herself to the dog with her tail carefully held to one side and her vulva working, and the dog goes on examining her scent marks. This form of mating requires patience. I, for my part, find it intensely interesting to watch the interplay, the changing roles, of the courting dogs. As long as no serious differences arise, they should be left to play.

It is important that the playground should never be too large, approximately twenty square metres (25 square yards) is an optimum size. If the dogs are given too much room, they may well dash at full gallop into a distant corner of the garden and disappear behind some bushes in order to be undisturbed. There is nothing wrong with this if the dogs are experienced, but it does deprive us of the chance to help if help is needed.

As a rule the process of mutual courtship leads the two dogs exactly to the point where we want to have them, the point at which the bitch willingly allows the dog to mount her, and a completely natural mating takes place. Now I shall have to confess that I take some action, which the firmly convinced ethologists would not approve of. I go to the united pair and assist them, in much the same way as was described at the beginning of this chapter. I see to it that the two are supported in their copulatory lock for the first two or three minutes, then turn the male carefully until the dogs are standing tail to tail, where they are held and comforted.

Yes, I am well aware it is not consistent to stipulate a natural mating on the one hand and then to go in and interfere. I have, however, been present at a number of natural matings in which the dogs did not tie. The bitch, trying to avoid the internal pressure, pulled away at the crucial moment and left the poor dog standing with all the precious fluid dripping on to the ground. The breeder, watching his puppies soaking away into the ground, was by no means pleased.

It is impossible to explain why in a high percentage of these natural matings a tie is not achieved. It may well be a sign that the moment is not right, but it is also possible that what is happening is really an indication of degeneration, since for a great many dog generations it has been the normal practice for human aid to be given in this situation. But to the credit of our dogs, it must also be said that we have had several dozen natural matings in which the tie was achieved, and the dogs subsequently separated, without any human aid whatever. This applies especially to matings between our own stud dogs and brood bitches. In those cases, everything was right: the dogs liked each other, they played the courtship game, and it was the right day.

When discussing these problems, it must be kept in mind that matings among pure-bred dogs are, in the nature of things, adversely affected by unfavourable circumstances. In the wild, animals

A NATURAL MATING
Photography E. Trumler.

Sniffing noses.

*Sniffing the
genital
region.*

*Playful
rejection by
the bitch in
the early
stages.*

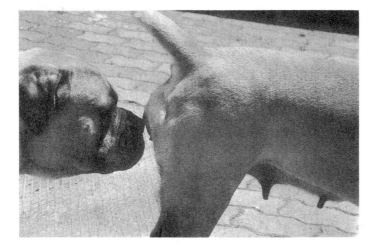

Sniffing the genital region. Note the typical tail position of the bitch, indicating readiness to mate.

Natural mating. The bitch mounting. An extra encouragement for the dog.

The dog, his penis erect, but still in the wrong position.

The tie.

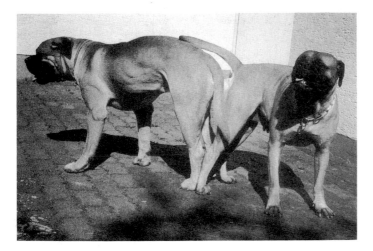

The copulatory lock.

mate instinctively with well-known members of their pack, the mating takes place according to an inbuilt timetable. We dog breeders often travel hundreds of miles and take our bitches to dogs that are complete strangers to them; we are always in a tearing hurry, and how often does our patience desert us? Have you ever checked up on this? Most matings take place on Saturday or Sunday! I wonder why? I simply cannot believe that the sexual cycle of the bitch can be reprogrammed according to the human calendar. It is, consequently, not at all surprising that matings between our domestic dogs turn out, at times, to be highly complicated.

I hope, therefore, that you will pardon my inconsistency in helping the dogs at the moment of copulation. I could have written quite different things here in order to keep in with the ethologists. But those who read this book would have wondered why in my natural matings the dogs do not pull apart, whereas in yours they always do!

The ethologists are quite right in using the behaviour of crossbred, wild dogs to discover the original pack behaviour of our domestic dogs. In the wild dog, the canine instinct is still very much intact, and this is, of course, also reflected in their mating behaviour. The Society for

Research into Domestic Animals has provided the nine interesting photographs of mating behaviour, which are featured in this book. These photographs illustrate natural mating behaviour right through the phases of mutual stimulation, the bitch playfully rejecting and then mounting the dog, and finally the tie. To complete the picture, it should not be forgotten that the pack is standing round like a crowd of inquisitive spectators – known in the human world as voyeurs-- whose presence in no way disturbs the mating couple. The first seven photographs are of one mating and the final two of a second. The final photograph illustrates quite clearly that the dog is not in the least upset when the bitch sinks to the ground. In fact, both dog and bitch appear to be quite content with this awkward position.

GETTING THE TIMING RIGHT

What is to be done if the two do not begin to relax and play, and do not show the slightest inclination to mate? You may observe that when the dog approaches, the bitch either sits down, lies on her back, or slides along the ground on her tummy. The diagnosis: it is not the right day. What should be done? I would advise waiting for at least six hours. It is also quite possible for the dog to show little or no interest, even though the bitch tries her best to stimulate him. Throughout the years, I have learned to put more trust in my dog than in the owners of bitches, or the vaginal smear taken by a veterinarian. The diagnosis in this case: the time is not right. What is to be done? Again, wait patiently. It should be a basic rule to separate the dogs after twenty minutes if they do not mate. Another attempt may be made six hours later. Experience will show that a longer break of at least twelve or even twenty-four hours is called for if the pair demonstrate obvious signs of not being ready.

Owners should not allow their dogs to over-exert themselves. Our own impatience easily transfers itself to the animals and makes them nervous or insecure, thus inhibiting the possibility of a speedy mating. I do know just how frustrating waiting can be. One very good bitch had been mated twice – both times unsuccessfully – to a stud dog abroad. She was mated the first time on the twelfth and thirteenth days of her heat, and the second time on the fourteenth and fifteenth days. The mating took place both times according to the procedure described earlier, with both animals on the leash and with a certain amount of assistance from their owners.

This bitch was brought to our stud dog on the sixteenth day of her heat, but the dog was not interested. Neither was he interested on the eighteenth day. But three completely unproblematic matings took place on the twentieth, twenty-second and twenty-third days, and the bitch subsequently had a healthy litter of eight puppies. The bitch's owner lived a good 200 kilometres (125 miles) away, and this meant a total of five different journeys before success was achieved. However, the breeder had a good idea as to how to breed his bitch successfully in future – although there is no guarantee that the bitch would always be ready at the same time.

It is a probability, but never a certainty, that a bitch's oestrous cycle will always follow a regular pattern. We have known bitches to be mated the first time on the sixteenth day, whereas on following occasions they reached their peak either a few days earlier or some days later. As a general rule, it may be accepted that, according to the progress of the previous heat, a bitch may reach her peak either between the ninth and twelfth days, or between the sixteenth and twenty-first days.

Let us take a look at this subject from a different angle. Our foundation bitch was mated with a young dog on the fifteenth day of her heat. Everything went well, and we felt very confident. On earlier occasions this had proved to be the right day. Five days later – that is to say on the twentieth day – our own stud dog gave the alarm. He showed quite clearly that this was the right day. Since I had already discovered that it was not wise to regard myself as brighter than my dog, I set off once again on a journey of 900 kilometres (550 miles). This mating went off beautifully too, but the whelping date and the size of the litter proved conclusively that the mating on the twentieth day of the heat was the one that had proved successful.

In fact, intelligent dogs that follow their instincts should be highly prized. We have owned two very successful dogs of this kind, dogs that mated only on the right day. Some dogs will mate everything that is put before them, and at any point of the heat! In such cases, it seems probable that instinct is subordinated to an over-active sexual drive. There are bitches, too, that will allow themselves to be mated at any time from the fifth to the sixteenth day of their heat, even though they have not reached their peak. Dogs with intact instincts only mate such bitches at the peak of their heat, which is, of course, of vital importance to fertilisation.

Dogs can demonstrate definite likes and dislikes. One of our very experienced stud dogs had a most beautiful bitch brought to him on several occasions, but for no obvious reason, he firmly rejected her. He just did not like her smell. When she was at the peak of her season and trying to stimulate him, he snapped at her quite fiercely and was totally unwilling to mate with her. This bitch was mated to another dog on the very same day and conceived! Other bitches kept together with a dog will only allow themselves to be mated with him.

There are dogs and bitches who live in close contact with their owners from an early age and have not been properly socialised with other dogs. These animals look upon people as their sole partners, and they are not willing to mate with their own kind. If an attempt to mate two dogs has to be called off because one or the other of the two makes it clear that it is not the right day, a second or third attempt – at an interval of between twelve and twenty-four hours – usually leads to a successful natural mating. Occasionally, it may prove to be too late and the peak may be passed. In this case, there is nothing to be done but wait until the next heat. However, in my own experience, out of around two hundred matings, using eight stud dogs owned by us, only about ten bitches went home unmated, although the time factor varied considerably in a number of cases.

I consider that matings should be repeated several times. More than ninety per cent of all bitches mated at our kennels were served at least twice. As a rule, the dogs appear to enjoy themselves, and the probability of success is considerably increased. The reason for this is quite simply biological. As has been seen, the decisive factor is the moment of ovulation, since only then are the ova ready for fertilisation. If the life span of the spermatozoa is taken into consideration, and two matings take place at an interval of thirty-six to forty-eight hours, it becomes clear that in the bitch's genital tract there are active, healthy sperm to fertilise the ova over a period of from sixty to seventy hours. A repeated mating helps to overcome the difficulty of determining the exact time of ovulation.

Now and again, however, a stud dog will refuse to mate a second time if the bitch is already past her peak. It is an interesting fact that in every case of this kind, the bitch conceived from her first mating. This is easily explained since the mating, forty-eight hours previously, had taken place when the ova were ready for fertilisation.

In this chapter, I have tried to explain the natural mating behaviour of our dogs, and to point out what has been made out of it by human beings. I would be delighted if as many dog owners as possible were to allow their animals to follow their own sound instincts when mating, and not to insist on the old, established routine. The undeniable advantage of a natural mating is that it takes place, as a rule, on the right day and thus increases the probability of conception.

FAILURE TO CONCEIVE

What happens if the bitch does not conceive? In all probability, there is a physical problem with one of the animals. In the case of the dog, this can easily be checked. An experienced veterinarian will extract some semen and examine it carefully. This is not particularly easy, as will be seen in the following section on artificial insemination, but the examination is considerably less complicated than is the case with the bitch.

What is the possible cause in the case of the bitch? I only need to give one example from my own experience. We once had a bitch who, when mated to two proven dogs, failed to conceive on two separate occasions. We then received an 'inside tip' from England, informing us that in such cases experienced English breeders had their bitches injected with a long-acting antibiotic, around twelve to twenty-four hours before mating. This was in the early sixties. Somewhat hesitantly, a veterinarian followed this recommendation, and the bitch went on to have a nice litter. In a sizeable small animal practice in Cologne, this became the accepted method for treating two-thirds of the bitches that had formerly failed to conceive. Later on, however, in Vienna, we went from one veterinarian to another and could find no one who had ever heard of this practice and none who was willing to inject an antibiotic, seemingly for no apparent reason. In the end, we managed to find one who was willing, and we had a fine litter of puppies from this mating.

Today an accepted practice is to examine the vagina for bacterial infection when taking a smear. Quite frequently, a high degree of bacterial infection is detected. This bacterial infection alters the vaginal secretion, and the semen ejaculated into the vagina is affected. An infection of the sexual organs of this kind is, in the normal way, treated with heavy doses of antibiotics. One thing should be made abundantly clear here; this treatment must be carried out prior to mating! I would also stress that any treatment involving heavy doses of antibiotics administered during pregnancy may easily lead to malformation in the puppies.

In addition to vaginal infections, there are other agents that may be the cause of infertility in the bitch:

a) Insufficient hormone production.
b) Excessive hormone production.
c) Inhibited ovulation.

At the University Clinic for Obstretrics, Gynaecology, and Anthropology at the University of Veterinary Medicine in Vienna, under the direction of Professor K. Arbeiter, a special service for breeders has been in operation since the early seventies. This service involves a systematic examination and treatment of brood bitches:

1. An initial examination at the start of the heat.
2. Determining the correct day for mating (i.e. vaginal smears as from day five at one or two-day intervals, and, at the same time, checking the hormone level.
3. Continued checks after mating up to approximately the twenty-eighth day, at which point the presence of a pregnancy may be ascertained with some certainty.

Happily, repeated checks of this kind are only needed in problematic cases. It may be an optimistic estimate, but I believe only about one bitch in ten is in need of this particular care. However, the service is absolutely ideal for complicated cases. There are, on the other hand, very many excellent veterinarians and clinics ready and able to offer expert advice and treatment. Admittedly, most veterinarians are unable to offer a service of this kind simply because their surgeries are not equipped with the necessary apparatus. The dog owner is well advised to ascertain what is possible and what necessary and to choose his veterinarian with care.

ARTIFICIAL INSEMINATION
THE PROS AND CONS

We have now arrived at a very controversial subject. Many breeders believe that it should be possible to make astronomical progress for their dogs with the aid of artificial insemination, since the semen from top-quality stud dogs may be used throughout the world. Others reject artificial insemination on the grounds that, with its aid, animals can reproduce themselves, even though this would have been an impossibility in the natural course of events.

As is the case with most things, artificial insemination has several aspects, both positive and negative. Let us examine the possibilities of its use, consider the implications, and then deal with its up-to-date technical application.

The University of Vienna considers it reasonable to employ artificial insemination in the following cases:

1. To overcome anatomical obstacles to mating.
2. Reluctance to mate on the part of the dog; refusal to mate on the part of the bitch.
3. Insemination with frozen semen.

It is an undeniable fact that owing to their excessive weight, some very large breeds have mating difficulties. Other breeds have developed such weak hindquarters, over the years, that many dogs find it anatomically impossible to mount the bitch. Where this is the case, it is, in my opinion, a culpable offence against the health of our dogs to make use of artificial insemination. It is the breeder's responsibility to breed healthy dogs. Healthy dogs are able to mate. Unfortunately, the human desire for novelty has produced extremes in size and shape in dogs, and has also produced dogs that are cripples. The responsible veterinarian should never allow artificial insemination to be used in order to reproduce animals that are so far removed from the norm.

I know of only one exception that might be made to the application of artificial insemination in the case of anatomical defects, and that is for a top-quality, prepotent stud dog that has been injured in an accident. I am thinking here of a stud dog that has lost a leg, but who is of great importance to a breed. An exception in this case is justifiable, since a leg lost in an accident is not an hereditary factor.

The pros and cons are less clear in the second case – reluctance and refusal to mate. I am quite prepared to recommend that artificial insemination should generally be rejected in order to assist animals that are unwilling to mate. In principle, animals of this kind serve to retard and not to promote a breed. Willingness to mate and ability to mate are two vital factors in the natural behaviour of every living creature. In nature, this lack of instinct prevents reproduction – human beings should subscribe to this wisdom and not trespass on nature's preserves.

There are, however, interesting borderline cases. We once had a ten-month-old youngster who had already successfully mated one of our white, brood bitches. The second bitch that came to him had already been mated in a previous season by another of our stud dogs. The young stud dog met his new partner full of expectations – and a terrible fight ensued. It turned out that the bitch, who was a brindle, had an obsession for white dogs! She subsequently behaved equally badly to all coloured Bull Terriers – our youngster had been her first victim.

I have already mentioned the disordered social behaviour among the fighting breeds; our young dog, despite his youth, gave as good as he got. The two of them rolled away down a densely planted thicket of rose bushes, and it took me a good five minutes to work my way through the thorns down to the battling dogs and to separate them. From that moment on, the dog was difficult to handle. He was willing enough to mate with friendly bitches, but the slightest sign of a growl called forth a ferocious fight. In order not to overtax our own nerves and those of the bitches' owners, we made it a rule to mate this dog solely by means of artificial insemination.

As has already been said, this was a borderline case, a concession to an excellent pedigree, an otherwise very good temperament, and a good anatomy. Today, I would definitely endorse the opinion that it is better for dogs – for entire breeds – not to reproduce themselves when, even at the peak of the heat, the fighting instinct overlays the sexual drive. Each individual case should, however, be considered on its own merits, taking into account all the advantages and disadvantages.

To sum up, I would say that, as a general rule, it is no more justifiable to make use of artificial insemination to overcome psychological problems than it is to overcome physical problems. We must have some guarantee that breeds will not suffer through the use of artificial insemination, and dogs with defects and those of poor temperament should never be used for breeding. I believe that in this sphere a great burden of responsibility rests upon clinics and veterinarians.

The use of the frozen semen is the last of the three points set out in Vienna. With the aid of frozen semen, use can be made of top-quality, well-proven stud dogs on a much wider basis. I am in full agreement with this point, provided it is ensured that the stud dog being used has the ability to mate in the normal way – i.e. that he possesses natural mating drive.

Consider for a moment the quarantine laws that block all interchange with a number of leading dog-breeding countries; just think about the distances from continent to continent. It is surely much simpler to transport deep-frozen semen in refrigerated containers than to transport our dogs. I am firmly convinced that science has made such great progress in the use of artificial insemination that it could, if properly employed, have a decisive influence on a number of breeds. The method has been so much improved of late that results with deep-frozen semen show a similar success rate (approximately 50 per cent) – a similar chance of a litter to that in the case of a direct mating.

It goes without saying that the strictest control is absolutely essential in all breeding carried out with artificial insemination. There must be definite guarantees that the dog living overseas, whose name is on the pedigree, is the actual father of the puppies. Fraudulent practices would otherwise become easier in this field than in normal direct matings. A great deal of experience has been gained in artificial insemination with other species of animals, and to this end, we might be able to learn how to solve such security problems. Fortunately, scientists have evolved methods of control for gene technology that make falsification extremely difficult, and they are also able to establish parentage beyond all doubt.

When seen from the viewpoint of making progress in dog breeding and overcoming the problems of time and distance, artificial insemination must be considered a valuable instrument. Thus, it is important to understand the method adopted in its use.

TAKING SPERM

The taking of sperm from the dog is a very much more complicated matter than is the case with the human male. I well remember one experience we had in the mid-sixties. We had imported a stud dog, who was said to have sired several litters. We even had some fine photographs of his offspring. Yet once he was with us, we had problems. He was not very willing to mate, and even when he had mated, there were no puppies. We took him to a renowned university clinic, where it was decided to extract some sperm from the dog. A very young veterinarian came along, bringing a vast apparatus known as an artificial vagina. With this he intended to collect the sperm. The poor dog had no idea what was going on. Despite several attempts, he did not produce any sperm.

The next day, he was introduced to a bitch in season, and a trial mating produced an ejaculate.

ARTIFICIAL INSEMINATION

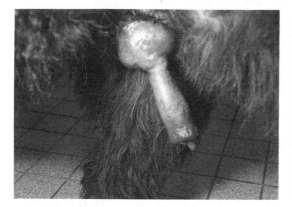

Extracting the semen.

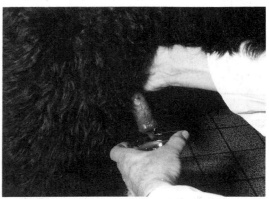

Collecting the semen.

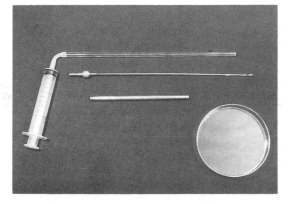

Technical equipment for insemination.

Introducing the semen fluid with a pipette.

This, and later examinations in two further institutes, showed with complete certainty that he had never at any time been able to produce fertile sperm.

One more example serves to illustrate the same kind of problem. After about twenty litters, one of our dogs appeared to fail. Despite trouble-free matings, three bitches in a row did not conceive. We decided to have his sperm tested. We took him to a well-known small animal specialist, 200 kilometres (125 miles) away. We had previously been assured that sperm testing was a routine matter at this clinic. The dog was taken into a small surgery and placed on the table. An assistant tried to obtain some sperm by manipulation. The surgery, however, appeared also to serve as a hallway, and every minute or two people kept coming in to fetch something or to ask a question. This did not help our dog, and he failed to produce any semen.

It is obvious from this that a specialist is needed to extract semen from a dog. If this is the case, it is really quite an easy task. The dog's mental state must be taken carefully into account, he must be sufficiently stimulated, and the required skills must be brought to bear. I should like to describe the procedure, as carried out at the Institute for Artificial Insemination of the University of

Utrecht. At the Institute, a bitch at the peak of her heat is always present when carrying out artificial insemination directly from the dog to the bitch. The bitch is encouraged to stimulate the dog, and the dog is given every opportunity to sniff at the bitch's genitals. At the same time, the expert massages the dog's penis quite slowly. The preputium enclosing the glans penis is worked slowly back, until it has been pushed right over the bulb of the penis at the end of the penile shaft. The penis is held above the bulbus and gently pulsated to stimulate an erection. This method leads to a full erection of the penis and ejaculation follows. The sperm is collected in a shallow glass dish. The end of the penis is tapped and rubbed repeatedly against the glass, a movement that clearly encourages ejaculation. As a general rule, approximately 0.5-1 cubic centimetres of the second ejaculate are recovered.

The ejaculate is examined, first its volume, colour and consistency, then – under the microscope – its motility, density and deviating pathological forms. Statistics collated by the University of Vienna show the normal values in the main secretion.

TABLE 4: NORMAL VALUES IN THE DOG SEMEN – MAIN SECRETION

Volume ml.	Colour	Consistency	Motility %	Density % /mm	Path.Forms %
0.5-1	greyish-white	milky	> 70	> 100.000	> 25

If the quality test of the semen proves positive, the ejaculate is diluted. This is done with one of various substances based on milk and egg yolk. This substance is a replacement for the amount of fluid normally stemming from the third ejaculate, which is essential to the progress of the semen up into the uterine horns and the fallopian tubes. The mixture of semen and fluid is then introduced into the bitch's sexual tract. It can also be shock frozen, transported in this condition, and used to inseminate another bitch in a different place.

THE PROCESS OF INSEMINATION

A pipette – from 25 to 40 centimetres in length, according to the size of the bitch – is required. The pipette is attached to a 10 millilitre syringe by means of a bent connecting piece.

The diluted semen, containing a minimum of 100 million motile spermatozoa, is drawn up into the pipette via the syringe. The syringe is then lubricated with a neutral ointment. The owner holds the bitch firmly in the standing position, and the veterinarian carefully slides the pipette through the vulva into the vagina and pushes it in as far as it will go. An exact knowledge of the bitch's anatomy is a very essential point, for the pipette has to be carefully manipulated past the clitoris and, on its way to the uterus, the orifice of the bladder must not be mistaken for the cervix.

If the vagina is roomy enough, a careful finger can help to find the way to the cervix. In the most favourable cases, it is possible to insert the pipette right up to the uterus, but – using this method – it is not always possible. When the pipette has been manoeuvred into the right position, a small portion of the seminal fluid is slowly discharged. Then, an attempt is made to insert the pipette still further and, finally, the remainder of the fluid is discharged slowly into the bitch's genital tract.

When all the fluid has been discharged, the pipette is slowly and carefully withdrawn. The bitch's hindquarters are raised, avoiding any pressure on her underside. Her vaginal orifice is closed by inserting a finger as deep as it will go. One hand strokes her back at the root of the tail, and gentle massage of the clitoris, with the free fingers of the other hand, serves to stimulate the bitch. The aim of this procedure is to imitate, as closely as possible, the normal tie. The manipulating finger brings about wave-like reflexes in the bitch, similar to those observed in a natural tie. These rippling movements are instrumental in propelling the sperm in the direction of the fallopian tubes. The success of the expert with skilful hands may easily be seen from the bitch's reaction after the slow, and careful, withdrawal of the stimulating and obstructing hands. I have seen some bitches as excited as though there had been a genuine tie, who – when returned to the car – let off steam in a riot of destruction.

In recent years the procedure has been improved, and it is now possible, via a vaginal tube, to insert the inseminate so deeply into the bitch that the seminal fluid is discharged into the uterus itself, via the cervix, thus enhancing the chances of success. An artificial insemination success rate of approximately 60 per cent is achieved with the pipette method. It is, however, advisable – depending on the stage of the oestrus – to repeat the insemination after an interval of twenty-four to forty-eight hours. The prospect of success is thereby considerably increased.

SUCCESS RATE

In calculating the artificial insemination success rate at Utrecht, it is important to bear in mind that the dogs primarily treated at this Institute are those that have considerable mating problems. Seen from this aspect, Professor Hendrikse's statement that a success rate of 60 per cent was achieved for all those cases in which both vaginal smear and semen quality were in good order is remarkable – especially as a success rate of 60-70 per cent is regarded as average for normal matings. At an institute of this kind, which by the way has been offering its services to breeders almost free of charge for many years, the human factor also has to be taken into account when calculating success rates. Vaginal smears show that around 25 per cent of the bitches are brought in on the wrong day, quite a large number of breeders were only willing to bring their bitches at the weekend, and many did not return for the second insemination, even though the vaginal smear pinpointed this as essential.

A total of 2,776 pairs came to Utrecht in one year, and from the artificial insemination carried out, there were 1,155 litters. This shows a success rate of 41.6 per cent. Despite the excellent and inexpensive services afforded at Utrecht, a considerable number of breeders failed either to send in the promised confirmation of success or to report a miss. Where no report was received, the mating was treated as a miss, but this remains an unknown factor.

TABLE 5: SUCCESS RATES FOR ARTIFICIAL INSEMINATION IN VARIOUS BREEDS

Breed	Success Rate	Breed	Success Rate
Staffordshire Bull Terrier	66.0	Boston Terrier	55.8
Whippet	57.0	Siberian Husky	55.0
Shih Tzu	53.0	Bull Terrier	39.7
Dachshund	52.3	Boxer	36.8
Bassett Hound	50.7	Old English Sheepdog	35.0
Cocker Spaniel	50.0	Airedale Terrier	31.8
Shetland Sheepdog	50.0	St Bernard	30.0
Yorkshire Terrier	48.0	Bouvier des Flandres	28.0
West Highland White	43.0	Samoyed	20.8
Miniature Schnauzer	40.0	Afghan Hound	9.0

On reading these figures, some breeders, maybe even some breed clubs, will become aware, possibly for the first time, that artificial insemination is actually carried out on dogs of their breed. It must, however, be remembered that the above list is incomplete, since it contains only those breeds that have fairly frequent recourse to artificial insemination at Utrecht.

In this connection, I should like to refer back to Table 3, already familiar to us in the section on sperm testing. This table supplies us with a survey of the semen quality of the various breeds tested. From the twenty-eight breeds of dog listed in the original table, I have selected ten from which stemmed most of the ejaculates examined in the test series. It would not be wrong to conclude that for these particular breeds, artificial insemination is of considerable significance.

TABLE 6: BREEDS IN WHICH ARTIFICIAL INSEMINATION PLAYS A CONSIDERABLE ROLE

Breed	No. of Ejaculates Tested	Breed	No. of Ejaculates Tested
Newfoundland	158	Rottweiler	81
Greyhound	146	Afghan Hound	79
Golden Retriever	129	Basset Hound	75
Boston Terrier	125	Dachshund	69
Bouvier des Flandres	84	German Shepherd Dog	65

These figures were published in 1984. I was concerned by Professor Hendrikse's statement that, in the case of the Newfoundland, for example, the inability of the dog to mount the bitch has frequently made the use of artificial insemination unavoidable. At this point, we should bear in mind that artificial insemination is carried out at this clinic almost exclusively directly from dog to bitch, and that the use of frozen semen from other countries, as mentioned earlier on, plays little or no role at all in these figures.

This extremely creditable research work is concentrated chiefly on fields in which anatomical or psychological anomalies are present. In Chapter Three: The Brood Bitch, I quoted the scientist M.J. Freak, who pointed out in the year 1962 that veterinarians and breeders bear a mutual responsibility for the fact that so many bitches today are unable to bear their young without a Caesarean section. Yet, the ability to bear young must surely be regarded as one of the most important features when selecting dogs for breeding. I should add to this: I am firmly convinced that the ability of dogs to reproduce themselves, without the aid of instruments, is of equal importance!

Let us say 'yes' to artificial insemination to help us span the great distances between the continents, or when quarantine laws prohibit a meaningful breeding interchange. A success rate of as much as 50 per cent may be counted upon today in the use of deep-frozen semen. Employing the vaginal tube and inseminate described above, this success rate might well be improved by a further 10 per cent.

In the interest of the health of our dogs, let us say a definite 'no' to all artificial insemination arising from anatomical or psychological inability to achieve a normal mating – unless we have complete assurance that the inability in question is not of an hereditary nature. Breeds of dogs in which artificial insemination has to be carried out on a large scale to ensure the continuance of the breed are in direct contrast to the highest breeding ideals, to breed healthy dogs!

Chapter Six

THE GESTATION PERIOD

We left our two dogs just after their copulatory lock had come to an end, and they had both withdrawn to enjoy a quiet hour's sleep. Our stud dog has now done his part toward producing offspring, and we shall not meet him again until he begins to take his share in teaching his puppies. But what will be taking place from now on in the genital organs of the bitch?

THE PROCESS OF CONCEPTION

Tests have proved that the first spermatozoa arrive at the upper ends of the uterine horns, at the entrance to the oviduct, only 25 seconds after the ejaculation. The interaction of sperm motility, contractions, and the flushing effect of the third ejaculate has already been discussed. The sperm and the ovum meet in the fallopian tube, the oviduct. The sperm penetrates the ovum - the head of only one spermatozoon drives into the ovum membrane. The tail of the sperm, which serves only to propel the spermato onward, is discarded at this point.

The ovum and the spermatozoon unite to form a zygote in which the genes of both the parents are united. The zygote divides to form a blastocyst. By means of cell division (mitosis), the embryo grows continuously. Within a period of approximately one week, the tiny embryo gravitates through the oviduct down into the uterus. On arrival there, it has attained the size of a minute mulberry, and is, therefore, known as a morula. In order to clarify this stage of development, although the morula is the result of numerous cell divisions, this compact agglomerate of cells is only very slightly larger than was the original minute unfertilised ovum. That is to say, it has a diameter of one hundred and eighty thousandth of a millimetre! The layman cannot help but be filled with amazement to discover just how far scientists have been able to go in studying all these individual developments!

On arriving in the uterus, the morula is now termed the blastula. The blastula implants itself in the mucous membranes of the uterus, a process that is known as the nidation. Nidation is completed approximately eighteen days after fertilisation, and it is at this stage that the actual pregnancy commences.

THE DEVELOPING FOETUSES

Up to the time that it enters the uterus, the morula is sustained by the oviduct's epithelial secretion; after nidation in the uterus, the blastula is directly connected with the dam's circulatory system. At this stage, the embryos lie in a row down the length of the two uterine horns. In the early phases of gestation, the uterine horns resemble strings of beads with each embryo lying separately, enclosed in its own individual foetal membranes. As the foetuses grow large toward the end of the pregnancy, the indentations gradually disappear, and the foetal membranous sacs end up touching

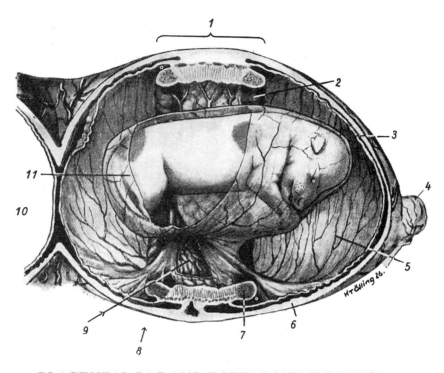

PLACENTAL SAC AND FOETAL MEMBRANES
Source: Zietschmann and Kroelling, 1958.

KEY: *1 = Zonary placenta, 2 = margo hematoma of zonary placenta, 3 = allantoic chorion, 4 = ovary, 5 = allantoic blood vessels, 6 = wall of uterus, 7 = margo hematoma, 8 = umbilical cord with blood vessels, 9 = umbilicus bladder, 10 = neighbouring placental sac, 11 = allantoic amnion.*

one another along the lengths of the uterine horns. The placental sac is, firstly, almost a circular form. As the pregnancy progresses, the shape alters until it become elliptical.

The individual foetus is enveloped in four embryonic membranes: the amnion is the puppy's immediate inner covering; the chorion forms the outer covering; and the allantois and the yolk sac lie in between these two. The embryonic secretion is transferred via the allantois to the dam's bladder, and via the yolk sac to her bowels.

Slender hair-like projections, known as villi, grow out from the chorion. These penetrate deeply into the membranes of the uterus and form a zonary placenta, thus establishing the connecting mechanism to the dam's bloodstream from which the embryo is nourished. After nidation in the uterine mucous membranes, the embryo is joined not only to the dam's blood circulation, but also to her bladder and bowels.

As the foetuses develop, the inner sac – the amnion – fills with a fluid in which the embryo swims. The urine that passes through the allantois forms a second, liquid cushion so that the foetus is very well protected against outside physical forces.

DURATION OF PREGNANCY

In every textbook, the duration of pregnancy for the dog is given as 63 days. This period does, however, vary considerably both for an entire breed, and also for one and the same bitch from litter to litter.   The research scientist, Naaktgeboren, evaluated 184 whelpings from various

Served Jan. Whelps March	Served Feb. Whelps April	Served March Whelps May	Served April Whelps June	Served May Whelps July	Served June Whelps Aug.	Served July Whelps Sept.	Served Aug. Whelps Oct.	Served Sept. Whelps Nov.	Served Oct. Whelps Dec.	Served Nov. Whelps Jan.	Served Dec. Whelps Feb.
1 5	1 5	1 3	1 3	1 3	1 3	1 2	1 3	1 3	1 3	1 3	1 2
2 6	2 6	2 4	2 4	2 4	2 4	2 3	2 4	2 4	2 4	2 4	2 3
3 7	3 7	3 5	3 5	3 5	3 5	3 4	3 5	3 5	3 5	3 5	3 4
4 8	4 8	4 6	4 6	4 6	4 6	4 5	4 6	4 6	4 6	4 6	4 5
5 9	5 9	5 7	5 7	5 7	5 7	5 6	5 7	5 7	5 7	5 7	5 6
6 10	6 10	6 8	6 8	6 8	6 8	6 7	6 8	6 8	6 8	6 8	6 7
7 11	7 11	7 9	7 9	7 9	7 9	7 8	7 9	7 9	7 9	7 9	7 8
8 12	8 12	8 10	8 10	8 10	8 10	8 9	8 10	8 10	8 10	8 10	8 9
9 13	9 13	9 11	9 11	9 11	9 11	9 10	9 11	9 11	9 11	9 11	9 10
10 14	10 14	10 12	10 12	10 12	10 12	10 11	10 12	10 12	10 12	10 12	10 11
11 15	12 15	11 13	11 13	11 13	11 13	11 12	11 13	11 13	11 13	11 13	11 12
12 16	13 16	12 14	12 14	12 14	12 14	12 13	12 14	12 14	12 14	12 14	12 13
13 17	14 17	13 15	13 15	13 15	13 15	13 14	13 15	13 15	13 15	13 15	13 14
14 18	15 18	14 16	14 16	14 16	14 16	14 15	14 16	14 16	14 16	14 16	14 15
15 19	16 19	15 17	15 17	15 17	15 17	15 16	15 17	15 17	15 17	15 17	15 16
16 20	17 20	16 18	16 18	16 18	16 18	16 17	16 18	16 18	16 18	16 18	16 17
17 21	18 21	17 19	17 19	17 19	17 19	17 18	17 19	17 19	17 19	17 19	17 18
18 22	19 22	18 20	18 20	18 20	18 20	18 19	18 20	18 20	18 20	18 20	18 19
19 23	20 23	19 21	19 21	19 21	19 21	19 20	19 21	19 21	19 21	19 21	19 20
20 24	21 24	20 22	20 22	20 22	20 22	20 21	20 22	20 22	20 22	20 22	20 21
21 25	22 25	21 23	21 23	21 23	21 23	21 22	21 23	21 23	21 23	21 23	21 22
22 26	23 26	22 24	22 24	22 24	22 24	22 23	22 24	22 24	22 24	22 24	22 23
23 27	24 27	23 25	23 25	23 25	23 25	23 24	23 25	23 25	23 25	23 25	23 24
24 28	25 28	24 26	24 26	24 26	24 26	24 25	24 26	24 26	24 26	24 26	24 25
25 29	26 29	25 27	25 27	25 27	25 27	25 26	25 27	25 27	25 27	25 27	25 26
26 30	27 30	26 28	26 28	26 28	26 28	26 27	26 28	26 28	26 28	26 28	26 27
27 31	28 1	27 29	27 29	27 29	27 29	27 28	27 29	27 29	27 29	27 29	27 28
28 1	29 2	28 30	28 30	28 30	28 30	28 29	28 30	28 30	28 30	28 30	28 1
29 2		29 31	29 1	29 31	29 31	29 30	29 31	29 1	29 31	29 31	29 2
30 3		30 1	30 2	30 1	30 1	30 1	30 1	30 2	30 1	30 1	30 3
31 4		31 2		31 2		31 2	31 2		31 2		31 4

Whelping chart: Calculated for a 63-day pregnancy.

breeds in which gestation periods fluctuated between 54 and 73 days. The greater majority of births took place between the 60th and 63rd days with the focal point on the 63rd day. The calculations in Table 7, a pregnancy calendar, are based on a 63-day period, although the average calculated by Naaktgeboren is 61.95 days.

The evaluation of 184 whelpings carried out by Naaktgeboren to establish length of pregnancy and number whelped in a litter (Table 8) shows a definite connection between the two. Small litters are born later, large ones arrive earlier. Naaktgeboren regards pregnancies of less than 58 days and more than 67 days as abnormal. His research results and those arrived at by Dr E. Hauck, Vienna, are in accord for the most part.

TABLE 8: THE RELATIONSHIP BETWEEN LENGTH OF PREGNANCY AND SIZE OF LITTER EVALUATED IN 184 WHELPINGS

Source: Naaktgeboren

No. of Puppies in Litter	Average Length of Pregnancy	No. of Puppies in Litter	Average Length of Pregnancy
1	70.4	9	60.6
2	65.8	10	59.6
3	63.3	11	60.8
4	62.5	12	57.7
5	61.8	13	59.0
6	61.7	14	58.1
7	61.1	15	59.1
8	60.9		

Other conclusions can also be drawn from these statistics, namely that large litters of ten or more are, as a rule, born before the 60th day and very small litters frequently go more than 63 days. The excessively long gestation period for a one-puppy litter of more than 70 days must be regarded as critical. I shall be dealing with this point in considerable detail in connection with whelping problems.

Just how extensive fluctuations in the gestation period can be in one and the same animal is documented by Naaktgeboren in a record kept of the six litters of a Chow Chow bitch. It is extremely difficult to find any conformity at all in this particular record. And, even though I may be in danger of repeating myself, there is only one explanation for it: animals are not machines! For the purpose of documenting this point I have added the following table:

TABLE 9: FLUCTUATIONS IN PREGNANCY LENGTH IN A CHOW CHOW BITCH

Source: Naaktgeboren.

No. of Litter	No. of Puppies	Length of Pregnancy in days
1	4	67
2	4	62
3	4	65
4	1	66
5	3	65
6	4	60

CARE OF THE IN-WHELP BITCH

The prospect of a pregnancy fills the human being with the feeling that he must now do all he can to take care of his bitch. He is certain that the in-whelp bitch must be very well fed in order to make quite sure that the puppies have everything they need for their optimum development.

Let me take you back to my description of what is going on inside the bitch. The foetuses grow only very little during the first weeks of pregnancy, and the "swimming embryos" are well-cushioned against outside influences by the fluids in their embryonic membranes.

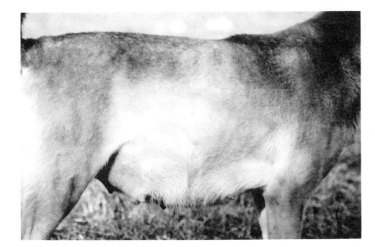

Bitch: Five and a half weeks pregnant. Photo E. Trumler.

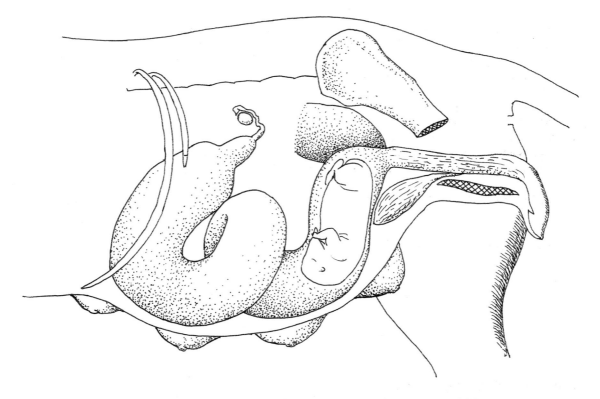

DIAGRAMMATIC VIEW OF A PREGNANT BITCH.
Source E. Trumler.
The approximate position of the left uterine horn at 50 days of pregnancy. The only part of the right horn shown is the section leading to the birth canal. One foetus is shown.

In the first four weeks of the gestation period, there is no need to worry about the tiny embryos. Allow the bitch plenty of space to move around, let her have plenty of exercise, and do not increase her normal ration of food! Pregnancy is not an illness; in the wild the daily struggle for existence goes on unaltered. The initial signs that the bitch may be pregnant are to be seen in an increased desire to sleep. By about the third week, she may show a tendency to vomit; her appetite may diminish, or she may go right off her food for a day or two. This sickness and loss of appetite coincide with the nidation of the ova in the uterus. It is easy to imagine that in this phase the bitch's entire metabolism is adapting to the new situation. In the parallel developmental stage of the foetus in the human fellow sufferer, a feeling of sickness and vomiting may also occur.

It is time to begin taking care of the bitch, in more than the normal sense, when her figure starts to spread. The early signs of increasing size do not become apparent in the abdomen, but immediately behind the rib cage in the loins. At around five and a half weeks, there is a bulge behind the rib cage and a clearly discernible swelling of the whole body. The teats will also have increased in size. When the bitch begins to show such obvious signs of pregnancy, then it is time for her to start to take things more slowly. By this, I mean the bitch should no longer exercise alongside a bicycle, go out with the guns, jump over hurdles, or do any other kind of very active sport. Over the years, we have learned to recognise early signs of a pregnancy by a slight vaginal discharge of a thickish consistency, which is colourless. This discharge commences about three weeks after mating and continues right up to the end of the gestation period. A slight discharge, colourless and thickish, is an excellent sign. We have never known a bitch with a similar discharge to have a pseudo-pregnancy. However, should the vaginal discharge turn white or even yellow, this is a very definite alarm signal. I shall be dealing with this subject later.

THE DIET

How should the pregnant bitch be fed? At this point, I should like to warn breeders never to over-feed. A little bit less is better for the bitch, and this applies to the time before and after her heat. The bitch carrying too much weight does not conceive easily, and she may frequently have problems both during pregnancy and at whelping time. The bitch is in the right condition if the vertebrae of the vertebral column and the ribs in their rib cage can just be either seen or felt. A bitch maintained in this condition should have no problems with her pregnancy or from whelping.

A healthy dog has a natural instinct for its nutritional needs. A well-trained dog licks the whole bowl clean in a matter of minutes. This dog, however, never actually gets as much as it could eat, but just that little bit less. In our own kennels, this is clearly the reason why we have never known a poor feeder. Never begin to entertain the idea that you should pander to your pregnant bitch! Continue to give her the normal ration after mating, if possible always just a little bit less than she would really like to have, and you will not encounter any feeding problems. Do not give way, even though the changes taking place inside the bitch cause her to lose her normal appetite for a day or two. Over the years, I have listened to the anxieties of owners, who, filled with concern for their bitches, have started frying top-quality meat, baking puddings, almost begging their dogs to eat! This is quite unreasonable and might even prove harmful for the bitch. If she prefers not to eat up her normal ration during the first few weeks, there are good reasons for this, rooted in her pregnancy. The breeder should see the situation for what it is and cease to worry.

Only one change is advisable at this stage, and that is a little more variation in the diet. The food industry claims, quite rightly, that their compound foods contain all the nutritional requirements needed by the dog. However, we have seen that a daily variation in the food put before our dogs pleases them. There is little difference in this respect between man and his dog. A varied diet sharpens the appetite. Fresh meat, cereals, milk products, fruits and vegetables, eggs, glucose, honey, fish, cod-liver oil – our dogs certainly love variety! The pregnant bitch should be given a diet containing plenty of vitamins, but the quantity of food should not be increased. From the fourth week, she should be having additional supplements such as calcium, phosphorus, trace elements, and vitamins. Pure cod-liver oil serves to enrich the vitamin intake, especially that of Vitamin D. Since this book is intended for the breeders of all breeds of dog, I cannot supply specific details of the additional quantities required. If you are using the proprietary supplements sold for pregnant bitches, it is essential to follow the instructions supplied by manufacturers. Always bear in mind that the addition of too much can do as much harm as the addition of too little. The breeder should make quite sure whether the basic foodstuff he normally uses already contains additives; he also needs to know roughly what its constituents are with regard to proteins, carbohydrates, fats, minerals, vitamins, and trace elements. This may sound very complicated, but there is no need to regard it as such.

Long before any publications appeared listing detailed tables of nutritional analyses, energy calculations, and so on, we put together our own food that proved its worth over many years. We have never had any deficiency diseases, either in puppies or in our brood bitches, let alone our adult dogs. The basic content of our foodstuff is 30-40 per cent raw meat, supplemented by cereals, vegetables, and fruit. Now and then, we put in a day with a diet of milk products, yoghurt, cottage cheese, supplemented by cereal flakes, egg, glucose, and honey. For more than thirty years, this diet has suited our dogs very well – as well as our pregnant and lactating bitches. There is nothing to be said against giving your pregnant bitch one of the compound feeds supplied by the commercial foodstuff manufacturers. You will be feeding her on a perfectly adequate, carefully compounded food, and it certainly makes feeding so much easier and avoids guesswork.

INCREASING THE FOOD RATION
When is it advisable for the breeder to increase the amount of food for the bitch, and when does she need additives to enable her to nourish her puppies properly? Let us go back to the migration undertaken by the fertilised ovum down to its nidation in the uterus; let us call to mind the time needed for this journey and the very slight amount of foetal growth in those first few weeks. It has been scientifically established that up till the 30th day of the pregnancy, the foetus has achieved a mere 10 per cent of its final birth weight. The remaining 90 per cent is gained in the second half of the pregnancy. It is no problem for the bitch to sustain the embryos perfectly adequately for thirty days after mating without any increase in her diet – even if it is a large litter.

From the 30th day onward the dog food industry advises increased quantities of food for the pregnant bitch. The requisite quantities are to be seen in Table 10.

TABLE 10: ADDITIONAL NUTRITIONAL REQUIREMENTS OF THE PREGNANT BITCH
Source: EFFEM Breeders' Advisory Service.

Weight of Bitch in kg	Normal requirements of the bitch per day in kj	Additional requirements per day from 30th day of pregnancy in kj	Additional requirements in relation to normal requirements in %
2	920	300	32.6
5	1825	750	41.1
10	3100	1500	48.4
20	5200	3000	57.7
30	7050	4500	63.8
40	8800	6000	68.2

Perhaps some explanation is required for this table. As a measure for the energy food requirements of the dog, science has introduced the term kilojoule, which means that we are able to calculate exactly the amount of energy the dog is being supplied with via the various foods. Up to a year or so ago, this was calculated in calories. The table tells us, in the first place, how much food we need to give our bitch (apart from the amount required for her own sustenance), and when we need to calculate the additional requirements for a litter as from the 30th day of pregnancy.

One interesting point is that the additional quantity required for a litter in small breeds is considerably less than in large breeds. A bitch weighing two kilograms (4.5 lbs.) needs only one-third of her basic diet, the ten kilogram (22 lbs.) bitch almost twice as much as normal, and the large breeds of over forty kilograms (88 lbs.) need an additional food amount of up to two-thirds.

These additional quantities of food are needed not only to produce energy, but also to supply the nutriment necessary for the development of the embryos. The calcium and phosphorus requirements of the bitch are doubled in the second half of her pregnancy, and those for magnesium, sodium, and calcium are even higher. Her diet must, in addition, also meet her supplementary vitamin needs. Vitamins E and D, the most important of these, have already been mentioned. But take care! Too much vitamin D can lead to a danger of calcification of the coronary vessels. I can only repeat the advice already given; when using proprietary products, it is essential to follow the instructions most carefully, and never to administer more than the recommended amount. As regards feeding times for the in-whelp bitch, for the first four weeks stick to the normal routine she was used to before she was mated. As a rule, this is one meal a day. After the first four weeks of the gestation period have passed, the additional amount (shown in Table 10) should be given in the form of a second meal. When the bitch begins to become heavy, at the latest in the seventh week, the food should be divided into three or four meals. When feeding several meals a day, it is very easy to vary the feeds, and, thus, sustain the bitch's appetite. In this way, the bitch is receiving a comprehensive and well-balanced diet containing all the necessary requirements. The instructions given in Table 10 should, of course, be adapted to suit the in-whelp bitch, since it is of vital importance to steer the amount of food given in the later stages of pregnancy in accordance with the size of the expected litter. If the bitch is still slender after the sixth week, so that it seems likely that she will have just a few puppies or perhaps no puppies at all, then quite obviously the increased amount of food given should only be slight, according to my own calculations about 20 per cent. One-puppy births pose particular problems for the dam. The excessive growth that takes place in single puppies should not be augmented by rich feeding. If, on the other hand, the bitch rapidly becomes very heavy and the litter looks like a very large one, the quantities of food recommended in Table 10 may be slightly increased. In my own experience, the bitch's food intake should be somewhat reduced. Many bitches, especially those carrying large litters, reduce their food intake of their own accord at this stage. In large litters, this should be compensated for by raising the quality of the food.

EXERCISE

Correct feeding is essential throughout the entire gestation period, but a proper balance between nutrition and exercise is of equal importance to the bitch. It is vital to keep the bitch in good physical condition for the approaching birth. She needs a sound heart, strong lungs, and well-toned muscles. It would be very harmful for her to lead a lazy life in the last few weeks of her pregnancy. Give her plenty of opportunity for exercise. Take her for good, long, but undemanding walks right up to the last week of her time, and you will be doing your best to prepare her for an easy birth. Even if, in the final week, our well-rounded lady looks at us with those soulful pleading eyes, we must still insist on her taking sufficient exercise.

DETECTING PREGNANCY

Now we come again to that constantly reiterated conundrum: is the bitch pregnant or not? This is, without doubt, the question most frequently asked in the world of dog breeding, and I have to admit that even after many years of experience it remains a most difficult question to answer.

Once we owned a very valuable brood bitch, recently imported, and she had missed twice for her previous owner. Was she going to miss yet again? We had reached the sixty-second day of pregnancy, and our experienced breed adviser came to see us. He had seen the bitch soon after her arrival, long before she was mated, and he stated quite definitely: "This bitch is not in whelp"! Rather hesitantly, I contradicted him, and his reply was: "If she has any puppies, my name is 'Willi'! The very next day she bore five healthy puppies and "Fred" had become "Willi". I must admit, Bull Terriers are sturdy dogs and much can be concealed beneath their rounded rib cage. Even veterinarians can experience difficulty in palpating the abdomen of these strong, particularly muscular bitches.

X-RAY DIAGNOSIS

If the breeder is either unwilling or unable to wait, there is always the option of finding out whether the bitch is in whelp or not by means of an X-ray. One objection to this is that the creatures of our earth are exposed to quite enough radioactivity already, without subjecting them, unnecessarily, to yet another dose. An X-ray is, however, a necessity if there is a question of a one-puppy litter. Most single-puppy births take place these days via Caesarean section, and it is essential, in these cases, to establish by means of an X-ray how the puppy is positioned. I shall be returning to this subject in detail in the section in the next chapter on whelping problems.

There are usually a number of personal reasons why it is considered necessary to discover whether the bitch is in whelp or not. The arrival of a litter of puppies makes it essential for the breeder to be able to allocate the time. If, after five to six weeks, he has come to the conclusion that the bitch has missed, it is understandable that he or she would like to make certain in order to be able to plan for the coming weeks. As regards radioactivity, there is no doubt at all that modern X-ray units give off only very little radiation, and the results show, with great reliability, whether our bitch is in whelp or not.

The skeleton of the foetus – a precondition for an X-ray diagnosis – is formed between the 40th and 55th day of pregnancy. The skeletal formation of the foetuses is recognisable as a white shadow. At the earlier stage around the 45th day, it is not possible, via an X-ray, to determine the actual number of puppies in a litter, but it is possible to ascertain whether the bitch is pregnant or not. By the 55th day, the expert is usually able to distinguish the number of foetal skeletons; the layman can at least see the heads and the skeletal bones.

An X-ray taken on the 60th day will show considerable detail. In a bitch carrying a large litter, the overloaded uterine horns take up practically the entire abdominal cavity, and will press on the other organs. In contrast, an X-ray for a single puppy taken in late pregnancy will show an excessively large puppy, with an entire skeleton which is clearly visible to the layman. For the veterinarian, the X-ray indicates the inevitability of a Caesarean section.

Looking at these four cases, it is clear to see just what radiography can achieve. Today, radiography has become an essential part of every small animal clinic's equipment. I recall a four-year-old bitch who had been mated fifty-nine days previously, and from her outward appearance, there was absolutely no sign at all of an approaching birth. Our veterinarian had gone away for a well-earned holiday, but it had been decided to let him X-ray her beforehand, just in case. The bitch was X-rayed, and the veterinarian shrugged his shoulders sadly – there were no puppies.

On the 65th day of pregnancy, our bitch appeared to be perfectly happy and comfortable.

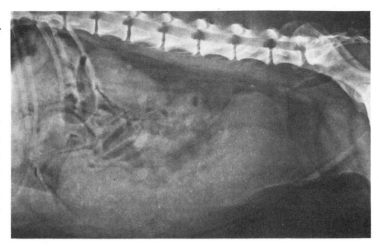

TOP: Sheepdog bitch, three years old; 45th day of pregnancy. Multiple birth. In the centre lower half of the X-ray, the uterine horns are visible. Within these, the foetuses are recognisable as a white shadow. At this stage it is not possible to determine the number of puppies in a litter, but it is possible to ascertain whether the bitch is pregnant or not. Photo: Dr Koeppel.

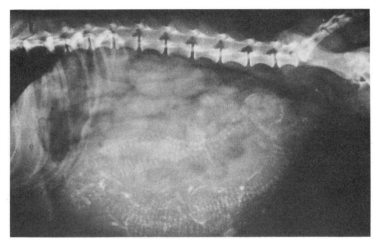

BOTTOM: Dachshund bitch, three years old, 55th day of pregnancy. By looking at the lighter shading in the central lower half of the X-ray, the expert is able to distinguish five foetal skeletons. Photo: Dr Koeppel.

Suddenly she began to pant. It could not possibly be true! She went on panting for an hour, for two hours. The first sign of a birth is often indicated by the bitch's continuous panting. Why should our bitch pant this much if she had no puppies? We called our veterinarian's assistant from her bed in the middle of the night, and when she arrived, we all sat around the panting bitch, quite unable to find an explanation for her behaviour. Perhaps just one puppy? The veterinarian was quite undecided: "Just imagine, my boss X-rayed this bitch himself! If I take her into the surgery, open her up, and there is nothing there, he will kill me!" she said. An hour after midnight, our bitch lay down and went to sleep. We gave the all clear; it was obviously a false alarm.

The next evening at around 7 p.m., the whole scenario began just as before. Again, we all collected around the bitch, trying to decide what had best be done. By this time, I felt I simply had to know what was happening. We phoned up a veterinary friend, who usually looked after our horse. He was tracked down at a party at the riding stables, and he arrived an hour later together with a noisy crowd of friends, just a little bit worse for wear. He bent over our bitch. He felt her abdomen, palpated her and declared: "There are two in there. Do you want me to get them out?" We thanked him, but decided to manage without his services. We packed our bitch into the car, and

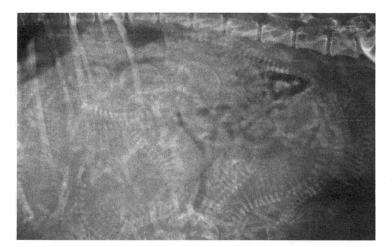

Boxer bitch, five years old, 60th day of pregnancy. With a large litter, the overloaded uterine horns take up practically the entire abdominal cavity and press on to the other organs.
Photo: Dr Koeppel.

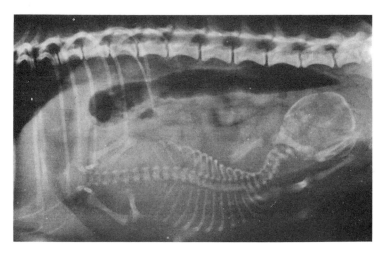

Poodle bitch, eighteen months old, 58th day of pregnancy. Single puppy. The large, single skeleton is clearly visible. In this case, a Caesarean section is inevitable.
Photo: Dr Koeppel.

drove, with the veterinary assistant, to the clinic. Two healthy puppies were born via Caesarean section, one of which went on to become a German Federal winner! And these two had remained mysteriously hidden from the X-ray's all-seeing eye!

This story illustrates a basic principle. Humans are not infallible – neither is our technical equipment. The probability of something of this kind happening is actually less than one per cent. Yet, even if a diagnosis is quite positive, the unexpected must always be reckoned with, and despite a definite diagnosis – "No puppies"! – the owner should remember to keep on studying his bitch's behaviour.

In 1986, a breeder described a similar incident to me. Six puppies had been born, and the bitch lay down, stretched out, and relaxed. The veterinarian present examined her, and said that all the puppies had arrived. Another breeder, who happened to be there, had such serious doubts that she insisted on having the bitch X-rayed. The result – there was no evidence of unborn puppies! Nobody knows where they came from, but two days later the bitch developed a raging temperature, and two dead puppies were taken from her by Caesarean section. This happened two days after an otherwise normal birth.

A considerable amount of practical experience is needed to make an accurate X-ray diagnosis and also remember that, in the operation of highly sophisticated radiographic units, mistakes are easily made.

PALPATION

This is a method of feeling the bitch's abdomen to detect the embryos in the uterine "string of beads". By means of palpation, the experienced veterinarian is able to locate puppies. The textbooks tell us that by means of palpating the abdomen, between the 18th and 21st day of the pregnancy, it is possible to detect the embryos. It is also stressed that this kind of diagnosis is possible between the 24th and 32nd day, but it becomes more difficult owing to the increasing girth of the bitch. In the literature on this subject, it is always pointed out that a great deal of knowledge and experience is required for palpation. Naaktgeboren expresses an urgent warning: "Let the layman be well advised not to feel around for the foetuses. It is better to wait for a couple of months in patience than by inexpert palpation to cause irreparable damage either to the embryos or to the bitch herself". In other words, the breeder and the layman should keep their hands off the abdomen of the pregnant bitch! In connection with the method of ultrasound diagnosis, I shall be describing the astonishing results that can be achieved by expert palpation.

THE STETHOSCOPE

The stethoscope is used in human beings to check the heartbeat of the unborn embryo. Can this instrument be used to diagnose pregnancy in the dog? It is possible from the final week of pregnancy to hear the puppies' heartbeats by means of the stethoscope. But the multiple birth in the dog naturally creates a certain amount of difficulty, and it is not possible to discover the size of the litter with this instrument. It is, however, an excellent means of distinguishing pregnancy from pseudo-pregnancy, since in pseudo-pregnancy there are obviously no heartbeats to be heard.

VISIBLE SIGNS

Kicking movements of the expected puppies are discerned by many breeders. Is this really evidence of a pregnancy? In the case of a large litter, the careful observer will be right. From the eighth week onward, with a little patience and the palm of the hand laid carefully on the bitch's abdomen, little twitching movements of the puppies may be felt. However, in my experience, there are a great many breeders with a powerful imagination! It is no exaggeration to say that, in my advisory capacity to many breeders, I could list at least ten who swore that they had felt these tiny kicking movements. This was not "perjury", since there is a lot of movement going on inside a bitch, and human beings have a very great sense of imagination, especially if something is desired very much. The fact is that in none of the above-mentioned ten cases did a bitch have one single puppy. We can therefore discard diagnosis entirely by means of kicking movements.

DIAGNOSIS BY WEIGHT

Naaktgeboren quotes yet another method, this time in relation to the weight gained by the bitch during pregnancy. He calculates the size of the expected litter from weight increases during pregnancy. However, in those cases in which only one or two puppies are born, this method does not afford us any great clarification. Naaktgeboren calculates a weight increase of a total of 5 per cent for a bitch bearing two puppies. A well-cared-for and well-fed bitch can, however, easily put on this amount of weight during a pregnancy period and does not require any puppies to assist her! In large litters, the weighing procedure becomes superfluous, so that I feel a little sceptical about this method.

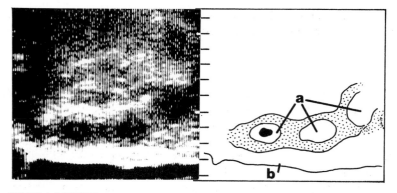

Ultrasound examination. Beagle bitch 32 days after mating. a = three placental sacs, b = the abdominal wall.

ULTRASOUND

There is one reliable method of early diagnosis. We are indebted for this method, on the one hand, to the expertise of practitioners in palpation and, on the other, to the bat. This little creature is the heraldic animal of ultrasonic diagnosis, a science that has brought about immense changes in the medical world in recent years.

As has already been stated, palpation – carried out by laymen or inexperienced veterinarians – does little toward diagnosing pregnancy in dogs. The matter looks quite different in the hands of a specially trained expert. This gives us an interesting parallel to the subject of semen extraction and artificial insemination already dealt with.

A very interesting treatise, once again from the Dutch University of Utrecht (published in October 1985), deals with the results of pregnancy tests carried out with palpation and with the ultrasonic system. The results are astonishing!

In 1983, 116 bitches of forty-two different breeds were examined by palpation. The majority of examinations were carried out between the 25th and 35th day after mating (i.e. after four weeks of pregnancy). In this research programme, existing pregnancies were diagnosed with an accuracy of 94.6 per cent, and the absence of a pregnancy with 82.8 per cent accuracy. The test method adopted is to stand the bitch on a table and to palpate her abdomen with both hands at the same time. One hand is laid flat on the abdominal wall and the other is pressed gently inward. The foetuses are perceptible as tiny rounded or oval bulges.

Why should the negative diagnoses be less accurate than the positive? It becomes clear from the statistics of this test programme that it was frequently a question of very small litters, and that examinations took place at an early date (i.e. around the 25th day of pregnancy). It is easy to understand that the minute bead-like structures are not easy to detect. Even so, the results of this test series afford convincing evidence of the efficiency of palpation as a test method for early diagnosis of pregnancy.

A further improvement in examination techniques is to be seen in the "bat technique" mentioned above (i.e. the ultrasonic examination of bitches). In this technique, sonic waves are emitted from a sonic generator on a frequency imperceptible to human beings. These sonic waves penetrate the body tissues. The individual tissues of the body are of varying density. The ultrasonic generator measures by means of reflections that vary according to the varying density of the tissues. These reflections become visible on a screen and are then documented as a film.

Before an ultrasonic examination of a bitch is carried out, all the hair in the area around her mammary glands has to be shaved off. The skin is slightly greased, and the scanner is laid upon the area. This particular examination technique is advantageous in that the bitch does not have to be anaesthetised and, in general, no sedation is necessary. A bitch with steady nerves is not in the least worried by an examination of this kind. An ultrasound examination at thirty-two days shows the embryos as black specks, and the bitch's abdominal wall is marked.

Examinations of this kind are carried out on a very large scale at Utrecht: in 1983 on 135 bitches, in 1984 on 97. Ninety-seven per cent of the pregnancies were accurately diagnosed, and 89 per cent of the diagnoses that the bitch had missed were correct. The Utrecht tests were carried out between the 25th and 35th day of pregnancy. Between the 30th and 35th days, the accuracy of the results proved considerably greater than those arrived at between the 25th and 30th days. The most interesting thing about ultrasonic examinations is the fact that, at this early stage (when an X-ray is unable to afford us any assistance), the ultrasonic method can provide us with a clear and comparatively reliable picture. It should also be remembered that an ultrasonic diagnosis involves no health risk at all for the bitch, and is thus an advance on the radiographic diagnosis.

Results have also been made available of examinations carried out in Scandinavia. In this test series 135 bitches were examined, and all examinations were made on the 28th day of pregnancy. The accuracy of the results amounted to 98.7 per cent. This is a most interesting development.

In conclusion, it may be said that ultrasonic examinations carried out in the early stages of pregnancy are more accurate than palpation. Another important point is that, hand in hand with improvements made in the ultrasonic units, costs have decreased considerably in recent years. An accurate pregnancy diagnosis is now possible at no great cost in most specialised clinics by means of palpation and subsequent ultrasonic examination.

All the same, we should not be content to let things rest as they are. As I have already said, tremendous improvements can still be made in the palpation methods adopted in small animal clinics. This is purely a matter of proper training in the skills which small animal specialists should possess. It is already possible to arrive at an accuracy rate of 90 per cent in diagnosis. On the other hand, it is clear that the investment in a good-quality ultrasonic generator can no longer constitute a great risk today for the small animal specialist with a large practice. The breeder may, therefore, both expect and hope that the veterinary services in pregnancy diagnostic procedures may improve even more in the coming years.

PROBLEMS IN PREGNANCY

To start with, let us remember that pregnancy is not a disease but a completely natural condition. The less fuss we make, the more naturally and easily these nine weeks will pass. However, during this period we should observe the bitch even more closely than usual. If we notice anything unusual, this might well be a sign of one or the other of the disorders I shall describe.

The widely accepted idea that bleeding ceases after mating is completely erroneous. We have always observed that bleeding continues from four to eight days after mating, and only then does it slowly abate. From bleeding – either pronounced or less so – no conclusions can be drawn as to whether the bitch is in whelp or not.

Hormonal changes within the bitch are of vital importance to the development of the foetuses. The oestrogen dominance prevailing on the day of mating is overtaken by a rapidly rising progesterone level. In the further course of events – approximately one week after mating – the blastocysts are approaching the uterus. There, after their migration from the oviducts, their implantation in the mucous membranes of the uterus takes place. A precondition for this pregnancy, however, is that the bitch's uterus has been prepared for this moment by hormonal changes.

The advice given here is intended exclusively for the owners of bitches that have repeatedly failed to conceive. In these cases, checks on the 3rd and 8th day after mating at a special clinic (such as the one at the University of Vienna) might well help. Vaginal examinations and hormone tests give an accurate diagnosis, and hormone treatment can assist in overcoming disorders. I am thinking especially of valuable brood bitches, whose puppies are urgently needed by breeders for the furtherance of the breed. Examinations and treatment are, in my opinion, justified in such cases. However, it should not be forgotten that, in all probability, in 98 per cent of these cases, disorders of the endocrine system are inherited and can therefore be passed on to the offspring. Nature is generally the wiser partner, and we should respect her methods of natural selection.

In Vienna, a third examination is recommended between the 18th and 25th day of pregnancy. As already described, the bead-like string of embryos can be detected by palpation from the 25th day. They have at that time – depending on the breed - grown to a size somewhere between a hazelnut and a table-tennis ball. The expert is also able to draw conclusions from an inspection of the vagina and mucous membranes, which will show any deviations from the normal clinical findings. If, for instance, the embryos are somewhat smaller or considerably larger than is usual at this stage, or if there is an increased cervical discharge, the specialist will describe this as hypoluteinism, an anomaly in which the loss of the embryos must be reckoned with. Even in this case, special treatment would be possible, but what was written in the previous chapter applies here, too – it would be unwise to attempt to save the situation.

PYOMETRA

I have learned, from my own experience, that it is imperative never to treat a pregnant bitch with antibiotics. Many readers know what a thalidomide child is. The use of antibiotics during pregnancy causes, with great probability, malformation among the puppies. In a litter of eleven, we had three severely malformed non-viable pups. Occasionally, a risk of this kind may well have to be taken. Our bitch was found to be suffering from pyometra (an inflammation of the uterus) three weeks after mating. The heavy, purulent discharge, accompanied by a temperature, left us in no doubt at all. We were, however, fortunate for it is only very rarely that pyometra can be successfully treated by high doses of antibiotics. In general, a veterinarian will advise an operation, a spay or hysterectomy (the removal of the entire uterine tract), since it is well known that inflammation of this kind recurs repeatedly.

The symptoms of pyometra are not always very clear. As a rule, the bitch is very thirsty, she occasionally vomits, and she seems depressed. A very high temperature is symptomatic. It is a good sign if the purulent discharge appears at once. In some cases the uterus is closed and, thus, fills steadily with pus. This leads to toxic substances entering the bloodstream, and the bitch poisons herself through the bacteria in her uterus. It should be mentioned here that an inflammation of the uterus can occur in a bitch of any age, even in a maiden bitch. It is, in my experience, very rare indeed for the litter of a pregnant bitch suffering from a pyometra to be saved; we were very fortunate with our eight healthy and only three malformed puppies.

FALSE PREGNANCY

Another problem, which sadly occurs very frequently, is the pseudo or false pregnancy. The worrying thing about this is that it can so easily be mistaken for a genuine pregnancy. There is hardly a breeder, hardly a veterinarian, who has not been taken in at one time. The bitch suffering from a false pregnancy shows all the signs the breeder so much desires in his mated bitch. She is tired, spends a great deal of time sleeping, she occasionally vomits, and her girth increases steadily. The mammary glands begin to show, and the nipples turn pink. The bitch has a good healthy appetite, which tends to make her put on even more weight.

I shall have to confess, at this point, that I have more than once prepared the whelping kennel, got the whelping box ready, and put everything else to rights to await the expected birth. The scales stood at the ready, and we have even begun to keep watch at night with our expectant mother – until we were forced to the conclusion that it had all come to nothing. And this was not just in our early days of dog breeding!

The frequency with which false pregnancies occur is one of the reasons why it is important to diagnose a proper pregnancy at as early a date as possible. I have already pointed out that in a false pregnancy the bitch's girth is considerably increased; the milk is even let down. From my own experience, I would go so far as to say that when a bitch produces milk between the 56th and 58th day, it is much more likely to be an indication of a pseudo-pregnancy than of a real one. Again, I must emphasise the fact that small amounts of a thickish, transparent vaginal discharge from the third week onwards, is the surest sign of a proper pregnancy. I have never observed any discharge of this kind in a false pregnancy. The breeder must, however, look very carefully, under certain circumstances even feel for it, especially if the bitch's genitals are pinkish or white.

It is perfectly normal for a bitch suffering from a false pregnancy to start digging large holes and making nests shortly before the prospective date of parturition. The bitch's body is being stirred by inner forces that compel her to act exactly as a pregnant bitch would. Not until the imaginary day of parturition is past do these forces subside. The organs and tissues then return to normal, lactation abates, and the bitch reverts to her normal life.

A famous writer on animals, Paul Eipper, in his book *The Yellow Great Dane Senta*, describes this phenomenon in an eight-year-old bitch very explicitly. I cannot do better than quote him here:

"The Great Dane moaned continually, she never barked, never whined. Her head was hot from the tips of the ears to the point of her feverish nose. The expression in her eyes was one of helpless anxiety. The nights were twice as bad as the days! Five, six, seven times her cries brought us rushing downstairs; there she sat; she had torn shreds out of the cushions, curtains, rugs, upholstery, and mattress and had gathered the rags together in a corner of her bed to form a nest for the unborn young. Unconsciously, the forces of destructive energy were at work; I don't believe Senta even recognised us at all.

"Suddenly she slid down on to her side, exhausted, and breathing heavily with a rattling noise. Next morning, milk was seeping out of her mammary glands while she lay peacefully on her bed. In an instant, her whole body was shaken by wild contractions; the contractions subsided in the course of the day, to return later, but no longer with such brute force. In the middle of the night, I heard the sound of a whirlwind and awoke with a start. It was 7 o'clock. I jumped out of bed, reached the door, opened it, and in pranced Senta, tail wagging brightly, ready to jump at me. I put both my hands on her Great Dane tummy, there was not the slightest sign of any thickening. A loving, demanding push brought my chin convincingly into contact with a healthy, cool, wet nose".

This complete metamorphosis of the Great Dane bitch took place exactly sixty-three days after the peak of her heat, at which moment she had escaped and gone off with a black shepherd dog.

The ethnologist, Eberhard Trumler, regards the biological function of the pseudo-pregnancy as regulative, by which means a bitch of the wild dog species reabsorbs the embryos in her body after mating. This happens in the wild state when weather conditions are extreme, or a shortage of food makes the bearing of a litter too difficult.

Foetal resorption of this kind has been scientifically established. In the early stages of the pregnancy, the foetuses may die, and they are then gradually dissolved within the bitch's genitals and absorbed without any sign of an abortion becoming apparent. Foetal resorption may take place up to the middle of the pregnancy. It can also take place even when the bitch bears a perfectly normal full-term litter. Professor Seiferle estimates that approximately 12 per cent of the fertilised ova die off in the early stages of development and are reabsorbed by the bitch.

There is one more thing that should be said about pseudo-pregnancies. If this occurs once in a bitch, it may well be regarded as an inherited, regulative mechanism and there are no actual grounds for concern. However, Eberhard Trumler points out, quite rightly, that in the present day dog-breeding world, false pregnancies occur very frequently indeed, and many bitches suffer from them after every oestrus without having been mated. Experts advise that such bitches should be taken out of breeding programmes. Even if they actually do become pregnant, it is highly probable that the tendency will be passed on. The advice, given by many veterinarians, that mating bitches that suffer from false pregnancies may act as cure must, in this light, be condemned. The only reasonable course of action is have a hysterectomy operation carried out on the bitch; firstly, so that she cannot pass on this tendency to her offspring, and, secondly, so that both she and her owner may be free from such disorders for the rest of her life.

ABORTION

Abortion can result from severe external effects such as a hard knock, jumping off a high wall, falling into a deep ditch, and so forth. A further factor might be an infection, such as bacterium brucella canis. This disease sometimes affects whole groups of dogs without the cause becoming easy to diagnose. When a member of the group is mated, the bacterial infection leads to an abortion between the 30th and 50th day of pregnancy. This is a very treacherous disease requiring careful observation and meticulous treatment.

Chapter Seven

WHELPING

Eberhard Trumler, quite rightly, regards whelping as the most important factor in the survival of individual dog breeds. For my part, I wish to impress on all those involved in breeding dogs that whelping is a perfectly natural process. Our dogs are ideally equipped by nature for giving birth. Despite certain undeniable signs of degeneration – for which we breeders must hold ourselves responsible – it is a proven fact that by far the greater number of births take place without the slightest signs of trouble.

There is, however, one serious danger to the normal progress of a birth, and that is the desire of the inexperienced human to help! From my many years of experience, I believe that more puppies are lost through lack of knowledge and skill on the part of the human being than through the effects of degeneration in certain dog breeds. It was for this reason that I felt compelled to write this book.

In the kennels of experienced and knowledgeable breeders, whelpings are 90 per cent trouble free. Any difficulties that may arise due to anatomical or psychological deficiencies in our dogs can, in most cases, be overcome by the knowledge of how to act. In the hands of the experienced breeder, scarcely more than 3 per cent of all puppies born should be lost.

I hope that this book as a whole, and this chapter on whelping and its problems in particular, will assist all breeders. Equipped with the necessary knowledge, the breeder may well be able to avoid problems in the great majority of births. If difficulties arise, and the vet is called in, expert knowledge will help you to assist in carrying out any procedures that are necessary.

NORMAL WHELPING

BUILDING TRUST
Absolute trust on the part of the bitch in her owner is of vital importance to the progress of a birth. As I see it, any aggression on the part of the bitch toward her owner is a sure sign of lack of trust. Unfortunately, we frequently hear accounts of bitches responding aggressively to any human approach in the first few days after whelping. These accounts document a serious failing on the part of the owners.

The excuse is sometimes put forward that the bitch is reverting to the behaviour of her ancestors. However, at the research station of the Society for Research into Domestic Animals, there have been numerous litters born throughout the years to wolves, jackals, dingoes, and wild dogs, and the female has always been willing to allow the person she trusted to assist at the birth. We also have various accounts of bitches whelping right in the middle of their own pack. But one report that really impressed me was that of Frau Kaiser-Golgojew and her famous pack of Borzois. Her bitches whelped, untroubled, right in the middle of their twenty pack-mates. Births of this kind were a perfectly natural procedure for the other dogs, and there was never any sign of aggression.

There is one vital piece of advice I will to give to all breeders. Devote plenty of time to the pregnant bitch, particularly from around the sixth week onwards. Stroke her growing tummy and the teats, and at the same time, the bitch can become used to gentle handling of the vaginal area. In this way, the bitch is being prepared to accept the touch of the human hand on any part of her body. The bitch will also happily lick the human hand, and this, again, is preparation for the licking of the newborn puppy. When whelping begins, the bitch trusts the human hand fully, and knows from experience that it will help her.

In almost every book on dogs, it is advised that the bitch should get used to the whelping box in good time, and that she should sleep in the whelping quarters for a good week before the birth. I believe this advice is totally wrong for the hobby breeder, who has from one to three bitches! It is correct that there must be a good whelping box, but it is wrong to leave the bitch alone in the whelping quarters, either in the daytime or at night. During the period before whelping, during whelping itself, and in the first few days afterwards, the bitch should be in close human contact so that she can be observed at all times. Shutting her away in a strange room would entail great cruelty. It would also be very tiresome for the owner to have to run along to the whelping quarters every few minutes to see what his bitch was doing.

In the final five days before whelping, we keep our bitches really close to us, thus ensuring optimum animal-human co-operation during the coming birth.

THE WHELPING BOX
The actual size of the whelping box varies, of course, from breed to breed, but it is of vital importance for the bitch to have adequate room for herself and her puppies during the first two or three weeks. This applies until such time as the puppies are able to crawl about, and move out of their den on their own.

An initial guide for measurements is the height and length of the bitch. The width and depth of the box should allow her to lie fully stretched and relaxed in the box. The height of the box should be slightly higher than her height at the shoulder. As regards the outer dimensions, the whelping box could prove detrimental if it is either too large or too small. If the floor space is too great, the puppies may stray and the bitch will become restless because they have got too far away from her. Should the box prove too large, a cardboard box can be fitted into it for the first few days to reduce the available space.

A five-centimetre (two-inch) batten should be fitted right round the underside of the box, forming an air-space beneath the box that serves as insulation. The rear wall and one side of the box are firmly anchored, whereas the other walls are flexible. A U-shaped guide rail should be screwed to the fixed side, and a second guide rail should be fixed to a supporting post fitted to the opposite corner. The front wall of the box fits into these guide rails. As a general rule, this front wall is not put into place until after whelping is over, as it would be in the way during the birth. The flexible side is connected to the rear wall and the supporting post, either by means of small bolts or hooks and staples.

Both the flexible side and the lid are hinged to enable them to be opened and closed as required. We always glue smooth narrow slats a few centimetres apart to the flexible side. When this side is let down later on, it serves as an exit and entrance for the puppies. The firmly glued slats provide the pups with a very good hold. The side should not be lowered until the puppies are three weeks old. From this time on, both the bitch and her pups come and go via the lowered side. The front wall with its outlet is replaced by a solid wall so that the bitch has to use the side entrance. When

THE WHELPING BOX

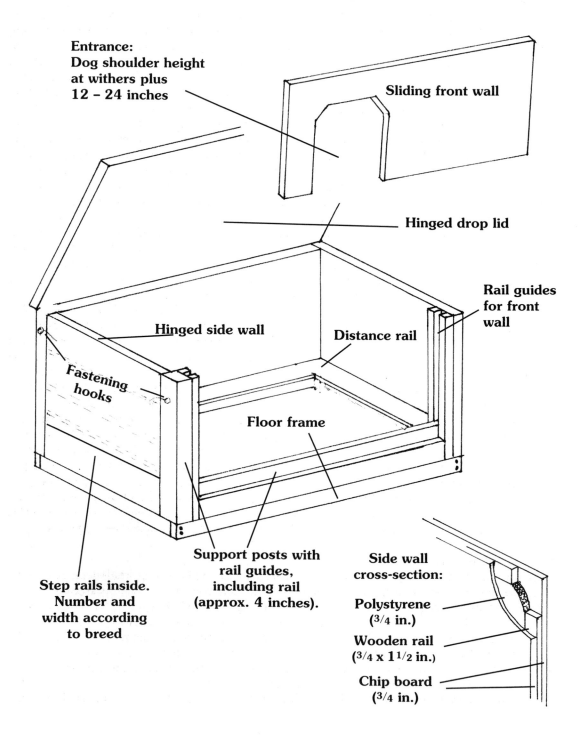

Entrance:
Dog shoulder height
at withers plus
12 – 24 inches

Sliding front wall

Hinged drop lid

Rail guides
for front
wall

Hinged side wall

Distance rail

Fastening
hooks

Floor frame

Step rails inside.
Number and
width according
to breed

Support posts with
rail guides,
including rail
(approx. 4 inches).

Side wall
cross-section:

Polystyrene
(3/4 in.)

Wooden rail
(3/4 x 1 1/2 in.)

Chip board
(3/4 in.)

the lid is shut down, the bitch is able to escape from her puppies, whenever she wants to, by jumping on to the roof.

In the case of large, heavy or clumsy breeds, it is advisable to fit rails round the inside of the box for the first two weeks. The rails prevent puppies that have strayed behind their mother from being crushed against the sides. Clearly, a puppy thus maltreated would cry, and most bitches react at once. If, however, the breed in question is a heavy one and the bitch is a bit insensitive and stolid, the puppy may well suffocate if there are no protecting rails. Accidents of this kind have happened with Bulldogs, Bull Terriers and Boxers. These rails are five to ten centimetres (two to four inches) wide, according to the breed, resting on corner posts ten to fifteen centimetres (four to six inches) high. They are put into place after the birth is over and can easily be removed for cleaning.

If the puppies are to be reared in a centrally heated room – which is, to my mind, the correct way – the box can be made of plywood, impregnated to resist moisture and acids. If the temperature is low in the kennel, then the box must be made of well-insulated material. We have had all the corners of our own whelping box, including those of the roof, covered with metal fittings. All the tiny little teeth marks in the metal plate go to prove that, without these precautions, our whelping box would have soon become no better than junk.

For more than ten years now, we have been using a special bathroom floor-covering of ribbed and impregnated soft rubber, or soft artificial fibre for the bottom of the box. The covering is cut larger than the floor of the box so that it extends upward two to three centimetres around the sides, thus preventing meconium, blood, and, later on, urine and faeces from soiling the box itself. A floor-covering of this kind is easy to clean and dries quickly after cleaning.

Well, the masterpiece is finished! Where are we going to put it? There are only two possible options. I prefer to have my bitch close to me, even during the night, from about the 58th day onwards. The whelping box is, therefore, placed beside my bed on the 58th day. This is very much more comfortable for me than sleeping on a camp bed in the whelping quarters. In this way, I do get a few more nights of decent rest. Unless I fall into a very deep sleep, any particular change in the bitch is easily perceptible. I consider it absolutely essential for the breeder to keep his bitch under close surveillance during these days. Unpleasant surprises can thus be avoided.

I know that I have already stated that the majority of births pass off without problems arising and without human aid. Why, therefore, am I making all this fuss? Well, you can never be sure that your bitch will be one of those that whelp without any difficulty at all. The amount of trouble involved in arranging everything so that one is fully prepared when the bitch begins to whelp is negligible compared with the risk of losing a puppy at birth, or of the bitch incurring an injury for lack of a helping human hand. To put it plainly, I regard it as an attribute of the genuine breeder that he looks upon the birth of his puppies as a personal experience that he would not like to miss. Those who consider a good night's sleep more important should not consider breeding dogs.

SIGNS OF IMMINENT WHELPING

Now we come to the vital question! What are the signs which indicate that whelping is imminent? In the section on phantom pregnancies, I have already mentioned a number of characteristics. As regards our own bitches, I can only say that one sure sign that a bitch is not about to whelp is the fact that she still enjoys her food. As long as she continues to eat her meals with a good appetite, she is not ready to give birth. We have only ever had one exception to this rule. In that particular case, the bitch ate a meal only two hours before giving birth. Otherwise, all our other bitches started to refuse food from eight to twelve hours before parturition set in. Since they were all very fond of their food, this, in itself, was a very clear indication.

The temperature guide, so frequently recommended (which I shall deal with in detail later on), has proved be somewhat unreliable, though we have tried it time and time again. Our bitches have often shown varying drops in temperature as much as four days before giving birth, but it has never been possible to ascertain any useful data.

The instinct to dig – to make a burrow in the ground – also varied very greatly among our Bull Terriers. A number of bitches never attempted to dig a hole out of doors, although their very large runs afforded every opportunity for them to do so.

There is one clear indication that whelping is about to begin, which is both obvious and reliable, and that is an increased restlessness interspersed with panting. This is the outward sign of the onset of the first stage of labour, the opening phase. This I have already dealt with in connection with the X-ray diagnosis that miscarried.

My own experience is largely confined to the German Shepherd Dog, Bullmastiff, and Bull Terrier breeds. This being so, I should like to use the research carried out by such well-known canine experts as Dr Cornelis Naaktgeboren, Dr Hans Raeber, and Eberhard Trumler, and to discuss their investigations.

Dr Naaktgeboren published a questionnaire for breeders in a Dutch canine periodical in the year 1963. In it, he asked breeders to supply detailed information about their bitches at whelping. The idea caught on and was taken over by periodicals in Germany, Austria and Switzerland. In all, Dr Naaktgeboren received detailed accounts of more than 700 births, an impressive amount of material which he then published in his highly commendable book, *Die Geburt bei Haus und Wildhunden* (*Whelping in the Domestic and Wild Dog*).

At this point, the thing that concerns us most is what breeders in all these countries had to say about signs of impending parturition. It is an interesting fact that the questionnaires produced 395 answers on litter size. As regards the questions on the approaching birth, it was possible to evaluate only 159 of the answers, a sure indication of the lack of preparedness, or inability on the part of breeders for close observation. Reports came in from a total of more than 700 births, but only 395 of these contained details of the size of the litter – that is, just over half (56.4 per cent); a mere 159 of the questionnaires returned gave clear details of the signs of approaching birth, and that is less than one quarter (22.7 per cent). Taking a closer look at these 159 answers, only around half the breeders had observed any restlessness in their bitches prior to whelping (57.2 per cent). Only 49 breeders were in a position to recognise the characteristic panting as a sign that whelping was about to begin. That was less than one third (30.0 per cent).

Sad though it is, an investigation of this kind merely goes to prove that the great majority of breeders have not the slightest idea of what is happening to their bitches, even though those breeders who actually answered the questionnaire were surely among the more active and interested of dog owners. As I have already said elsewhere, lack of knowledge on the part of the breeder constitutes the greatest danger to whelping.

Advice about checking the bitch's temperature is given in most books. The basic idea here is that, towards the end of the pregnancy, the progesterone dominance in the hormone level declines. This pregnancy hormone has a positive influence on body temperature, and as it declines the body temperature sinks by as much as 4 degrees Fahrenheit (2 degrees Centigrade), and sometimes even further.

Clearly, some use can be made of this to predetermine the approximate time of whelping. To take the temperature, insert a normal thermometer deep into the bitch's anus. Only if it is inserted deep enough can a really accurate reading be acquired. The thermometer should be lightly greased beforehand either with oil or Vaseline. The normal temperature in the dog is from 101-102 degrees Fahrenheit (38 to 39 degrees Centigrade), higher, therefore, than that of the human being. Regular checks about every four hours are necessary. We are looking for the lowest reading, which should be round 99 degrees Fahrenheit (36.5 degrees Centigrade). The theory tells us that after reaching its lowest point – from approximately 12 to 24 hours before parturition – the temperature will begin to rise again towards the normal reading of 101 degrees Fahrenheit (38 degrees Centigrade). However, all the data that I have collected over the years does nothing to confirm this theory.

Naaktgeboren drew up four temperature charts, in which temperatures were taken four times a day. In none of them does a reading of 99.5-100 degrees Fahrenheit (below 37 degrees Centigrade) appear, and, far from confirming the above theory, the charts show nothing more than a fluctuation of body temperature. I am indebted to Eberhard Trumler for the following temperature table of the Pug, Tilli. The table contains a number of readings, and it is interesting to see that they were taken at short intervals. Here again, there is no evidence of a rise in temperature from 12 to 24 hours before whelping begins. To sum up: from my own experience and from documentation available from other sources, I am only able to confirm that some days before parturition the bitch's temperature falls by one or two degrees. In my opinion, however, temperature checks afford no clear indication of the actual time of whelping.

TABLE 11: FLUCTUATION OF TEMPERATURE BEFORE PARTURITION
Source: Eberhard Trumler

Temperature Table of the Pug Bitch, Tilli

61st Day		62nd Day	
Time	Temperature	Time	Temperature
0950	99.7 F	0920	98.0 F
1140	99.7 F	1020	98.4 F
1300	99.0 F	1120	98.2 F
1400	99.0 F	1300	98.4 F
1530	98.8 F	1430	98.2 F
1640	99.1 F	1500	first puppy born
1830	99.0 F		
2000	99.0 F		
2230	99.1 F		

Eberhard Trumler lists, as follows, the typical characteristics of the first stage of labour, the period of dilation:

1. Increasing restlessness
2. Retiring to whelping box
3. Scratching and tearing at her bedding
4. Increasingly frequent licking of her vulva
5. Vaginal discharge
6. Licking floor of box
7. Rapid breathing
8. Worried expression
9. Frequent getting up and lying down
10. Turning around
11. Repeated turning toward her tail.
12. Panting
13. "Faraway" look in her eyes
14. Little response when spoken to
15. Violent digging
16. Intensive swallowing
17. Trembling
18. Preliminary contractions
19. Pressing in of elbows when sitting
20. Whining (seeking protection)

Trumler stresses that these characteristics, from number four onward, really do follow one after the other. Thus, we have a number of behavioural aspects forming a picture, but we must never make the mistake of supposing that every case will follow exactly the same lines. The above listed behavioural characteristics should merely be regarded as an indication that parturition is about to take place.

All the visible changes in the bitch, both in her anatomy and in her behaviour, are brought about by hormones. This applies to the swelling of the milk glands and the vulva, the falling out of hair around the teats, and the secretion of milk, as well as to the heavy panting and the desire to dig. Around the final day before whelping, the flanks of the bitch fall in, her belly appears to hang lower, the hip bones protrude, and the muscles in her pelvis and uterus slacken. Controlled by the birth hormones, all these muscles become softer and more pliable, as does the part of the uterus called the cervix. There is an increased mucous secretion in the vagina. This all serves to gradually prepare and smooth the way for the passage of the puppies – the birth is about to begin.

The panting of the bitch, clearest sign of the approaching birth, shows us that in the coming 4 to 10 hours we must concentrate solely on her and her litter. If the whelping box is in the bedroom, then it is there that the birth should take place. If the bitch has slept in a basket beside the bed, now is the time to move with her into the whelping quarters.

HEATING THE WHELPING QUARTERS

There has always been a great deal of discussion about the desirable temperature of the whelping quarters. According to some, all that is required is adequate protection for the bitch and her puppies against damp. Those who advocate this method stress that the domestic bitch may well bear her puppies and raise them in a temperature at or below freezing. At the research station, Wolfswinkel, the famous foundation bitch, Baba, whelped in frost and snow and reared her puppies out of doors. Beware though, we are told that heated quarters are unnecessary, and any additional source of warmth for the puppies is superfluous. All that is needed is some protection against wetness. Puppies must be hardened! Our domestic dog continues to degenerate ever further, thanks to the lack of common sense in human beings.

So, are we to do without heated whelping quarters? I fear I am quite unable to follow the apparently logical arguments of researchers. There is no doubt that wild dogs have to adapt to their environment; for them it is absolutely essential. But for hundreds of canine generations, we have bred the domestic dog to suit our own requirements and, making use of the dog's broad mutation scale, we have brought about a multiplicity of changes. There is no question that, today, there are still a considerable number of dog breeds that are able to withstand the dangers of inclement weather quite as well as their wild ancestors were. But is must be equally clear that, in the great majority of cases, dogs have been bred with very different aims than the resistance to cold. Breeders' aims have been to develop certain qualities in a breed, and only in a few cases have these aims included adaptation to extreme cold as, for instance, in the Nordic sledge dogs.

The aims of other breeders have been to develop a domestic dog, in the closest sense of the word, and such dogs are not equipped for demonstrating their hardiness by bearing and rearing their puppies in icy kennels. Admittedly, these days, survival courses are run for people in which tough sportsmen can prove their adaptability to tropical jungles and icy, Arctic wastes. However, the great majority of our fellow humans are highly susceptible to damp, cold, and other kinds of inclement weather.

For my part, I come down firmly on the side of those who rear their puppies in a heated room at the temperature recommended by veterinary experts. I can already hear the accusation that I am promoting degeneration and softening of our domestic dogs, but I will only listen when it comes from those who are willing to spend the winter in a cave that affords them sole protection from wetness.

I am making a special point of this because, in the course of my life, I have come across a number of kennels in which breeders, owing to fear of degeneration, reared their dogs in a manner close to nature. Later on, I had occasion to listen to the endless tales of woe from the unfortunate puppy purchasers who had bought their dogs from these spartanly-run kennels. Although the warning about not allowing our dogs to become too soft is founded on honest and well-meant intentions, it is frequently adopted and practised by those who, from sheer greed, inefficiency, and slovenliness, allow their dogs to become neglected.

Must we praise those things that make our dogs hard? No, let us damn those things that make our dogs sick! Protection against cold and wet, heated kennels, cleanliness and hygiene are not, for me, signs of softening up or degeneration. They are an absolute precondition for the correct rearing of domestic dogs.

WHELPING EQUIPMENT

What have we done to prepare for the coming birth, to ensure that we have the right item at hand when it is needed? The suitable design for a whelping box has already been presented. To give the bitch something to do when she is overcome by a compulsion to dig, it is best to put an old sheet into the box. Newspaper, so often recommended in books, is definitely not a good idea. Admittedly, if used in large quantities, it absorbs the mass of fluid involved in a birth. But how do you get rid of all those soaking newspapers in an age of oil and electric heating, and in the face of the environmental restrictions laid down today?

And are old newspapers really all that hygienic? Just consider how many hands they have passed through, and where they may have been stored. If you have a white or light-coloured breed, the black of the printing ink leaves nasty stains on damp coats. Newspapers retain all the moisture we are trying to avoid. So hand over all those papers you have gathered to the paper collection before the birth takes place. You are not going to need them!

I recommend a good solution of detergent for your puppies (one bucket of water and two tablespoonfuls of a mild disinfectant) and, in addition, a good-quality absorbent cloth. A good-quality cloth will take up a great deal of moisture and can easily be wrung out. For the first few weeks, these cloths are quite indispensable. With their aid, meconium, amniotic fluid, blood and urine can quickly be removed from the whelping box, and, together with the detergent solution, they afford optimum disinfecting of the floor of the box on which mother and puppies are lying. The bitch can also be easily cleaned and dried with this cloth.

A cardboard box, approximately 12 to 15 inches (30 or 40 centimetres) – larger or smaller according to the breed – is the next requirement. This should be fitted out with two hot-water bottles, the water temperature being around 107 degrees Fahrenheit (42 degrees Centigrade), and well-covered over with a thick towel. A second towel should be draped over the top of the box. As the birth continues, the firstborn puppies can be laid into this box should the bitch be either restless or somewhat clumsy. Whether this is likely to be the case or not is something that you cannot foresee. Puppies that have been licked dry and have had their first drink of their mother's milk will lie peacefully in this box, protected from stray draughts by the covering towel, and they will enjoy a little sleep.

Those who have seen the amount of moisture involved in whelping and know how restless a bitch may become when she is having contractions, will realise how important it is to have this snug, warm place for those puppies that are dry and have drunk their fill. If complete trust between the bitch and her owner has been built up, she will readily accept this care for her puppies. The cardboard box is close at hand, so that when there is a longer interval between the birth of puppies, the firstborns can be put to their mother again to be cleaned up and given a second drink.

If a suitable hot-water bottle is not available, the cardboard box can be placed beneath an infra-red lamp. The most important factor in the use of such lamps is the correct adjustment above the puppies. Place a thermometer where the puppies will be lying. If the thermometer reads between 24 and 28 degrees Centigrade, the puppies will be comfortable under the lamp. If the lamp is positioned correctly, the puppies will lie relaxed beneath it, neither avoiding the direct rays nor bundling up together. In the former case, the lamp is too low and in the latter, it is too high. The bottom of the box should be covered with a piece of towelling or a bit of old blanket.

A good, sharp pair of scissors and some thread will be needed in case anything goes wrong with severing the umbilical cord. The scissors are for cutting the thread, which may be required to tie the umbilical cord. The cord itself must never be cut. It should be compressed between two fingernails and torn off. I will come back to this subject later.

Another requirement is a pair of scales, and a notepad and pen for recording times of birth and weights. The best type of scales to use are those that respond instantly to pressure. On this type of scale, weights can be quickly and easily read. The type of scale used for weighing babies, where the weights have to be adjusted, is too intricate. Puppies are not known for keeping still, particularly as they get bigger, so it is preferable to go for the easy-reading scale.

If you need to assist with the birth of a puppy, you will need a tube of sterile lubricant to rub on your fingers. Sterilised gloves, as used by veterinarians, are recommended. If these are not available, then the hands must be well disinfected, and to avoid injuring the bitch, the fingernails should be cut short and filed. Hot water, nail brush, and soap are, of course, also required.

When planning for the birth, it is worth bearing in mind that the bitch may not have any milk. This can occur even if she is literally 'swimming' in milk up to the moment of whelping. Owing to the strain of giving birth, the milk may temporarily dry up, and it is also possible for the number of puppies to be too great for the actual flow of milk. One of the excellent proprietary puppy milk products that are on the market should, therefore, be at hand, together with a supply of puppy nursing bottles or tube-feeding equipment, and an electrically heated bottle warmer should be available to keep the milk warm.

SETTING THE RIGHT ATMOSPHERE

Keeping calm is the first essential at a birth! Try to keep calm and to give your bitch the feeling that you are there to support her. Your motto should be: "We are going to get through this together".

Strangers should not be permitted to come into the whelping quarters during the birth. Their presence is disturbing, and the bitch might easily become upset. If she happens to be a good watchdog she might even suddenly remember this responsibility! Whelping will progress more easily the less the mother is distracted from the matter in hand.

It is, however, unnecessary to be over-cautious. In the pack, the bitch would be surrounded by her pack-mates. Remember the Borzoi pack of the Kaiser-Golgojew group, which watched the progress of the birth with interest. Bitches who are well used to people, to other animals, and to their surroundings, are not usually easily upset. This also applies to those cases where it is necessary to call in the vet. Most vets approach bitches in such a way that they do not become worried.

However, I am strongly opposed to taking the bitch to the veterinarian when complications arise. I believe this is very stressful for the bitch. If it is merely a question of giving the bitch an injection to stimulate contractions, or of manipulating a puppy that is apparently stuck in the birth passage, then the vet should come to the whelping quarters. If a Caesarean section is called for, then the technical equipment and hygiene of a well-furnished surgery are essential.

As regards the presence of spectators at a whelping, this is a matter for the breeder to decide. I have allowed children in my house to watch this miraculous happening. I have been able to enjoy this wonderful event together with the child, without any of our bitches being in the least upset.

WHEN DO MOST BITCHES WHELP

Now we come to an important aspect of nature's laws, and one that has been observed in numerous mammals. As a rule, parturition takes place at a time when the animals would normally be resting. The reason for this is the automatic (involuntary) nervous system. The parasympathetic portion, which slows involuntary functions, determines the time of rest, and the sympathetic portion, which accelerates them, determines the time of activity. It therefore follows that the parasympathetic promotes contractions, whereas the sympathetic impedes them. All of this would be straightforward if we had regular times of rest for our domestic dogs. But just consider the watchdog whose main activity lies in the night, and the family dog that has had to adapt its own activities to suit those of its family.

Nothing conclusive can be accrued from Naaktgeboren's investigations into more than 268 whelpings. These were distributed evenly throughout the 24 hours of the day and night. Strangely enough, there was a slight rise in the number between the hours of 6 and 8pm. Raber, on the same subject, found that his bitches also gave birth throughout the 24 hours, but with a slight focal point (maximum frequency) in the early hours of the morning, between the hours of 2 and 3am. I can confirm these observations. Most of our litters were born in the early hours shortly after midnight.

It has frequently been observed that the bitch seeks human companionship when she is about to whelp. If the breeder is away, she may even delay giving birth and wait until he returns home – even if he is absent for several days. The absence of her own well-trusted human partner appears to act as an impediment to contractions, a clear indication of how urgently our dogs need their closest social companion when giving birth. This fact alone should surely make all breeders aware of how serious their obligation is to their bitches.

THE LABOUR BEGINS

Let us return to our own bitch. When we left her, she was plainly panting, a sure sign that the cervix was beginning to open. Panting indicates the onset of the first stage of labour, an outward symptom of internal muscular relaxation, especially in the region of the uterine cervix. The vulva, the outer end of the female genital tract, is also considerably enlarged, moist and soft. There is a white mucous discharge from the vagina. This colour is quite in order, it is completely normal, and there is no cause for concern. Within the bitch, muscular movements are taking place throughout the whole uterus, and the cervix is beginning to dilate. The unborn puppies, encased in their membranous sacs, are being slowly conducted towards the opening of the uterus, which continues, as though under hydraulic pressure, to dilate.

The process of birth is controlled mainly by hormones. It is set in motion by the hormone oxytocin. This hormone also activates lactation. The puppies lying in the two long horns of the uterus are pressed by muscular contractions toward the uterine opening. The fact that mothers afflicted with paraplegia can bear children, proves that these contractions are not controlled by the central nervous system. They are contractions of the smooth muscle fibres, which cannot be voluntarily activated. The muscle fibres contract behind the unborn puppies and drive them on.

The bitch has an outstanding internal guidance system, in which a number of muscular centres interact to form a perfect pacemaker. A carefully co-ordinated mechanism guides the delivery

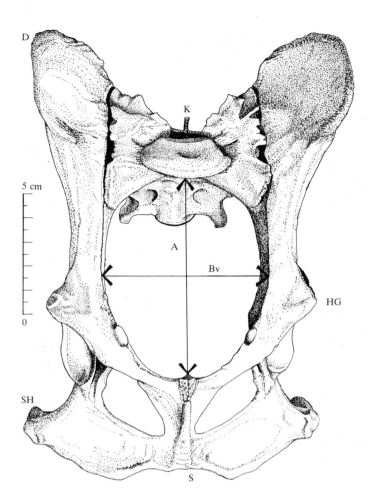

Sacrum and pelvis of the bitch (crossbred Irish Wolfhound ex East Asiatic Wolf) viewed from the front.
Source: E. Trumler.

KEY: *K = Sacrum, D = Wing of Ilium, HG = Acetabulum, SH = Ischial tuberosity, A and Bv = Inner measurements of pelvis (78 mm and 66.6 mm), S = Sciatic notch.*

from each horn in turn. And here we come across yet another phenomenon. If there is a dead puppy in one of the horns, this interplay is interrupted, and the puppy in the other horn has the right of way! Researchers believe that this is due to the fact that living puppies rotate of their own accord while being born.

These wave-like, muscular contractions from the ends of the uterine horns press the foetuses in the direction of the body of the uterus, in readiness for being born. During this process the bitch is panting very heavily – 100-120 breaths per minute have been counted during this opening phase.

The first-stage contractions have brought the unborn puppies into the right position. Naaktgeboren compares this to people queuing at the two entries for one gate to a platform. What happens next? At the uterine cervix, there is a kind of threshold, across which the puppies have to pass before they can enter the vagina. A considerable amount of muscular contraction is needed to overcome this particular point.

The first stage of parturition – the opening stage – can last for several hours. According to Naaktgeboren, the breeder is unable to ascertain the actual onset of this stage, and he quotes an

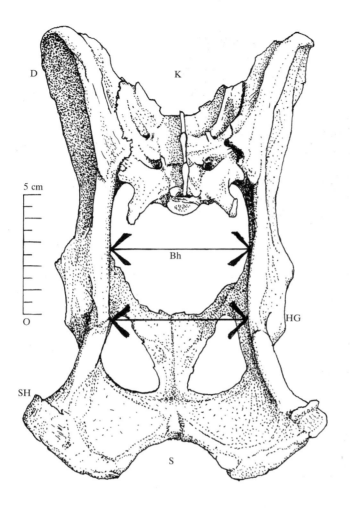

Sacrum and pelvis of the bitch (crossbred Irish Wolfhound ex East Asiatic Wolf) viewed from the rear.

Source: E. Trumler.

KEY: *K = Sacrum, D = Wing of Ilium, HG = Acetabulum, SH =Ischial tuberosity, S = Sciatic notch, Bh = The greatest inner width at the rear of the pelvic girdle – the narrowest passage the puppy has to pass (63 mm).*

average time of 12 hours for the duration of this phase. Only the expert, equipped with a vaginal speculum, would be able to ascertain how far the cervix has dilated. To me, this all seems somewhat theoretical. What we really need to know is the general time lapse from the moment the bitch begins to pant to the delivery of the first puppy.

Eberhard Trumler recommends informing the veterinarian after the bitch has been panting for three hours, in order that an injection can be given to stimulate stronger contractions. Frankly, I am not happy with this suggestion. It is a well-known fact that a number of strains, in some cases, whole breeds have whelping problems. I believe these are disquieting signs of degeneration that should be corrected by planned breeding. The ethnologists are right when they say we should breed from those bitches that give birth easily. Ease of giving birth is not merely a question of the pelvis, but also a question of hormonal stimulation. The breeder should, therefore, select not only for anatomical but also for hormonal breeding qualities. In my opinion, a bitch should be taken out of the breeding programme if she fails at this decisive moment, since she will, in all probability, pass this fault on to her offspring.

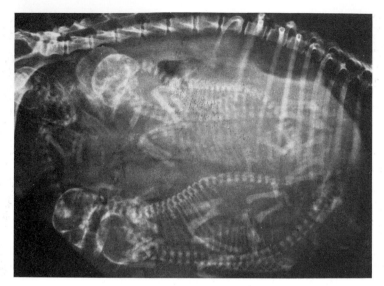

Fox Terrier bitch, four years old, giving birth. One puppy, correctly positioned, has already entered the birth canal. Its head is already in the pelvic opening. Note how the extremities, the legs, are lying close to the puppy's body. In this way, the diameter of the whelp is kept as small as possible, and birth is made easier.

Photo: Dr Koeppel.

German Shepherd bitch, five years old, giving birth. The puppy has entered the birth canal in posterior presentation. The puppy's back lies parallel to the back of the bitch, and, in this way, it is best adapted to the birth canal.

Photo: Dr Koeppel.

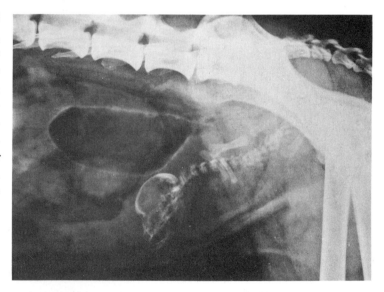

THE SECOND STAGE

When the first puppy reaches the threshold of the uterus, the bitch will begin straining hard. In this, the second stage of labour, the bitch bears down with considerable force, and the puppy is driven slowly onwards. Even for a layman, the change from the first to the second stage of labour is very obvious, as wave-like contractions are clearly visible along the bitch's abdomen. A considerable number of vigorous contractions are needed for the remainder of the foetus. The puppy not only has to pass out of the uterus, but also has to pass through the mother's bony pelvis. This bottleneck is the most critical point along the whole birth passage, and it will be dealt with later in the section on whelping problems.

It is, therefore, easy to understand why Eberhard Trumler advises breeders to check the pelvis of

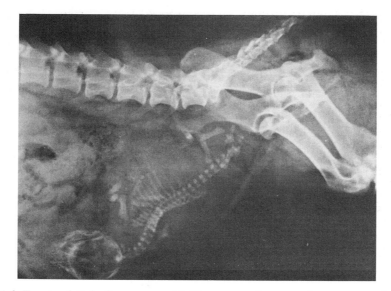

Scottish Terrier bitch, five years old. The puppy in posterior presentation is lying on its back. It is just about to enter the birth canal. The mother's backbone and that of her puppy are not parallel but opposite to one another. This position can lead to a lengthy time in the birth canal. In this case, the birth proceeded without any complications at all, but it could well happen that delivery from this position becomes very difficult. Depending on the circumstances, an attempt must be made to turn the puppy in the birth canal, and this is, of course, a matter for an experienced vet.

Photo: Dr. Koeppel.

every brood bitch most carefully. Trumler is of the opinion that a puppy's head is never too large, but that a bitch may have too narrow a pelvis. This, however, depends very largely on the angle from which you view the problem. The subject will be dealt with further in the section on whelping problems in one-puppy litters.

The first puppy is in the uterus and is being pressed onward by vigorous contractions. Its passage leads from the uterine horns through the cervix and into the vagina. The bitch's behaviour should now be closely observed. Towards the end of the first stage of labour, the opening phase, she has been digging and tearing at her bedding, turning round, lying down, and getting up. She has been licking her vulva and cleaning up the mucus from the floor of the box. She is very restless. All these actions occur instinctively. They ease the movement in the uterine horns and, later on, the passage from the uterus to the vagina.

The bitch may frequently ask to go out. She needs to urinate but often only passes a few drops. At times, she humps her back as though she would defecate, although, since she is unlikely to have eaten recently, she is unlikely to pass faeces. The breeder should be aware that the bitch often adopts this humped position when she is having a strong contraction. Special care should be taken at night during these expeditions into the garden. Good lights and an additional flashlight are absolutely necessary. A puppy can be delivered in this way, and it happens so quickly. We have actually experienced this only twice in more than 250 births. We helped the bitch to attend to the puppy, and it came off well in both cases.

Throughout the entire progress of the birth, the bitch requires adequate exercise. Movement eases birth. Even in the first stage of labour, repeated short walks are advisable. Obviously, when the bitch is carrying a large litter, she will need persuasion. It is her natural instinct to cling to her whelping quarters. The advisability of short walks applies even more to the second stage of labour. Repeated exercise shortens the intervals between each birth and, thus, the entire duration of the whelping.

Most bitches bear their puppies either lying down or sitting, or in a position that might well be described as halfway between lying and sitting. Between contractions, the bitch constantly moves to a fresh position, turns around, and digs at her bedding. During second stage contractions, she frequently presses her hind legs against the side of the whelping box as though seeking support.

In general, easier births take place lying or half-sitting. The so-called defecation position is seen, for the most part, in difficult births. In my estimation, two-thirds of all puppies are borne by their mothers either lying down or half-sitting. Do not attempt to influence your bitch if she continually changes her position during the birth. The only thing of importance is to see that she does not injure newborn puppies when she is turning around or digging. This is why it is so important to have a warm, cardboard box ready to hold the puppies in safety.

The most difficult point, the narrowest part of the passage the puppy has to negotiate is the mother's pelvic brim. The bitch's behaviour shows us when it has reached this position. She raises her tail high, spreading it from the root; the tail is not held straight up in the air but is bent downward like a bow. This typical position of the tail is quite obvious. The spreading of the tail at the root appears to widen the narrow passage through the pelvis a little.

The first puppy to be born has the greatest difficulty, as its body must dilate the birth canal and this birth prepares the way for the other puppies. Due to the muscular pressure on the uterus and vaginal walls, the amniotic sac – the membranous bag encasing the puppy – bursts, and a greenish fluid is discharged from the vagina. This clear, greenish-coloured fluid is a positive indication that the delivery stage has begun. The fluid lubricates the birth canal, the muscles of the vagina relax and the canal widens. When the sac bursts, the puppy is left lying unprotected in the birth canal.

For a short time, this presents no danger to the puppy, as it is still being supplied with oxygen from the mother's circulatory system via the umbilical cord and placenta. However, if too much time elapses, the situation may become critical. If the puppy is lying in an unfavourable position, the umbilical cord may become wrapped around it, or too narrow a pelvic opening may make the puppy's passage impossible. It is, therefore, advisable to call in the veterinarian no later than fifteen minutes after the bursting of the sac and the ensuing release of fluid. Action that the breeder can take will be dealt with in the section on whelping problems.

Frequently, the delivery of the first puppy to be born is heralded by the appearance of a small, dark bubble. If the membranous sac has already broken, then the first thing to emerge may well be a nose or even a foot. Another vigorous contraction or two, and the puppy is born.

THE NEWBORN PUPPY

If the puppy is still enclosed in the membranous sac, the bitch will instinctively break this with her incisors. She will lick the puppy thoroughly, massaging the newborn creature, and thus stimulating circulation. The first little squeak, sometimes a real cry, draws oxygen into the puppy's lungs. The first cry is the breeder's hoped-for signal that the birth has gone off well.

In licking the puppy, the bitch massages it with her strong tongue and, at the same time, she conveys the membranous sac via her tongue into her stomach. Frequently, the placenta (afterbirth), to which the puppy is attached by the umbilical cord, appears at the same time as the puppy. The bitch then severs the cord. She does this with her back teeth, the premolars, and not, as is often believed, with her incisors. Once the placenta has emerged, the bitch will consume this, together with the umbilical cord hanging from it. There is nothing wrong in this. She should never be prevented from doing so, even though it may not seem very pleasant. The placenta provides the bitch with a food that is particularly rich in hormones, and nature has decreed that the bitch's first meal after giving birth shall be the placenta. She needs all the vitamins, hormones and nutrients, contained in the afterbirth, for her puppies. The placental hormones also promote contractions and milk production.

It may well be that a maiden bitch is so overcome with all these new events that she looks at her firstborn puppy and does not know what to do with it. It is now the breeder's turn to act. He should hold the puppy to the bitch and try to persuade her to lick it. All our preparations now come into their own. The bitch licks the hand with its interesting scent, licks the puppy and, as a rule, her instincts awaken and she cleans away the sac and begins to wash the puppy.

Should the bitch be so dazed that her instincts fail to function for the moment, then the breeder must do her work for her. There is no time to lose! The newly-born pup is no longer connected, via the placenta, to the mother's circulation, and so the supply of oxygen is broken off. There is also the danger that, in taking his first breath, the puppy will draw fluid into his nose and mouth and suffocate. The breeder must act and act fast!

The puppy should be held in the hand in a head-down position, and the membrane should be broken at its throat so that the amniotic fluid can drain sideways and not get into the puppy's mouth, nose, or lungs. The membranous sac should be removed upwards like a glove and, at the same time, the umbilical cord should be firmly pressed between finger and thumb. Again, the breeder should try to interest the bitch in the puppy, and encourage her to sever the umbilical cord. If she is still not interested, this task will have to be performed by the breeder, pressing the cord firmly between two fingernails and breaking it off about an inch (two centimetres) from the puppy's navel.

If the puppy is not showing signs of life, it should be rubbed with a warm towel. Vigorous massaging often produces the first, longed-for cry. This should come soon, as time is running out! Shake the puppy – head down – a few times to get any remaining fluid out of its lungs. If necessary, the breeder can hold the puppy to his or her own mouth and try to suck the fluid from the mouth and nose, and then commence breathing into it. To do this, the puppy's entire muzzle must be held in the mouth, and the amniotic fluid gently sucked out. After spitting this out, a few breaths can be gently exhaled into the puppy. Great care must be taken as too much pressure could injure it.

Some breeders swear by administering a drop of diluted brandy on to the puppy's tongue. However, in my experience, it is the rubbing and shaking, clearing the puppy's nose and respiratory passages, which are considerably more effective and, above all, quicker.

This race for time to hear the first cry is sometimes really hair-raising. It is important to appreciate that a newborn puppy is not nearly as fragile as it might appear. It can tolerate quite vigorous handling. Take a look at the instinctive action on the part of the bitch, who goes to work quite roughly when she dries off her puppies. If the bitch has failed to take an interest and you are trying to bring the puppy to life, never give up too soon. We have had puppies who have been stuck in the birth canal outside their sac for half an hour. They have arrived blue and apparently lifeless, but my wife has managed to bring them back to life. Sometimes this has taken as long as five minutes.

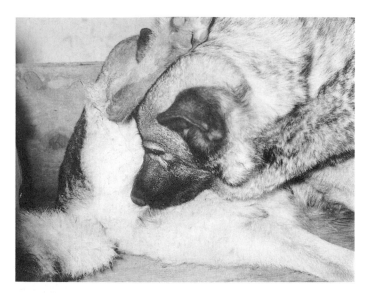

THE BIRTH PROCESS

Before the birth of the first puppy.

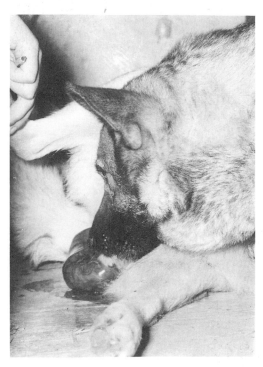

Just born.

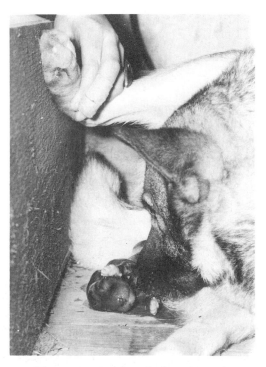

The puppy is already free from the placental sac.

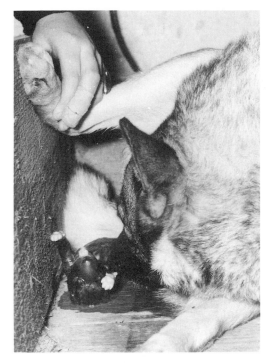

The mother licks the puppy, stimulating it to breathe.

The newborn puppy searches for a teat.

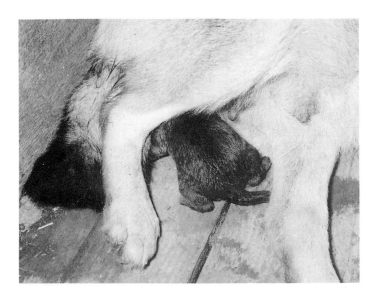

At first, it goes in the wrong direction.

Instinctively, the puppy changes course and finds its way to a teat.

The first vital drink.

The normal rhythm of a birth: While number three is still being licked clean, number four arrives.

Opening up the placental sac.

The puppy emerges from the sac.

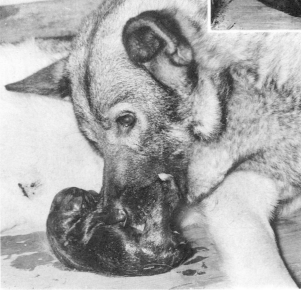

Severing the umbilical cord.

Licking the newborn puppy.

While the mother deals with this puppy, number three finds its way to a teat.

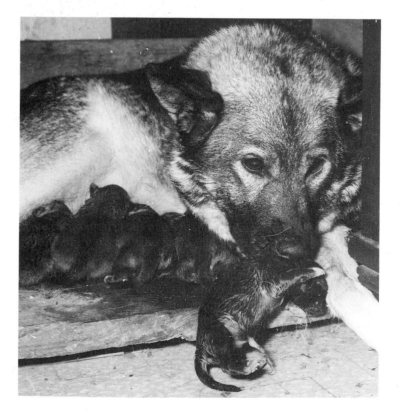

The bitch moves a puppy. Sometimes she may appear quite rough in her handling, but, in most cases, her maternal instinct will guide her.

The mother tends her new family.

Fresh water is offered to the bitch.

Another possible course of action is to hold the puppy under the cold tap for a few seconds, rub it dry, and try breathing into it. The ribs can be depressed and released, as in first-aid administered artificial respiration. Slight pressure is exerted on the chest and then released. A little salt placed on the tongue can also act as a stimulant.

These skills may be urgently required in the case of a Caesarean section. The anaesthetised mother is in a deep sleep and cannot care for her puppies. Worse still, the anaesthetic will have entered the puppies' circulation via the mother's bloodstream, and they will be slightly anaesthetised. Additionally, the pups will not have had to make their way through the narrow birth canal, in which pressure and stress definitely have an animating effect. Puppies surgically removed from the uterine horns require immediate intensive care, of the kind described above. In the case of a Caesarean section, it is not only the skill of the surgeon that matters but also the skill of those attending to the puppies. The number of live puppies delivered by Caesarean section depends equally on the skill of both parties.

DURATION OF THE BIRTH PROCESS

How long does the delivery of a puppy take? As we already know, the first one has the hardest time and, therefore, needs a little longer. As a rule, from four to six contractions are required to express a puppy, and the delivery of an individual puppy takes approximately three minutes. Naaktgeboren analysed the delivery phase of thirty-nine births. Six puppies were born in less than one minute, and sixteen arrived within three minutes. One dubious fact ascertained by this investigation appears to be that ten puppies took more than ten minutes to be delivered, with times of ten, fifteen, twenty-five, thirty, and even forty-five minutes! These slow deliveries occurred most frequently in small breeds and in Bulldogs. I shall return to this subject when dealing with whelping problems. Let us go one step forward and deal with the duration of a whole whelping. A decisive factor here is the intervals at which the puppies are born. From his experience with wild dogs, Eberhard Trumler reports an average of two hours duration for a litter of six. This would be one puppy every twenty minutes. Eberhard Trumler considers it reasonable to double this time for the domestic dog. This means that the average bitch would require four hours to give birth to her six puppies, and we could expect one puppy to be born every forty minutes.

Naaktgeboren worked out the average interval between the birth of two puppies on the basis of documentation collected at 172 whelpings. He concluded that the interval between the birth of puppies was forty-five minutes, which largely coincides with Trumler's conclusions. As a rule, however, the second puppy is born more quickly than the first, and that from the seventh puppy onwards, intervals may become longer, probably because the bitch is growing tired. In Naaktgeboren's statistics, the intervals between the eighth and ninth puppy were, on average, seventy-seven minutes.

Naaktgeboren concludes that puppies are born at similar intervals owing to the fact that the horns of the uterus begin to shorten as they are vacated. During the birth, the puppies are being steadily forced towards the cervix, and, thus, the distance each puppy has to cover is approximately the same.

Prolonged rest periods may occur during whelping. In general, I would advise calling the vet if the interval is more than two hours. In the case of some bitches, this may be due to uterine inertia – lack of the hormones that promote the birth process – or a dead puppy blocking the passage (more about this under whelping problems).

It is sometimes not easy to be certain that all the puppies have been born. A short walk is useful here, with close observation of the bitch's flanks. Experienced breeders have an eye for this and can tell when all the puppies have arrived. The beginner needs some assistance at this point, either from an experienced breeder or a veterinarian.

BREECH BIRTHS

Many breeders are haunted by the idea that rear presentation (breech birth) is dangerous. Clearly, and quite mistakenly, they transfer the difficulties arising in the human medical world to the breeding of dogs. As a general rule, a breech birth – hind feet and tail appearing first – is no more complicated than a normal birth, in which the puppy comes into the world head first. A look at statistics makes this quite clear.

Naaktgeboren has researched this subject in great detail. From 768 puppies, 511 entered the world head-first and 257 feet-first, which is very nearly a ratio of 2:1. In an evaluation of the giant breeds (Great Dane, St Bernard, Leonberger) and equally, in the Toy breeds with a shoulder height of up to ten inches (twenty-four centimetres), half the puppies were born in the rear presentation. In the large breeds such as the German Shepherd and Greyhound, working dogs and gundogs, about a quarter of the puppies were born breech.

BREED AND SIZE OF LITTER

This book is intended, in the first place, for breeders of purebred dogs, and it is, therefore, important to highlight the relationship between the size of the breed, the number of puppies in a litter, and whelping difficulties. It is a fairly well known fact that big breeds have, as a rule, a larger 'quiverful of children', and that parturition usually proceeds much more easily. The smaller the breed, the fewer puppies, and the more potentially complicated the birth. Why should this be so?

U. Sierts-Roth made an interesting calculation in 1953, in which he expressed in percentages the birth-weight of the puppy in relation to the weight of the bitch. I consider these figures very informative:

TABLE 12: BIRTH-WEIGHT OF PUPPY IN RELATION TO WEIGHT OF MOTHER
Source: U. Sierts-Roth.

Great Dane	1.03 %	**Skye Terrier**	2.80 %
Rottweiler	1.05%	**Whippet**	2.89 %
St Bernard	1.14 %	**Dachshund**	3.34 %
Greyhound	1.70 %	**Welsh Terrier**	3.48 %
Boxer	1.78 %	**Pekingese**	3.60 %
German Shepherd	1.78 %	**Pinscher**	4.20 %
Chow Chow	1.87 %	**Pomeranian**	4.34 %
Hovawart	1.94 %	**Brussels Griffon**	4.59 %
Pointer	1.99 %	**Miniature Pinscher**	6.12 %
Afghan Hound	2.34%		

It is not difficult to see that puppies born to bitches of the breeds in the first column are tiny in comparison to their mothers. No wonder that these litters are, as a rule, large and the puppies born much more easily than those in the second column. Puppies of larger breeds are small in comparison to their mothers, and according to breeders, births are relatively simple.

There are some more interesting statistics concerned with the medium-sized litter and its relationship to the size and breed of the brood bitch. Naaktgeboren evaluated 395 litters with a total of 2,321 puppies. This works out to a medium-sized litter of 5.87 puppies. Thus, the average size of a litter for these breeds is around six puppies, a number that breeders have come to accept as normal.

This material becomes really interesting when it is broken down into groups according to size. Naaktgeboren used a tape-measure to differentiate between sizes. Personally, I think that weight might be a better basis, since so many Breed Standards have made it their aim to shorten the legs of large breeds. However, Naaktgeboren's breakdown of breeds affords us some interesting information.

TABLE 13: THE RELATIONSHIP BETWEEN LITTER SIZE AND SIZE OF BREED
Source: Naaktgeboren

Height at Shoulder in cm.	Number of Litters	Number of Puppies	Average size of litter
up to 24 cm	18	72	4.0
25-40 cm	118	540	4.6
41-50 cm	127	728	5.7
51-70 cm	125	918	7.3
over 70 cm	7	63	9.0
Total	395	2,321	5.87

Naaktgeboren also used the results of this research to investigate whether there was any difference between the size of litters in maiden bitches and those bitches who had previous litters. He found no indication to confirm this point. It is, however, a definite fact that the size of the litter increases in relation to shoulder height. This research also confirmed that in litters of the same breed, the larger the litter, the lower the weight of the individual puppy. Where there is only one puppy in a litter, this can lead to considerable difficulty, which will be dealt with later.

CARING FOR THE NEW FAMILY
The newborn puppy's first, and most important, objective is to get to a teat in order to receive nourishment, and it shows great energy and determination in getting to the source of the supply. In contrast to the behavioural pattern of the piglet, which always uses the same teat, the puppy takes any teat it can reach. Having arrived at its objective, the puppy takes firm hold of the teat and begins to work on it with its front paws. The suction in the puppy's mouth, and the paws working alternately against the teat stimulate the let-down of milk.

Even while the puppy is nursing – or immediately afterwards – the bitch will wash the tail end and genitals with her broad tongue. This massage with the tongue is vital to the puppy. From the nourishment it has received through the placenta, the black faecal matter that remains in its bowels must be evacuated. The massaging tongue removes this meconium, and the bladder is emptied at the same time. In the first few days after birth, the puppy is not able to pass urine or faeces without the aid of the mother's tongue. If the bitch does not lick her puppies or licks them too little, this can lead to constipation and can endanger the lives of the puppies.

Sometimes a bitch may show a peculiar lack of instinct. We once had a bitch who very busily cleaned the anus, but if she happened to get urine on her tongue, she was so disgusted that she gave up all further effort to clean her puppies.

If the bitch does not do this job or does it rather carelessly, the breeder must intervene. The bitch massages the puppies' tummies as well as the area round the anus. The breeder must copy this action, using a piece of soft flannel, cotton-wool, or a small sponge. This should be moistened in warm water (body temperature around 101 degrees Fahrenheit, 38 degrees Centigrade), or a little oil can be used. If you massage in a circular movement on the naked tummy and round the anus, this serves to relieve constipation, and urine and faeces are discharged. Some puppies are very sensitive and do not relish being rubbed with a sponge or a cloth. In this case, a finger dipped in salad oil usually does the trick. Never forget that constipation can cost a puppy its life. As a rule, puppies clearly show their discomfort by crying and restlessness. It is important to keep a close check on the navel area. The bitch has usually severed the umbilical cord with her premolars, and a short end, around an inch (two centimetres) long, remains. The umbilical cord carries vessels for arterial and for venous blood, which enabled the puppy to be joined to the mother's circulatory system. If the breeder has to intervene and cuts the cord with scissors or a knife, a serious loss of blood would be unavoidable, unless the cord was tied with thread prior to cutting. However, squeezing the cord between the nails of the forefinger and thumb closely simulates the severing action of the bitch's premolars. It is only necessary to bind up the cord if the bitch has been over-zealous and has severed it too close to the puppy's body, thus causing bleeding. If the cord ends are bluish-pink when checked, everything is in good order. Within 24 to 36 hours, the umbilical cord will dry, shrink, and fall off.

If the bitch severs the cord too close to the navel, this can lead to bruising of the skin on the stomach. However, these small lacerations usually disappear when licked by the bitch. In extreme cases, injuries can be inflicted – the skin of the stomach may be torn, and the intestines laid bare. This is usually the cause of canine cannibalism. The bitch herself disposes of puppies injured in this way via her own stomach. In any case, the puppy cannot be saved, and should be taken from the bitch and released from its suffering.

It is most important to make sure that the placenta is delivered for every puppy. This is simply a matter of counting. It can happen that when the last puppy in one of the uterine horns is born, a placenta may be retained because a puppy from the other horn is starting. This can easily lead to a severe infection. Twenty-four hours after parturition is completed the placenta will begin to putrefy. If a placenta has been retained, the veterinarian will have to give the bitch an injection to stimulate contractions, which should produce the afterbirth.

As long as the bitch wishes, she may consume all the afterbirths. If there is a large litter, she may well bring up the placenta again after swallowing it. If she does this and does not attempt to consume it a second time, the placenta should be removed.

In the intervals between the births of the puppies, the bitch should be given a drink of fresh water. She usually takes this avidly as it helps to wash out her mouth. She can also be given glucose in her water, but never make it too sweet. We have never needed to give other restoratives during parturition, since the bitch takes too much in any case with the afterbirths, the amniotic fluid, and cleaning up her puppies.

It is advisable to keep on cleaning the whelping box during the birth with the detergent solution (mentioned earlier) and a good, absorbent cloth. The amniotic fluid, blood, meconium, and urine, must all be removed. To clean the bitch (around her genitals and tail), fresh supplies of lukewarm water should be used. We use two cloths and two buckets, one with the mild disinfectant solution for the whelping box, and the other for cleaning up the bitch. The sheet on the bottom of the box is also frequently replaced.

If the puppies have been removed from their dam during the advent of a new arrival they should, of course, be put to her again between births for her to clean and suckle them. Bitches that have confidence in their owners do not object to being helped in this way. Each puppy should be weighed immediately after it is born and has been cleaned up. Detailed notes should be made on each birth, giving time and birth-weight. If your puppies are uniform in colour, they should be marked immediately after they are born to avoid getting them mixed up later on. The best way to mark them is to snip away a little hair with a pair of fine scissors. For example, if there are three puppies of exactly the same colour, leave one unmarked, snip a little hair from behind the right ear of the second puppy, and from behind the left ear of the third puppy. The coat grows very quickly so that the markings need repeated renewal. Marking with a felt pen or spots of colour appear to be useless, for under the dam's rough tongue these marks very quickly disappear. In addition to time and birth weight, these markings are entered in the record of the birth; thus an accurate account can be kept of each individual puppy.

The birth is over, and the bitch is tired. After a short outing, she returns to her puppies, which are all dependent upon her for a constantly repeated cycle of feeding and cleaning. Many books recommend a good meal of beef juice, eggs and cereal flakes to strengthen the bitch. This advice is good. If the bitch will take the food, she should be fed. I advise against milk foods, so frequently recommended, at this point. In consuming the afterbirths, the bitch has absorbed a great many substances that can lead to diarrhoea, and adding milk can only make matters worse. My dogs are accustomed to meat meals from early life onwards. So we give raw meat, which does act as a laxative. Afterwards, they sleep peacefully while their little family feeds.

ASSESSING INHERITED DRIVE

The newborn puppy is entirely the product of the parents' genes; at this early stage, environmental influences have not yet begun to work. That is the reason ethnologists try to ascertain, at this particular point, what psychological characteristics the puppy has inherited. Then, and only then, is it possible to discern the inherited qualities. The nerve centres convey impulses that propel the puppy to carry out individual, co-ordinated actions, and from birth, the puppy is filled up by a single drive – the drive to reach the source of nourishment.

Based on these deliberations, Eberhard Trumler has developed a "biotonus test". He considers that, if a puppy does not attempt to find the mother's teat within the first few minutes of life, it is not genetically sound. Defective genes cannot be cured; the only course of action is to cull or exclude such animals from the breeding programme.

In order to illustrate this more clearly, I should like to quote from Trumler's book, *Mit dem Hund auf Du: (On Best Terms with your Dog)*:

"I consider the first few minutes of life to be vital. Without the slightest experience of life, propelled simply and solely by his inherited genes, the puppy is set in motion. It is possible to measure the strength of this drive fairly reliably, since it is expressed in the first few minutes of life in the liveliness of the movements of the newborn puppy, in his energy and the speed with which he finds a teat and begins to suck. It is now, within the first hour of life, that differences among individual puppies are made clear. These are distinct differences, not caused by environment, by chance or learnt from experience, but simply and solely the result of inherited characteristics. These first few minutes of life afford us the opportunity, never to be repeated, to assess clearly the inherited vitality of the puppy and future dog".

Let us take a look at our puppy, the way it moves its head from side to side, searching, the mouth poised upwards, the plaintive cry for nourishment. The inborn energy is steered instinctively in its search for warmth and sense of perception. While searching, the lifted head swings to one side and then the other, head and shoulders bend first to the left then to the right. The back legs are braced against the floor of the box. These are all purely instinctive movements. If an external stimulus occurs, it will take over the role of steering. The mother's coat exerts a warmth stimulus, the little head works forward along the coat and, lifted up, comes to the teat. Again, instinctively, the little mouth opens, the tongue envelops the teat like a funnel, and, then with the tiny paws treading the teat, sucking commences.

In the biotonus test, the puppy is placed in the centre of a board over which rough linen has been stretched. The linen is marked off in circular segments. Weaker puppies just lie where they are put or move very little, whereas stronger ones crawl around with drive, putting all their energy into their search for warmth and nourishment. The observer notes the way the puppy moves and the speed, and the marked-off circles and segments act as a measure. It is also possible to make deductions during the birth to supplement the biotonus test. Trumler writes that top marks should be given to a puppy that searches vigorously for nourishment once freed from its membranous sac, and to one that begins to struggle even when still within the sac. Trumler gives lower marks to the puppy that first rests a while and then goes actively on his search. Lower marks go to the puppy that is drawn to the mother's warm coat but is unable to find the teat and has to be helped before it begins to suck, and the puppy that finds the teat, sucks just a little, and then lets go, is similarly evaluated The inactive puppy that has to be placed on the teat but does not suck vigorously, and has to be kept alive with the aid of a feeding bottle or tube should be given bottom marks. Trumler recommends not attempting to rear such puppies but having them painlessly destroyed. The same applies to abnormally small puppies.

Although I fully recognise that this is the right attitude, I should like to add something to it. The actual progress of the birth is decisive for the proper assessment of the situation. We had one, very large puppy that was stuck for more than half an hour in the birth canal after the sac had broken. We removed the membrane covering his mouth as he lay in the vagina, enabling him to breathe. This strong puppy had turned blue over half his body during his thirty-minute sojourn in the birth canal. For the first few minutes, he lay in a completely exhausted state. I believe that he had expended a great amount of energy in order to arrive alive in the world. I readily admit that we had difficulty in getting him to nurse, and he had to be put to his mother's teat repeatedly, where he sucked but little in the first hours, due to exhaustion. However, this puppy was the pick of the litter at seven weeks. All his life he remained a powerful dog with a distinctive personality. He gave his owners endless pleasure and became a valuable stud dog. His progeny were also outstanding for their excellent temperaments.

As to the very small puppies, the breeder must exercise individual judgement on this point, but weight alone should not be the main criterion. We have had a tiny pup that weighed 150 grams less than his siblings at birth – about half the normal birth-weight. In the biotonus test at birth, this puppy achieved top marks. This puppy also developed well, even though he was unable to catch up with his brothers' and sisters' weight in the first seven weeks. He went on to become a good, sound, and very active dog. However, if a very light birth-weight coincides with a poor biotonus reaction, the puppy would appear to have very little chance of survival.

Even though I fully acknowledge the value of the biotonus test, I have to admit that, now and again, I have helped puppies weakened by a difficult birth to take their first feed at the teat. To do this, use the finger and thumb to lightly press open the puppy's jaws, and place them round the slightly massaged teat. Hold the puppy in this position, if necessary, until it props itself up on its hind legs and the front paws begin their treading motion. We have put these puppies to the teat several times a day during the first few days, and have taught them to hold their own among the other members of the litter. I can make no excuses to the ethnologists, who believe that only the fittest puppies should survive, and the weakest should not be aided by the breeder. The only excuse I can put forward is that for more than twenty-five years we have had very even litters, and that when our puppies left us at seven weeks they have always been of sound temperament and full of vitality. Our dogs have frequently been well placed in breeders' and progeny groups. It is inevitable that the breeder's feelings take over now and then, and common sense is relegated. Feelings do, after all, play a role in dog breeding.

MALFORMATIONS AND INJURIES
Each puppy must be closely examined for any possible malformation. I have already written about puppies harmed by antibiotics. In one case, the top of the skull was not closed; in two others the

joints of the hind legs were doubled, and the legs hung down loosely like those of a rag doll. Clearly, such puppies are not capable of living. In quite a number of breeds, cleft palates and also harelips occur occasionally as hereditary defects. More frequently, puppies are born with cleft palates. In this case, the roof of the mouth has a gap in the centre. This means that when the affected puppy sucks, no vacuum is produced and it cannot, therefore, suck at the teat. If the puppy is fed with a bottle, the milk runs through the gap and out again through its nose. Sometimes puppies are born very weak or under-sized.

Throughout the years, experience has sadly shown us that however hard you try, it is hardly ever possible to rear affected puppies successfully. Puppies with cleft palates are anatomically condemned; the weak, soft puppies are usually suffering from congenital heart trouble, and the harelip is a real malformation. Sometimes you come across a puppy whose abdomen has been torn open, and sometimes the dam treads on a puppy so clumsily that a leg is broken. In all these cases, the best solution is quick, painless death administered by your vet. It is an interesting fact that a bitch, as a rule, instinctively rejects such puppies. She may push them aside or carry them out of the whelping box. The quicker the breeder acts, the better it is for all concerned.

Unfortunately, even after the whole litter has been born, we cannot be sure that no further problems will arise. There are a number of risks concerning the bitch and her ability to cope with her puppies. There is the bitch who leaps into the whelping box and, depending on her weight, causes severe injuries to her pups. Others lie on their puppies and do not react at all, however loudly they squeal. (Again, fitting the whelping box with rails to cope with this problem will usually suffice.)

I have to admit that Bull Terriers are often poor mothers. Some bitches will only allow their puppies to suck when physically compelled to do so; others bite their puppies to death; and again, others trample around roughly on their babies. We have been left to deal with puppies with broken bones, one with a torn lung, and a semi-paralysed puppy. Close supervision of mother and her litter, is therefore essential, at least for the first twelve days. This supervision entails keeping watch day and night without interruption, ready to act at the slightest sign of danger.

This is a particular problem relating to the Bull Terrier breed, and it results from past breeding when selection was never based on good maternal qualities. It is probable that these poor maternal qualities reflect the misguided emphasis formerly placed on breeding for the so-called fighting dog heredity. This breed is an extreme case, yet, all the same, it is important to maintain close observation of dam and puppies of whatever breed during the first few days. I should like to repeat that in 90 per cent of cases all goes well, and there is no necessity for the breeder to intervene. I have always envied those breeders whose bitches of good, sound instinct save them so much care and worry. If the scientist were to tell me now that it would probably be better to allow dog breeds to die out in which bitches show such severe deficiencies that they have to be watched day and night to avoid injury to the puppies, then I cannot raise any positive objections. Most probably, my love of the Bull Terrier breed, has made me somewhat blind to the problem. It is therefore incumbent upon me to agree unconditionally with the demands of the ethnologist to eliminate those strains in which the maternal instinct is lacking.

WHELPING PROBLEMS

GATHERING KNOWLEDGE
Naaktgeboren is quite right when he says: "The most dangerous thing is for the breeder to be overcome by panic!"

Knowledge is the best means of combatting any form of panic. In order to be able to provide

The mother is the puppies' first teacher, and they learn much from her example. This German Shepherd bitch shows a lovely, calm temperament as she lies with her playing puppies.

Photo: Steve Nash.

The mother will be quick to reprimand a puppy if it steps out of line.

Photo: Steve Nash.

ABOVE: For the first few weeks, puppies, like these Greyhound pups, rely on their mother for security.

BELOW: Puppies also learn a great deal from playing with each other.

Photos: Steve Nash.

Through play, a pecking order is established among the members of the litter.
Photos: Steve Nash.

ABOVE: At feeding time, the strongest most determined puppies will get the lion's share. Note the puppy who is missing out on the action!

BELOW: Puppies are always ready for a game, and licking out this empty milk jug provides great entertainment.

Photos: Steve Nash.

By six weeks of age, the puppies are beginning to emerge as individuals with their own distinct personalities.

Photos: Steve Nash.

ABOVE: Swift to react, this Shetland Sheepdog puppy is learning from every new experience.

BELOW: It is important to give the puppies plenty of human contact while they are at their most receptive.   *Photos Carol Ann Johnson.*

Puppies must also learn to get on with other animals.

LEFT: Children and puppies enjoy a special relationship.

BELOW: A beautifully reared Border Collie puppy ready to take his place in the world.

Photos: John Sellers.

readers with this vital, basic knowledge, I shall deal with whelping problems in the order in which they are listed in Professor K. Arbeiter's book *Clinic of Canine Diseases*. I shall try to express, in my own words and from my own experience, the causes of these problems and the possibilities of dealing with them. I am much indebted to the leading veterinary surgeons at the universities of Vienna and Utrecht for their most excellent suggestions and illustrations.

Anyone who undertakes to write a book on dog breeding must, of necessity, assemble their material from the research and expertise of many specialists. No one should ever presume to believe themselves capable of providing readers with a full picture solely out of personal experience. I am, therefore, both willing and happy to admit that a considerable part of this book documents the knowledge of others, to whom I should like to express my gratitude for allowing me to make use of their knowledge, research and experience. It is reasonable to suppose that in many ways this book documents the standard of knowledge on dog breeding arrived at today.

The fact that whelping problems arise, and will always arise, does not indicate that the birth of puppies is, in general, a difficult matter. I am quite certain that if the breeder adopts the right attitude and breeds only with bitches of sound instinct, approximately 90 per cent of all births will proceed with no trouble at all.

Many of the complications I am about to describe force one, of necessity, to the conclusion that false breeding stock selection policy is at the root of many of these problems. I am in complete agreement with the English scientist, Freak, who condemns all those physical abnormalities – and psychological defects – that inevitably lead to complications at parturition. It is my candid opinion that all those breeds that, owing to anatomical or psychological abnormalities, are either unable to reproduce themselves or else do so only under great difficulty, come under the heading of crippled breeds. It remains to be hoped that this book may help those responsible to recognise these problems and thus take steps to solve them.

WEAKNESS IN LABOUR CONTRACTIONS

The problem of weak contractions has already been mentioned earlier in the section on normal births. Inadequate contractions, or weak labour, is due to an hereditary, functional failure of the hormonal regulatory system. In my own kennels, I have always been able to predict, with considerable certainty, which of our younger brood bitches was likely to require veterinary aid at parturition and which would not. We have also had lines that were completely free from this problem. This gives me a clear indication that careful breeding selection is important for overcoming this disorder.

Apart from the hereditary disposition, a so-called primary labour weakness – apparent right from the start of the birth – may occur if there is a very large number of puppies in the litter. In these cases, the abdominal wall is excessively stretched, and there is also, frequently, the additional danger of eclampsia. A weakness in labour can also arise if the foetuses are unevenly distributed in the uterine horns, or if the uterine musculature has been previously damaged by difficult births.

Characteristic of labour weakness is the fact that (despite the discharge of vaginal mucus and sometimes even placental fluid) the birth does not commence, and the bitch does not strain. The only way to overcome this problem is for the veterinarian to administer a hormone injection to stimulate contractions. It is of vital importance to calculate the dose very carefully indeed, since an overdose can call forth a uterine spasm (uterus spasmus). If repeated injections do not have the desired effect, a Caesarean section is the only possible solution.

It has already been mentioned that, during the birth of a large number of puppies in one litter, the good, strong contractions seen at the beginning gradually dwindle after a time. This constitutes a so-called secondary labour weakness, and it is a normal occurrence in a large litter. The probable cause is hormonal exhaustion. This weakness can also be overcome by the injection of hormones. Should injections not prove successful, again the only remaining alternative is a Caesarean section.

NARROW PELVIS – SINGLE-PUPPY BIRTHS

As has already been seen, Eberhard Trumler regards the narrowness of the pelvis in many dog breeds as the cause of the most difficult births. The mother's pelvic outlet forms a kind of bottleneck through which the puppy has to pass. This problem occurs most frequently in Toy dogs, in Bulldogs, and related breeds. The British scientist, Wright, studied this problem in detail as early as 1934.

Normally, the pelvic cavity of a bitch is longer than it is wide. In his large mongrel bitch, Trumler measured a length of 78 millimetres (3¼ in.) and a width of 66.6 millimetres (2¾ in.). Wright's research results established the fact that small breeds have a rounder and therefore shorter pelvic cavity, instead of the longish oval one seen in larger breeds. Parturition problems are considerably more pronounced in bitches with this small, round pelvis. To add to this difficulty, it would seem that breeders of small breeds appear to feel the need to compensate for the small size of their dogs by requiring, in the Breed Standard, a particularly large head.

Naaktgeboren points out that in small breeds such as the Toy Poodle, the Dachshund, the Papillon, the Maltese, and the Lhasa Apso, births are, as a rule, perfectly normal. However, he has, at times, registered horrific births in the Chihuahua, the Griffon Bruxellois, the Boston Terrier, the French Bulldog, and the English Bulldog. Dr Emil Hauck quotes from the anatomical measurements established by his fellow countryman Fritz Kess in the year 1924. In this study, fluctuations in the measurements of French Bulldogs are given between 28.8 and 43.6 millimetres. The heads of the mature foetuses measured between 30.3 and 38.6 millimetres. Advanced mathematics are not needed, in this case, to perceive that a number of puppies are quite unable to leave their mother's body via the pelvic opening.

For many years, I have known a number of Bulldog breeders who have directed all their efforts toward breeding for natural births, and who have taken every bitch that had a Caesarean section out of their breeding programmes. There is, in fact, no possible alternative. Trumler is perfectly right when he condemns systematic breeding with bitches prone to Caesarean births as cruelty to animals.

In addition to the far too frequent incidence of the narrow pelvic cavity, the single-puppy birth, occurring as it often does in individual breeds, plays a considerable role in problem whelpings. Dr

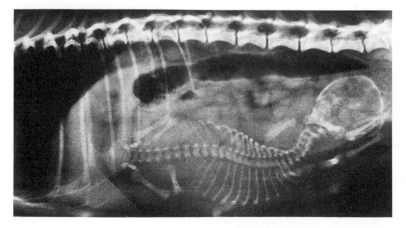

Poodle bitch, eighteen months old; 58th day of pregnancy, single puppy.
The foetus is much too large, and so a Caesarean section is necessary.

Koeppel states: "Brood bitches of those breeds in which single-puppy litters are common – for the most part, bitches of Toy breeds – should be examined by a veterinarian in the sixth week of pregnancy at the latest. Single puppies lead, in many cases, to problems both during pregnancy and at whelping, and this makes constant veterinary control essential".

Looking at an X-ray of a single puppy, taken in late pregnancy, it is easy to see the reason for Dr Koeppel's concern. It has benefited exclusively from all that nourishing food its mother has been provided with. When a single-puppy litter has been diagnosed, it is essential to control the dam's food intake in such a way that there is little surplus left for the foetus. Thus, it is clearly of great importance to have the bitch checked early enough by an expert veterinarian. When matters progress too far, it is quite impossible for the puppy to be born in the natural way. In the case of relatively narrow pelvic openings and single puppies, Caesarean section is nearly always unavoidable.

FOETAL MALFORMATION

Despite good, steady, powerful contractions, a normal pelvis and well-opened birth passages there are occasions when a birth does not take place. The cause is generally found to be a foetus that is too large, malformed, or incorrectly positioned, or a dead foetus that is blocking the birth canal. An example of this is when the puppy's head is bent at the neck and, with its chin resting on its breastbone, the puppy has become stuck in the canal. A puppy with its head bent forward in this way takes up approximately twice the amount of room as a normally positioned puppy. We have had one or two cases of this kind in our own kennels. The puppy was always dead and had to be removed by Caesarean section. I have not been able to discover any reason for this particular faulty positioning.

With foetal malformations of this kind, there are two options. Although a Caesarean section is almost always called for, the alternative would be to use forceps to extract the puppy. (More about this method in the following section.) In principle, I believe that the best solution in such cases is always a Caesarean section.

MANUAL OBSTETRICS – FORCEPS BIRTH

These two methods come under the heading of conservative obstetrics. A distinction must be made when determining the position of the puppy:

1. The puppy is stuck in the dam's vulvar cleft (vestibule or introitus vaginae).
2. The puppy is stuck in the dam's pelvis.

When the puppy has passed through the mother's pelvic passage, it has overcome the most difficult stage of birth. If it then becomes stuck in the vulvar cleft, a skilled veterinarian should be able to assist it on the rest of the way. In dealing with normal births, I have already advised the breeder to call in the veterinary surgeon if a prolonged interval between births occurs.

If the veterinarian comes to the conclusion that the puppy has become stuck in the birth canal, he will feel for its head or hindquarters with his left hand. After raising the bitch's vulva, the index and middle finger of the right hand will grasp either the puppy's head or the hind legs. Manipulating the vagina in this manner usually induces massive straining on the part of the bitch. When a contraction occurs, the foetus is slightly turned and withdrawn, while the left hand continues to stem the bitch's perineum. This obstetrical method requires a great deal of skill and experience, as well as an excellent knowledge of anatomy.

If the puppy has been driven further along the birth canal by the contractions, the experienced

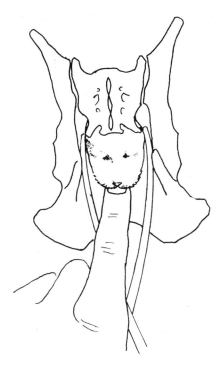

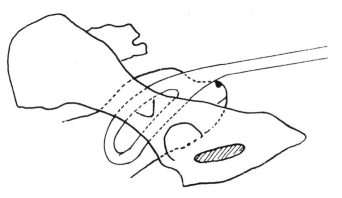

LEFT: Forceps birth I: The forceps, controlled by a finger, is placed carefully around the puppy's head.
                                    Source: Vienna 1986.

ABOVE: Forceps birth II: The forceps is closed around the puppy's head in the mother's pelvis. The forceps must be correctly applied if injury to bitch or puppy is to be avoided.   Source: Vienna 1986.

breeder with skilled, slender fingers, is well able to assist it, working in conjunction with the bitch's contractions. For this purpose, a first-class quality surgical glove is essential. With slender fingers, the puppy is gripped by two folds of skin, either at the side of the neck or hindquarters. When a contraction occurs, the puppy is slightly turned and extracted. As a rule, it is released from its unfortunate position by the very first contraction.

Apart from the Caesarean section, the only other method of releasing puppies that have become jammed is by means of forceps, in the hands of a skilled veterinary surgeon. Before attempting this method, a careful check must be made to ensure that the puppy is not too large to be born with the aid of forceps. The veterinarian must also ascertain whether other puppies are waiting to be born behind the one that is stuck. If this is so, a Caesarean section is, as a rule, the better solution for the puppies. Forceps are only advisable if it is the last puppy that has become stuck.

In a forceps birth, the index finger of the left hand is inserted into the vagina to locate the puppy. The forceps is then introduced beneath the finger in such a way that its broad jaws clamp over the puppy's head or hindquarters. The left index finger keeps steady contact with the puppy, while the right hand gently withdraws the forceps holding the puppy, in conjunction with a contraction. It should be possible to extract the puppy even if it has become jammed in the dam's pelvic passage. The puppy is held with the left hand, through the mother's abdominal wall, and gently pressed toward the forceps, which is being held in position in the vagina by the right hand. Anyone following this procedure will surely agree with me that a very high standard of veterinary skill is essential.

It is not difficult to imagine the strain that this kind of birth puts upon the sexual organs and nerves of a bitch. The danger of injury in the entire vaginal area cannot be precluded. In small and dwarf breeds, the amount of room in a bitch's anatomy would make such a procedure appear extremely doubtful. The success achieved in Caesarean section operations today means that surgery, as a general rule, is preferable to a forceps birth.

CAESAREAN SECTION

A general anaesthetic is administered for this operation. The choice of anaesthetic and the dosage are of vital importance, since the puppies are still connected to their dam's circulatory system and are, thus, also affected by the anaesthetic. The veterinarian must assess the dosage necessary to ensure freedom from pain for the duration of the operation and, at the same time, a minimum of danger to the unborn puppies. A birth by Caesarean section makes great demands on the speed and skill with which the veterinarian works. Despite the weak dosage, the operation must be completed and the incision sutured before the bitch begins to come around. This makes the Caesarean section one of the greatest tests of surgical proficiency.

A Caesarean section should be carried out in a small animal practice, properly equipped for these emergencies. A very desirable piece of equipment is an apparatus that keeps a constant check on the bitch's heartbeat throughout the operation.

The incision is usually made centrally, between the mammary glands and from a point just below the navel toward the vulva. Today, however, the incision increasingly is made to avoid the bitch's right flank. This method means that the puppies do not have to suckle in close proximity to the healing wound. Both uterine horns are extracted from the abdominal cavity. The surgeon then opens one of the horns, grips the nearest puppy and removes it from the uterus. Easing of the umbilical cord (tension) in conjunction with massage on the outside of the uterine horn, serves to loosen the placenta from its anchorage. The puppy is then freed from its foetal membranes, and the umbilical cord is severed by firmly squeezing it, and then breaking it off.

One puppy after the other is removed from the uterine incision and treated in the same manner. When one horn has been emptied, the second follows, if possible via the same incision. Should this prove impossible, an incision will have to be made in the second horn.

When all the puppies have been born, the uterine incision is sutured, the entire operative field is treated with bactericide, and finally the abdominal wall is stitched. When the incision is made between the mammary glands, a tampon is placed along the wound and stitched in such a way that the puppies' sharp little claws are quite unable to penetrate the area around the wound.

While the surgeon is carrying out this operation at all speed, his well-schooled assistants are dealing with each of the newly-freed puppies and encouraging them to breathe. (This point was dealt with in detail in the section on normal births.) All that remains is to emphasise once again that the success of a Caesarean section depends not just on the skill of the surgeon, but also on the manual dexterity of his assistants in stimulating the puppies to breathe. Given these conditions, all healthy puppies removed by Caesarean section should, as a rule, be able to live.

When faced with a Caesarean section, and bearing in mind the need to eliminate bitches with whelping problems from a breeding programme, you will see that it is advisable to have the bitch's uterus removed in this same operation. In this way, both you and your bitch will be spared a repeat performance of such a stressful episode. Needless to say, there are exceptional cases in which your veterinary surgeon can give you the assurance that the bitch is unlikely to have a second Caesarean the next time around. In these very few cases, it worth leaving the bitch intact. In general, the veterinarian works on the precept that it is possible for a bitch to undergo a birth by Caesarean section twice, and, on occasion, even three times. This may well be correct from the medical point of view, but it is definitely wrong from the breeding angle. Make up your mind, and take the proper decision! My advice is to avoid breeding with a bitch after a first Caesarean section.

Some breeders learn from the unfortunate, sometimes tragic, experience of others – and few

CAESAREAN SECTION

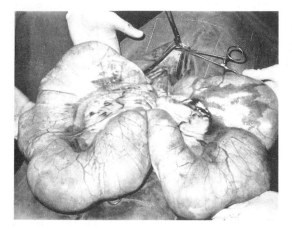

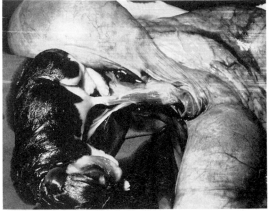

Both the uterine horns have been extracted from the abdomen and are about to be opened.

The first uterine horn has been opened. The puppy is still attached to the placenta by the umbilical cord. The foetal membranes have already been removed.

After the Caesarean section: operational incision in the right flank.

breeders are free from making errors. One of our best brood bitches, whose first two litters had been born perfectly normally, had to undergo a Caesarean section at her third whelping. The fact that she had whelped normally, twice previously, encouraged us to believe that this was exceptional. However, at her fourth whelping she had to be given an injection to stimulate contractions and, although the first puppy was born without undue difficulty, she then laboured for over two hours to expel a second puppy, which finally arrived dead. A further long wait made a Caesarean section unavoidable. The result was one live puppy and two dead foetuses removed from her uterus. At that moment, I made a very dreadful mistake – a mistake that was to cost the bitch her life. Thinking of her outstanding progeny, I failed to insist on her uterus being removed. Five weeks after the Caesarean section, the operation scar ruptured, and a general anaesthetic had to be administered. Only a month after this, she developed a pyometra, and a hysterectomy had to be performed. On this last occasion, it proved impossible to save the bitch. Three operations in short succession, accompanied each time by the administration of antibiotics, proved too much. The pyometra infection failed to respond to the antibiotics and, despite all our efforts, we were unable to save our Lisa. I hope you will be able to make the right decision at the right moment.

When you know a Caesarean section is inevitable, it is essential to make preparations for the puppies you will be bringing home. Make sure to take the well-warmed cardboard box with you, and before undertaking the return journey, the hot-water bottles must be refilled and their temperature checked. Remember that, according to her condition after the Caesarean, lactation may well be delayed in the bitch. When you get home with the mother and her puppies, you must first check whether the bitch is able to feed and clean her puppies in the first few hours, since the colostrum, the first milk secreted after parturition, is of such vital importance to the puppies. (Should bottle feeding become necessary, you will find this dealt with in the following chapter.)

THE FREQUENCY AND CAUSE OF WHELPING PROBLEMS

In his book, Naaktgeboren quotes M.J. Freak's research results. In 1962, this scientist studied 272 cases of whelping problems, and these are listed here in the following table.

TABLE 14: CAUSES OF DIFFICULT BIRTHS
Source: M.J. Freak, 1962

Foetus too large in relation [to pelvis]	77	28.3%
Foetus too large (single puppy)	15	5.5%
Malformation of a puppy	2	0.7%
Incorrect presentation	12	4.4%
Pelvic presentation	35	12.9%
Abnormally soft birth canal	4	1.5%
Pathological pelvis	1	0.3%
Soft abdominal wall (Bulldog)	3	1.1%
Weak primary labour contractions	41	15.5%
Weak secondary labour contractions	44	16.2%
Disorders due to nervous restlessness	17	6.3%
Eclampsia	7	2.6%
Abortion	2	0.7%
Puppies dead before parturition	10	3.7%
Other causes	2	0.7%
	272	100.0%

Taking a close look at the causes listed in this table, it will be found that this material provides an interesting supplement to the various causes already described. It will thus be seen that primary and secondary labour weaknesses contributed to eighty-five (i.e. 31.3 per cent) of all the problem cases. The conclusion has already been reached that the relatively large puppy and the pathological pelvis are only two different aspects of the same problem and that – except in the case of the single-puppy litter – the narrow pelvis is the sole cause of such problems. In these statistics, this is shown to be the cause of seventy-eight (i.e. 28.7 per cent) of the whelping problems. It is clear, then, that these two most frequently occurring factors amount to 60 per cent of all parturition complications. In his study, undertaken by questionnaire, Naaktgeboren investigated a total of 120 litters in which parturition problems arose. His research results are shown in the following table:

TABLE 15: CAUSES (IN PERCENTAGES) OF PARTURITION PROBLEMS IN 120 LITTERS
Source: Naaktgeboren

Exhaustion in the bitch	30%
Dead puppies	25%
Weak contractions	13%
Breech presentation	10%
Too large puppy	7%
Fear	5%
Anterior presentation	3%
Unknown	7%

When considering these statistics, it should be remembered that they constitute the results of research by questionnaire and are not the results of Naaktgeboren's own experience. It would appear that Mrs Freak's statistics are not only given in greater detail, but they are also more comprehensive. The exhaustion factor, on the part of the bitch, may well be the result of a number of anatomical agents leading to this exhausted condition. Our interest here lies mainly in discovering these causes. This also applies in the case of the dead puppies. Why is it that these puppies were dead?

I have, in fact, only incorporated Naaktgeboren's statistics in this book to draw attention to the fact that it is quite natural for a bitch to become exhausted when parturition is difficult, or when she is bearing a large litter. Nature usually regulates these problems by allowing considerable intervals to arise between individual births. Eclampsia is a problem that arises after the birth is over. (I shall be dealing with this subject in the next chapter when we come to the condition of the bitch once the birth is over.)

Chapter Eight

THE NURSING BITCH AND HER PUPPIES

THE NURSING BITCH

Whelping and the suckling of puppies put a very considerable strain, both physically and psychologically, on the brood bitch. After the first deep sleep, she will be facing a constantly increasing risk during the next eight weeks. Raising a litter of orphans makes it very clear indeed what a tremendous amount of nourishment six puppies consume – as well as the task of cleaning up after them. This is a full-time job for the bitch, with hardly a break. Tirelessly, the puppies seek their nourishment and, just as tirelessly, the mother's tongue takes care of cleanliness and stimulates digestion.

The large intake of placentas usually causes some digestive trouble in the bitch. A loose, blackish stool is often passed in small amounts. Do not be worried if, during the first three to four weeks, there is a thickish vaginal discharge consisting of blood and mucus. This reflects the natural regeneration of the bitch's uterus. In time, the blood content diminishes, but it is perfectly normal for the discharge to continue for the entire duration of the lactation period (i.e. for from five to six weeks). There is no cause for concern, unless the discharge becomes purulent or the bitch's temperature continues to be raised over a longish period.

In the first three days after parturition, the bitch's temperature is quite high, usually over 102 degrees Fahrenheit (39.2 and 39.8 degrees Centigrade). If it goes above 103 degrees Fahrenheit (40 degrees Centigrade), it is advisable to call in your veterinarian. This also applies if, after three days, the bitch's temperature is still over 102 degrees Fahrenheit (39 degrees Centigrade).

After whelping, the bitch's nutritional requirements increase rapidly. Naturally, the additional food requirement is in direct proportion to the number of puppies she has to feed. Four puppies mean at least double the normal ration, increasing to treble the ration with six puppies. Due to the intensive metabolism and lactation, the bitch's liquid intake is increased many times, and plenty of fresh water must be available all the time.

Through the milk, considerable quantities of protein, fat, minerals and vitamins are transferred to the puppies, and these have to be replenished in the bitch's own food. Most breeders have little or no idea of how rich the bitch's milk is. The following table is a comparison between the contents of bitch's milk and cow's milk in percentages, and it gives a good impression of the richness of a bitch's milk. The calorific content of bitch's milk is more than twice as great as that of cow's milk.

TABLE 16: A COMPARISON OF BITCH'S MILK AND COW'S MILK, IN PERCENTAGES

Contents	Bitch's Milk in %	Cow's Milk in %
Dry Matter	21-23	13.5
Fat	9.0	3.8
Lactose	3.1	4.8
Protein	8.0	3.3
Casein	3.5	2.8
Albumin	4.5	0.4
Mineral matter	0.9	0.7
Calcium	0.28	0.12
Phosphorus	0.24	0.10
kcal/kg	1261	600

The above table is arranged in accordance with the statistics issued by the *Basic Guide to Canine Nutrition* (New York, 1965). The fat content in canine milk is of special importance, and all the other contents are higher than those in cow's milk. This is the reason why cow's milk is quite unsuitable for rearing puppies by hand.

The scientists Strasser and Leibetseder calculated the average calorific requirements of a puppy per day, per body-weight, in kilograms. This increases, naturally, from birth to the fourth week of life – during this period of rapid growth – and decreases again from the tenth week.

TABLE 17: CALORIC REQUIREMENTS OF A PUPPY IN KCAL/KG BODYWEIGHT

1 week	195 kcal/kg	from 4 weeks	265 kcal/kg
2 weeks	220 kcal/kg	from 10 weeks	200 kcal/kg
3 weeks	245 kcal/kg	from 14 weeks	140 kcal/kg

The above table does not make allowances for the different sizes of puppies or for the breed. The calculations should be taken as average values for medium-sized dogs. In very large and very small breeds considerable additions and reductions will become necessary.

To avoid misunderstandings, the above calorific figures are given per kilogram of body weight. It thus becomes clear that the nutritional requirements of the puppies are very great in the third to the tenth weeks. In the first three weeks, the nursing bitch covers the tremendous nutritional intake of her puppies all alone; and after this, she covers partially, according to how much we hand-feed the puppies. It is of vital importance to meet the mineral matter and vitamin requirements of both the bitch and her puppies. Proprietary food additives are, as a rule, needed here. (This subject has already been discussed in Chapter Six.) Throughout the entire lactation period one of the proprietary puppy milks should be fed to the bitch and, later on, to the puppies themselves. These puppy milk products promote lactation in the bitch, and they contain vital additives for both mother and babies.

One basic rule must always be observed. Even if the bitch has ten teats – frequently, a bitch has only nine or maybe eight – this does not mean that a healthy bitch can feed more than six puppies on her own. Without exception, larger litters require a helping human hand. These days, bottle feeding is a fairly straightforward business, and it is an absolute necessity for rearing large litters. In Toy breeds, the limit to the number of puppies a bitch can feed is even lower; at most, she can

The nursing bitch must be fed a top-quality diet.

Photo: Steve Nash.

manage four puppies, after which additional feeding becomes necessary. Every breeder should be aware that the puppies draw off all they need from the bitch. Unfortunately, there are some people who find it a lot easier to feed their puppies via the bitch's teats than to bottle-feed. The result of this is a poor, skinny bitch constantly under siege from hungry six-week-old puppies. This type of rearing amounts to real cruelty, and puppy purchasers are well advised to avoid breeders of this kind. Breeders who want to see their bitches in good shape after whelping, make sure she is helped as early as possible by hand- or bottle-feeding the puppies as soon as this becomes feasible.

A well cared for and correctly fed nursing bitch, who has been assisted with feeding the puppies until such time as they are ready to go to their new homes, can be in very good condition when her puppies leave her. Eleven weeks after whelping, we took a bitch that had reared eight puppies to the World Dog Show. In the face of strong competition and under a very experienced judge, she took the title of Vice-World Winner. She was in first-class condition.

ECLAMPSIA
The most dreaded disorder that can befall a nursing bitch is eclampsia. The greatest requirement of a foetus growing in its mother's womb, and of the puppy hanging on to its mother's teat, is calcium. Thus, excessive demands made on the dam's body during pregnancy and an intensive withdrawal of nutrients during lactation can lead to the collapse of the bitch's metabolism. Scientists regard eclampsia as a severe disturbance of the body's calcium metabolism and of the vitamin and hormone reserves.

The outward signs of eclampsia are similar to an epileptic fit; they differ, however, in that the bitch does not lose consciousness in an attack of eclampsia. The first sign that something is wrong is usually shown by restlessness and whining, progressing to muscular spasms. In severe cases, the bitch adopts a characteristic attitude, standing with all four legs stretched stiffly out and her head bent toward her back. She runs a very high temperature, her heartbeat is very fast, and her breathing is rapid. An attack of this kind may last for several hours, and a veterinarian must be called in immediately. This situation has potentially fatal results. If the veterinarian is contacted at the onset of the first symptoms, the bitch usually responds well to intravenous injections of calcium and, if required, to tranquillisers.

After an attack of eclampsia, the bitch must be kept in a darkened room, and she must, of necessity, be separated from her puppies. The puppies have to be weaned in order to avoid a deterioration of the bitch's condition by further secretion of milk. Cold compresses (ice-bags or a solution of aluminium acetate) laid on the mammary glands will help to alleviate the condition. Separating the mother from her puppies means that the breeder must, for the time being, take over the feeding and care of the puppies. It is for the veterinarian to decide how long the dam must be kept away from her puppies. The earlier the condition is treated with calcium injections the better. Veterinarians do not like giving intravenous injections, especially when the dog is excited, since the introduction of the needle into the vein, and the burning associated with the calcium administration, can make the bitch very restless. However, this is the only way in which immediate aid can be given. The question as to whether adequate calcium additives, prior to and after whelping, can prevent eclampsia is debatable. One important factor to remember is that calcium and phosphorus must be administered in a ratio of 1.2 : 1.

MASTITIS

Mastitis or inflammation of the mammary glands in the nursing bitch is a condition which is feared by all experienced breeders. The cause of mastitis is primarily the retention of milk resulting in mammary engorgement. It is therefore absolutely essential to make sure, throughout the entire lactation period, that all the teats are suckled by the puppies. Milk retention occurs especially when only two or three puppies have eight or even ten teats at their disposal. In the case of a large litter, it is usually possible, when the hardening is only slightly advanced, to clear the gland by putting a strong, active puppy to the teat. It is essential to check each mammary gland several times a day. If a hardening is observed, the teat should be gently milked and the milk should be checked for appearance and taste. If there is no sign of infection, a strong-sucking puppy is usually the best solution. If, however, instead of the expected milk, a mixture of milk and pus appears, this is generally a sign of a bacterial infection. From unclean bedding, bacteria can penetrate the mammary glands, a danger that once again emphasises the need for hygiene in kennels. There is also the danger of infection from the claws of the puppies.

Acute mastitis is usually accompanied by a high temperature. In most cases, only a few of the glands are affected, not the entire mammary area. It is advisable to treat the disorder at the very first signs of hardening. In this way, real trouble can generally be avoided. For many years, we have used a camphor-based lotion, which is dabbed on the affected place. It should be allowed to air dry and be left for at least an hour – longer, if possible. Before putting the puppies to the bitch again, the lotion should be carefully sponged off. The treatment should be repeated several times a day after each time the puppies have had a good, long drink. With the aid of strong-sucking puppies and this lotion we have, up to now, been able to avoid any severe cases of mastitis.

However, if the inflammation has spread, affecting considerable areas of the mammary glands, and if the teats are secreting a yellowish-brown discharge, sometimes containing blood, then the puppies must be weaned at once or their health will be endangered. They will, for the time being at least, have to be bottle-fed or tube-fed. The bitch requires veterinary attention, and the infection usually has to be treated with antibiotics. The fluid in the mammary glands has to be massaged or pumped off several times a day and the whole area cooled with compresses (aluminium acetate). Later, moist, warm compresses and ointment rubbed into the skin to stimulate the circulation will help to diminish the engorgement.

During the course of the illness, the bitch should be given little to drink and should be fed easily digestible, non-constipating foods. If and when her puppies may be put back to her remains for the veterinarian to decide. In particularly severe cases, abscesses may have formed in the mammary glands, and these will probably have to be lanced to evacuate the pus. Mastitis is a critical illness, and only speedy and proper treatment can help to avoid irreparable damage.

Eclampsia and mastitis have one thing in common; if the disorder takes a severe form the puppies not only lose their mother as the source of milk but also become dependent on man for their care and hygiene. More will be said about this in the section on hand-rearing puppies.

THE FIRST TWO WEEKS

For the first two weeks after whelping, the bitch will be concentrating on caring for and feeding her puppies. This is a period in which a bitch, whose instincts are intact, requires no human aid at all with her puppies. She will save you a great deal of work in these two weeks as will be seen later on in the section on hand-rearing puppies. The main tasks of the breeder during the first two weeks are to see to cleanliness in the whelping box, keep a check on the mammary glands, and look after the bitch's own hygiene and nourishment needs.

The heavy post-natal discharge of the first few weeks leaves its mark on the bitch's coat and tail. Lukewarm water is a simple well-tried means of keeping the dam clean. During the first few weeks, the mammary glands should also be washed with lukewarm water several times a day.

A very important task is trimming the puppies' nails. If the nails are not cut back, starting from when the puppies are a week old, they will scratch the mother's mammary glands. Using nail-scissors, only the sharp point of the nail should be cut back.

THE MATERNAL BOND

Do not get so involved with looking after the puppies that you forget to look after the bitch. She needs exercise, even though she will need gentle persuasion since she will not want to leave her puppies or the whelping box in the first few weeks. All the same, a short walk in the fresh air is called for every three to four hours. This helps to stimulate circulation and will assist her to pass urine and faeces. When the puppies have reached the age of two to three weeks, this strong bond becomes slightly loosened, and the bitch may go outside if she wants to for half or even a whole hour, or she may choose to lie somewhere in the house with her people. Before she comes into the house, it is a good idea to check her for vaginal discharge and, if necessary, wash her down.

Three weeks after whelping, the bitch should leave the whelping box several times a day for an hour or two. She also needs a bed in the whelping room where the puppies cannot reach her. Step by step, the bitch begins to leave her puppies for ever-lengthening periods and gradually returns to her status as a family dog. However praiseworthy these maternal tasks may be, covering as they do not only feeding and care of her puppies but also playing with them and at the same time training them, she deserves some rest. Just watch how four or maybe six little ruffians tear and bite at their mother. This is quite as it should be; it is part of their lives, and even their mother seems to enjoy it. At this stage, however, the puppies need a great deal of sleep and, while they are sleeping, we can help the bitch to find her way back into her old life.

It is possible that, in this respect, I am again adopting an attitude that does not accord with the opinions of the behaviourists. It is true, the wild dog family is cared for in the first seven weeks by the mother and after that by the father, and this is a full-time job for both parents. However, it should not be forgotten that, in the wild, whelps will be left alone for considerable periods while their parents are out hunting for and capturing the required source of food. I am of the opinion that in breeding pure-bred dogs we are rearing family dogs – dogs for people. Therefore, between the fourth and eighth weeks man undertakes a whole range of imprinting and leadership tasks, sharing the training of the puppies with their dam. (This subject will be dealt with in detail in the following chapter in the section on rearing puppies in the fourth to seventh weeks.)

DISEASES IN PUPPIES

LACK OF COLOSTRUM – SEPTICAEMIA

Scientists are in agreement that by means of the colostrum, the milk secreted by the dam in the puppies' first two days of life, the puppies are provided with their mother's immunity to disease. Although the pups in their mother's womb have been connected via the placenta to their mother's circulatory system, through which harmful agents such as toxins and roundworm eggs are continuously transferred to the puppies, immunity is passed on only through the colostrum. The immunity imbibed with this milk is so strong that it serves to protect the puppy almost entirely for the first seven to ten weeks of its life – that is, if it has been able to obtain some of the colostrum.

This brings us to two important points. Firstly, the constitution of the mother's milk undergoes continual changes throughout the entire lactation period, and at all stages it is perfectly adapted to the puppies' development. This means that the milk of a foster mother, who may have whelped two or three weeks previously, although better for the newborn pups than a commercial product, is not totally suited to their requirements. The closer the whelping dates of the foster mother and the foster pups, the better.

The second important point is that it is advisable to give the brood bitch a protective booster prior to mating, thus ensuring the effectiveness of the immunity passed on to the puppies via the colostrum.

If a puppy has not obtained protection through the colostrum, either because the bitch has died or has become seriously ill, it will, unfortunately, be exposed to all sorts of infection. The danger of an infection cannot be stressed enough. Infections can occur even in the most hygienic of kennels, perhaps through the bitch herself coming into contact with her kennel mates who have, themselves, been in contact on their outings with other dogs. Every visitor and even the owner of the bitch and his family are all potential sources of infection.

The pharmacological industry has gone to some lengths to develop a temporarily effective medicament for puppies that have not obtained any colostrum. This is the so-called gamma globulin, which is administered if the puppies develop that most dangerous of all puppy diseases, septicaemia. Septicaemia is caused by a severe, pathogenic, bacterial infection of the blood: more simply blood poisoning. The causal agents are mostly pyococci, streptococci, staphylococci, and coli bacteria. Infections may occur in the first few hours after birth, up to the age of around two weeks. Outward signs shown by the puppy are: apathy, distended stomach, a tight abdominal wall, whimpering, and unwillingness to suck. There may, in addition, be difficulty in breathing, inflammation of the navel region and purulent diarrhoea. The infection is usually transmitted to the puppies via their mother's milk, but it can also be caused by a skin injury (for example a docked tail).

The infected puppies become rapidly weaker and are at great risk. Immediate veterinary attention is absolutely vital. Just as important is the temperature of the room, which must be kept between 80 and 85 degrees Fahrenheit (25 and 30 degrees Centigrade). The veterinarian injects gamma globulin preparations beneath the skin. If there is any indication of milk infection, the puppies must immediately be separated from their mother and will, from then on, have to be fed on proprietary foods. If they are unwilling to suck, the pups are given polyionic electrolyte solution with a 5 per cent glucose supplement. It is also advisable to give the puppies antibiotic drops by means of a feeding tube.

Unfortunately, the chance of survival for such puppies is very slight. As a rule, the infected pup dies within eight to twelve hours. Frequently, one of the litter will die every 12 to 24 hours. When the first one dies, an immediate autopsy is called for. If it is possible to diagnose the infection exactly, steps can be taken to attempt to save the remaining puppies. It is therefore essential that your veterinarian carries out the autopsy as soon as possible. According to present-day findings, the puppies do not pass the infection from one to the other but are all exposed to a common source of infection. In most cases, the bitch refuses to lick and care for her sick puppies, she disregards them entirely.

Early prophylactic treatment is of utmost importance. The manufactured para-immunity inducer is used to inoculate puppies that have not received colostrum for any reason (Caesarean section, death of the bitch, lack of lactation, etc.). It is injected beneath the skin immediately after birth, and again twelve hours later.

On various occasions, we have reared puppies after a Caesarean section and, on one occasion, we had a severe infection in the puppies before hearing about the immunity inducer. Nevertheless, we were luckily able to save the whole litter, treating them as described above. Since that time, however, we have always used the prophylaxis and have been very satisfied with it.

HERPES CANIS INFECTION

This virus disease first made its appearance in the United States in the most virulent form in 1964. It has, in the meantime, spread throughout Europe and is considered one of the most common causes of death in puppies. In the UK, this disease is known as 'fading puppy syndrome'. In the United States, the term 'fading puppy syndrome' refers to neonatal septicaemia.

There is a distinct difference in the course run by the herpes virus infection and that of septicaemia. It is assumed that the herpes infection takes place before birth via the placenta, or else at parturition in the vaginal passage. The incubation period is thought to be one week, and the disease is contagious. The disease has not been observed in puppies of over three weeks of age.

The infected puppies show no particular signs of illness in their first few days of life, and their weight gains are perfectly normal. The first indication of trouble is a yellowish-green diarrhoea, often overlooked since the puppies continue to feed well and are bright and lively. Some puppies, however, either retch or vomit immediately after suckling. One or two days before they die, the puppies refuse all nourishment, they whimper miserably, breathing is accelerated, and the stools contain blood. Puppies hardly ever come through this disease alive, and should one actually do so, it generally suffers continuously from diarrhoea and does not thrive. An autopsy – which is advisable for every puppy that dies – will reveal that considerable internal bleeding has taken place in various organs, particularly in the digestive tract.

Present-day science does not provide a successful treatment of this disease. A three-day course of inducer injections is recommended to increase the gamma globulin protection. I understand that too low a room temperature favours the outbreak of the disease.

NON-TOLERANCE OF MOTHER'S MILK

Now and again, when pups have reached the age of between three days and two weeks, non-tolerance of their mother's milk may occur. The signs of this are: constantly crying pups, wind (gas), greenish diarrhoea, and a reddened and swollen anus. As a rule, this is an indication that all is not well with the mother's milk. It may contain poisonous substances – toxins. The veterinarian must arrange for the milk to be tested without delay, as the puppies are at risk.

They will have to be bottle-fed with one of the commercial simulated bitch's milk products. This should be carried out for at least 24 hours. They can be given a 10 per cent glucose solution (for example, in fennel tea) until the wind (gas) has been cured. When the results of the milk test become available, it is for the veterinarian to decide how to proceed. If he or she comes to the conclusion that the puppies must be hand-fed, the measures described in dealing with mastitis in the bitch must be applied in order to avoid inflammation of the mammary glands due to milk retention. The cause of 'fruitless sucking' is a very different one. This occurs, as a rule, within the first 24 hours after birth. The puppy sucks at the nipple, but it appears to be exhausted and also seems to lack appetite. These symptoms become apparent in pups whose lung tissues have failed to develop fully, possibly due to lack of oxygen before birth. The prescribed treatment is oxygen, warmth, and a glucose solution, although this is, in my opinion, a wasted effort.

DIARRHOEA IN PUPPIES

It is of vital importance for puppies' stools to be constantly checked, and the responsible breeder should look upon it as one of his most important tasks. Early diagnosis of trouble can lead to a speedy recovery from what could otherwise turn into a potentially lengthy and critical illness.

The most frequent cause of diarrhoea in puppies seems to me to be a complete lack of knowledge about the composition of canine milk. It has obviously not yet become clear to many dog owners that milk and milk are not always alike, especially when they stem from two different animal species. Even if this basic fact has been registered, it does not appear to prevent people making foolish mistakes. Sometimes the proposal is heard that cow's milk should be diluted with water to make it more easily digestible for the pups!

The differing constitutions of cow's and canine milks are clearly shown in table 16. Taking into account the double calorific content of bitch's milk, it is clear that cow's milk should certainly not be thinned down but, in actual fact, it should be enriched. Cow's milk can be used in this way as an additional food, but it must be supplemented by one of the proprietary milk powders, where ingredients correspond to those of canine milk. Cow's milk, without this supplement, will most certainly cause diarrhoea in the pups. It is also advisable when feeding a mixture of dry meal and milk to add a finely grated apple. If you follow these suggestions carefully, you should be able to avoid digestive troubles in your puppies.

Most digestive troubles are due to feeding. Mother's milk is perfectly adapted to the digestive properties of the puppy's internal organs. If diarrhoea occurs during the period when the pups are being fed entirely by their mother, this is a sure sign of one or the other of the diseases described above. When the puppies are weaned and their food is changed to something different, this means that the puppies' digestive organs have to adapt themselves considerably. The constitution of the intestinal contents is altered, thus also altering the conditions for the intestinal flora which itself has to undergo a change. It is, therefore, of vital importance to feed the puppies with the right kind of food throughout the entire rearing period. This is by far the safest way to avoid digestive troubles.

The new foodstuffs must be easily digestible for the pups. If, for instance, the puppies are fed proteins that have either been over-heated or incorrectly stored, they cannot be easily broken down in the small intestine. Similar difficulties may occur if the starch in carbohydrates is not broken down. Cereals fed to dogs have to be made digestible, either by cooking or else by special treatment at an industrial level. Feeding too much unrefined sugar, either in the form of sweets or in too large amounts of lactose (milk sugar), invariably leads to diarrhoea. Lack of hygiene in preparing food, feeding leftovers, or serving ice-cold food straight from the refrigerator are potential causes of digestive trouble.

It is, therefore, clear that in order to prevent digestive troubles arising, foods must be prepared with the utmost care. Those people who find it difficult to mix the food in the correct proportions should make use of special diets, scientifically manufactured by the fodder industry. A feeding plan will be given later in this book, which should assist breeders in preparing and mixing the best possible puppy food themselves.

Once diarrhoea, due to incorrect feeding, occurs in a puppy, a short (but firmly adhered to) fast is the best possible cure. Fresh water can be replaced by weak tea, and milk must be cut out entirely. It is much better to let the puppy go without food for from twelve to fourteen hours than to begin to feed too soon. After this period of fasting, the puppy should be fed fresh, raw, lean ground beef of the best quality. If this is digested without any trouble, gradually start feeding meals of milk and cereal.

If the diarrhoea persists, then a veterinarian must be called in. Special care must be taken to ensure that puppies suffering from persistent diarrhoea do not dehydrate. The veterinarian will prescribe special medication.

DWARFISM

According to Professor Dr Walter Schleger, genuine dwarfs carry a lethal gene that leads, in the normal course of events, to the dog's early death. It is necessary to make a clear distinction between very small puppies who, if their biotonus is in order, have a good chance of survival, and those of dwarf growth that are suffering from a disturbance of the pituitary gland (hypophysis). At times, dwarf puppies are rather lethargic and make little attempt to suck. Eberhard Trumler would certainly give them very poor biotonus marks, and he would be quite right in adjudging their chances of survival as slight. A good breeder would not attempt to rear such a puppy by hand. All his efforts would, very probably, be wasted.

In order to be able to make a more careful study of this disorder, we nursed along a dwarf puppy born in our kennels some years ago. He gave us a good deal more work than all his four siblings put together. His weight gains fell well behind theirs, and at the age of eight weeks he weighed only a third as much as they did. His hindquarters showed an extraordinarily pronounced cow-hocked stance, he was badly out at elbows, and his pasterns were weak. One of the characteristics of this disease is limited movement, occurring, at the latest, around ten weeks. In the reports I have received on similar cases, there was always a pronounced eczema between the toes. In coloured animals suffering from dwarfism, there is a significant loss of colour due, according to present-day findings, to an inability to absorb zinc.

My own experience in raising such a puppy coincides, in general, with the tests made by Dr Andrea Schleger of Vienna. The majority of puppies suffering from dwarfism have to be put to sleep at the age of from three to four months, owing to their steadily increasing debility. Our own puppy, Tiny, died of acute heart failure at the age of four months. I have given this particular example in some detail in order to emphasise how problematic matters may become when man disregards the clear warnings of nature and decides to take a hand where it would be better to let events take their course.

THE NEED FOR RESEARCH

In the majority of cases involving dying puppies, veterinary advice is given and treatment for the individual case prescribed. Suggestions may also be made to the breeder as to how, by special treatment (before mating, during pregnancy, and before birth), similar disorders may be avoided in future whelpings.

My most urgent request to geneticists is that they should investigate these disorders and the disposition to such disorders in order to establish to what extent they are genetic – that is, in what degree are they hereditary. It would probably be advisable to take all bitches, in whose litters numerous deaths occur, out of the breeding programme. Personally, I would never buy a young bitch from a litter in which puppies had suffered such disorders.

I am well aware that research is expensive, and the dog does not come under the species of animal whose health and heredity can be researched with the aid of large state subsidies. However, it is an area which concerns all breeders of purebred dogs, and some form of co-ordinated investment by breed clubs would undoubtedly prove to be worthwhile.

HAND-REARING PUPPIES

In recent years, great strides have been made in the hand-rearing of puppies at both national and international levels. For many years hand-rearing was condemned, and the breeding regulations of most breed clubs in Germany refused to register hand-reared pups since they were expected to be of poor quality and both physically and psychologically weak. More advanced breeding regulations permitted the rearing of puppies with the aid of a foster mother.

It must be admitted that up until the sixties, hardly any suitable canine milk was produced by the dog food industry. Tremendous advances have been made in this respect in the past twenty years. It is only really possible to evaluate this if it is compared with the situation in countries where such foods are not available. The number of excellent commercial brands of high-quality puppy milk throughout the entire Western world is really amazing!

On two occasions, I have been obliged to use artificial milk for my puppies. On the first, at the end of July 1971, our brood bitch was hit by a car, whose driver was tearing along at top speed. She was dragged along over loose gravel for at least 90 yards (80 metres), and she suffered broken bones, broken ribs, fearful abrasions along her flanks, and a torn abdominal wall – and this bitch had a litter of two-week-old puppies at home! This story goes to show just how tough Bull Terriers are. Our veterinarian said he would have euthanased a bitch of any other breed. We, however, had not just got a severely injured bitch to care for, we also had eight hungry puppies! We very quickly learned how to bottle-feed!

The next time we mated this excellent brood bitch, it became clear that she was going to produce a large litter. At that time, in Germany, the highly controversial question of a litter being limited to six puppies was under discussion. After a certain amount of dispute, we were lucky enough to obtain an exemption from a rather broad-minded breed committee, and so we did not need to put any puppies down. It was, therefore, in 1972 that we raised a complete litter of ten for the first time. Our objective was to be able to show perfectly normal weight gains throughout the entire rearing period, and especially at the time when the litter was finally checked over. The breed adviser wrote in his report: "Very well reared, even litter, brood bitch in tip-top condition, breeder exhausted!"

It must be emphasised that only the full, personal commitment of two adult persons made this positive outcome possible. It was hard work the entire time and if we were to calculate the working hours we put in, our wages would have been meagre; in fact our household help told us that she would never be prepared to undertake such hard work. Our reward, on the other hand, was great, with two youth world winners in 1973 from this litter. Summing up, I can say that, in my own experience, raising puppies with commercially manufactured puppy milk can be just as successful as natural rearing.

Hand-rearing becomes advisable under the following circumstances: death of the dam, complete or partial lack of lactation, supplementary feeding in large litters, mastitis, eclampsia, infectious diseases in the dam, accidents, and rejection of puppies by aggressive dams, thus endangering the pups.

ACCOMMODATION

Let us suppose that the dam is no longer available. This makes the breeder's task (together with his helpers) very clear! All the puppies need in the way of a "nest" is a cardboard box (mentioned as temporary quarters in the whelping chapter). This, of course, applies only to small litters of small breeds. In fact, the normal whelping box can also be used: the only vitally important point is to make quite sure, especially in the first few days, that the temperature is high enough for the puppies.

Experts give the temperatures required as 85-90 degrees Fahrenheit (30-32 degrees Centigrade) for the first two or three days, 80 degrees Fahrenheit (27 degrees Centigrade) for the following fortnight, and 75 degrees Fahrenheit (23 degrees Centigrade) for the next two weeks. These temperatures are fairly easy to maintain in the first few days in the cardboard box, with the aid of two hot-water bottles (which must, of course, be refilled every two hours). This is better than using a whelping box with under-floor heating. If an infra-red lamp is used, this must be positioned high enough above the pups to ensure adequate air circulation; otherwise, the air around the pups will become too dry.

As soon as the pups begin to crawl, they need more room and should be transferred to the whelping box. The bottom of the whelping box should be fitted with a piece of bathroom floor covering made of soft rubber or artificial fibre. This is very easy to clean, and its rough surface enables the puppies to crawl around. Absorbent cloths now come into full use: it is absolutely essential to keep the whelping box clean. The grooming, cleaning motherly tongue has to be substituted by yet another damp cloth. This should be at body warmth, and is used to rub down every puppy several times a day.

FEEDING AND CLEANING

But how do we get this milk into the puppies in the first place? The instructions for preparing the mixture of water and powdered milk concentrate are clearly laid down by the manufacturers. The ingredients of the product, and the mode of preparing the feed, must never vary. Make quite sure that the puppies are fed milk, freshly prepared, in exact accordance with the manufacturer's instructions. Older dogs will be glad to consume any leftovers.

As a rule, the milk is fed to the pups in a normal baby's bottle. Glass bottles break easily; plastic bottles are hard wearing. Make use of a baby bottle-warmer, in which one bottle can be warming up while another is being used for feeding. We have always selected a teat shaped much like a mother's nipple, and we have tried out a number of systems. There are always a few difficulties to be surmounted. The puppy must take to the teat, the hole must be neither too large nor too small, and the consistency of the milk changes continually in accordance with the instructions given for the various ages of the pups. If the hole is too small, the puppy gets too little; if too large, it may choke on excess amounts. The milk should not flow too freely or the tiny tummy will be filled too quickly. Patience, and a choice of teats, are needed to get everything right.

It is not difficult to get the pups to accept the teat. The puppy is hungry, so it takes the teat, which must be at body temperature, as would the dam's nipple. It goes without saying that the milk must also be body temperature. The vacuum formed in the puppy's mouth enables it to suck strongly. The puppy is held, according to its size, either in your hand or on your lap. The pup should be lying on its back, and there is a certain resemblance here to a human infant. The puppy will instinctively attempt to work on the bottle with its front paws. This is a good sign and shows that it is behaviourally intact. When sucking begins to flag, pull a little on the bottle. This wakes the puppy up; it will take another big mouthful or two and be quite replete. Do not put the pup back in the box at once, as it will certainly have to bring up some wind (be burped). All this soon becomes a routine matter for both puppy and puppy feeder.

Once the puppy is fed, it will need to be cleaned. However, we must check how much it has drunk. This is an easy matter, thanks to the markings on the bottle. Some puppies give the impression that they are sucking properly, and air-bubbles can even be seen rising now and then in the bottle. If the volume is checked in the bottle, it will be seen that the pup has only been chewing the teat. It is easy to learn from observation whether a pup is sucking or merely chewing.

Some breeders prefer stomach tubes for puppy feeding, but, using these, the pup does not need to suck and can choke if the feeder is careless. In these cases, it is better to make use of the small feeding bottles with a proper teat, which are produced by the pet food industry.

The next task is to perform the mother's job of cleaning the puppies after every meal. This can be done with a moist, warm ball of cotton-wool (cotton), with tissues, or with a small sponge. A circular, massaging technique should be used on the pup's tummy and around the anus. It is of vital importance for the meconium to be passed within a few hours after birth. Urine is usually easily passed, but faeces generally require longer, patient massage. When one puppy has been fed and cleaned up, it is the turn of the next one!

We reckon that it takes between fifteen and twenty minutes to feed and clean a puppy. If there are six puppies to be cared for, one single feeding session lasts for two hours. In the first few days, the puppies have to be fed every two hours, and from the third day, every three hours – and this goes on around the clock, day and night. This timetable makes it clear that at least two people are needed for rearing a litter. One person alone could not possibly manage. The work must be split up into alternate day and night shifts – alternating only for the 'nursing staff' – for the puppies have to be cared for on a regular schedule. In no time, you appreciate what a wonderful job brood bitches, with their sound instinct, do for us – and they manage with a lot less trouble than we do!

From the twelfth day, a break of four hours is possible in the night, and this can be extended from the fifteenth day to as much as six hours – but not longer. From the eighteenth day, the intervals between daytime feedings can be extended to four hours.

When hand-rearing puppies, it is not a matter of getting as much liquid food into their stomachs as possible. In some breeds, there are pups with an excellent biotonus, and they are inclined to take as much as they can get from the bottle. The pup's tummy should be full after the feeding, but not too distended. The best way to check how much to feed is always the weighing scales. There should not be any difference in weights between hand-reared puppies and those reared naturally. It is a generally accepted rule that the healthy puppy, according to breed, should at least double its weight in the first ten days. (In the next chapter, you will find a weight chart, which gives some rather interesting data.)

As is the case when rearing puppies in the normal way, hand-reared puppies are given their first solid food on the evening of the twelfth day. In small breeds, this may be postponed for another day or two. This first solid food we offer is a tiny ball of best, ground beef, held and kneaded in your hand until it has become quite warm. The pup is fed this, its first meat, in tiny portions, and it usually takes this avidly. Sometimes, a puppy may find this a bit difficult at first, sucking and munching on the meat until it is well saturated with saliva and the pup can swallow it. Once more, there is nothing for it but patience and yet more patience.

When the puppies have had their first meat meal, the first feeding interval of four hours can be introduced. The meat meal is more satisfying and is, therefore, given as the last meal of the day.

If the puppies being hand-reared have not lost their mother, and it is a question of supplementary feeding for a very large litter, the pups should be put to the dam at the end of the day for a good drink before the four-hour feeding interval. They appreciate this night-cap very much indeed. If the dam is not available, the pups should be bottle-fed after their meat meal.

It is a tremendous help if the dam – even if she has no milk – can assist with the care of the pups. If she is well and her instinct is sound, she could undertake this care on her own, which would reduce the breeder's workload by at least half. However, a careful check must be kept to see that she is really cleaning them up and grooming them. Constipated pups become restless and begin to cry; if the bitch does not do the job, then you will have to see to it yourself.

In a kennel there is a good chance that one of the other resident bitches will undertake the work of the sick dam. A suckling puppy frequently touches off an intensive nursing drive in many bitches, and this not always only in the grandmother rediscovering her youth.

I have described in detail in the last section just how important it is to keep a constant check on the puppies' stools. This applies in particular to hand-rearing. We were once feeding a commercially-produced puppy milk that was causing very hard stools. The puppies had great difficulty in passing the tiny, dry, yellowish particles that appeared – a clear case of constipation. The best remedy is a drop of edible oil, placed on the puppy's tongue. If this does not clear the matter up, a little lactose should be added to the bottle-feed. This can be obtained from any pharmacist. Patience is, once more, called for in massaging the pup's tummy and around the anus. At the slightest sign of inflammation of the skin, the anal region and the tummy should be lightly smeared with baby oil. If, after using edible oil and lactose, you cannot manage to get the puppy to evacuate its stools, the veterinarian should be called.

The normal faeces are slightly formed, pulpy, and yellowish. If the movements are thinnish, dark, and slightly fermented, try giving a little kaolin powder, dissolved in a small amount of water. This should be placed on the puppy's tongue in such a way that he has to swallow it. If the diarrhoea becomes persistent, remember the dangers previously described, and call in your veterinarian. It is to be hoped that your puppy had colostrum or at least gamma globulin at the right time.

The remainder of their rearing period runs much the same course as that of puppies reared by their mother. In the next two weeks, the food normally supplied by the dam is replaced by bottle-feeding at four-hourly intervals. From the fourteenth day, the puppies are able to pass their urine and stools unassisted, which relieves the breeder of a lot of work. As with mother-reared pups, supplementary food begins to take the place of milk. (This transition will be described in dealing with the individual rearing phases in the next chapter.)

Chapter Nine

REARING THE LITTER

DEVELOPMENTAL STAGES

THE FIRST TWO WEEKS (VEGETATIVE PHASE)

To begin with, the puppies' lives are geared to a rhythm of sleeping and nursing. Now and again, their dam gives them a gentle push with her nose, they fall over on their backs and get thoroughly licked. Their mother's tongue washes and massages, helping the pup to pass faeces and urine. She cleans up the waste, and the pups go back to the teats until such time as they fall asleep again.

The temperature in the whelping box should be kept constant during this period at over 70 degrees Fahrenheit (20 degrees Centigrade). This is much lower than the temperature needed for orphan puppies. In their whelping box, the pups are in close contact with their dam, the floor is heated, and the pups can snuggle up to their mother to keep warm. If they begin to crawl and push together into a heap and press themselves close to the bitch, it is advisable to raise the temperature by several degrees. Puppies lying stretched out quietly, side by side, are a sign that the temperature is right.

Lying in close contact in order to find warmth.

Photo: E. Trumler.

WEIGHT GAINS

In the first few weeks, the weighing scales are a great asset. With their aid, it is possible to check the growth of each individual pup. Weigh them every day for the first three weeks, always at the same time of day and, if possible, just before they have nursed. In this way, a clear picture will be obtained of their daily progress. In Table 18 the weight gain of a litter of Bull Terrier pups is shown. Each individual puppy is listed with his name and markings. In this way, it is possible to avoid mixing up the puppies when weighing them.

TABLE 18: WEIGHT CHART FOR PUPPIES (WEIGHT GIVEN IN GRAMS)
J.Litter, Alemanneutrutz

Name of Puppy	Colour & Markings	Weight at birth 19/12.	20.	21.	22.	23.	24.	25.	One Week 26.	27.	28.	29.	30.	31.
JILL	Pure-white	300	330	350	390	420	490	530	600	670	720	810	840	980
JOY	White, red marking	340	330	330	380	435	490	550	640	680	790	900	930	1030
JETTE	Pure-white	320	310	330	350	410	450	480	550	590	700	750	780	880
JUWEL	White, ear mark	340	350	380	400	450	520	560	640	720	780	910	910	1050
JUDY	White, ear mark	320	310	340	370	420	490	520	630	700	750	850	870	1010
Weight per week		324							528					

Name of Puppy	Colour & Markings	Two Weeks 1.1.	2.	3.	4.	5.	6.	7.	8.	Three Weeks 9.	11.	13.
JILL	Pure-white	1010	1070	1150	1260	1330	1410	1520	1570	1660	1800	2000
JOY	White, red marking	1160	1220	1300	1360	1480	1560	1630	1700	1750	2000	2250
JETTE	Pure-white	950	1030	1060	1170	1210	1270	1410	1460	1490	1720	1930
JUWEL	White, ear mark	1150	1150	1190	1330	1420	1520	1580	1640	1710	1960	2090
JUDY	White, ear mark	1020	1120	1150	1280	1360	1380	1460	1500	1560	1800	2000
Weight per week		1048								1574		

Name of Puppy	Colour & Markings	Four Weeks 15.	16.	20.	Five Weeks 22.	27.	Six Weeks 29.	3.2	Seven Weeks 5.2
JILL	Pure-white	2200	2250	2650	2950	3350	3800	4300	4600
JOY	White, red marking	2480	2600	3020	3220	3850	4250	4820	5200
JETTE	Pure-white	2130	2200	2620	2800	3300	3820	4150	4550
JUWEL	White, ear mark	2110	2320	2750	3000	3520	3920	4500	4800
JUDY	White, ear mark	2180	2280	2600	2850	3310	3750	4200	4460
Weight per week		2220			2964		3908		4722

One-week-old Bull Terriers puppies instinctively lie close together.

If the birth-weight in the table is compared with that of the second day, it will be seen that three out of five puppies have lost weight; they now weigh less than they did at birth. This is perfectly normal. The transition from nourishment absorbed via the placenta to an independent intake brings about a slight check. After that second day, however, the puppies' weights must increase steadily. If on two consecutive days one of the puppies has not gained, this is probably a sign that the pup had just had its fill the previous day before being weighed, and was very likely about to nurse again when taken to be weighed. Given the very slight weight increases in the first week, this is perfectly normal – yet it is an indication to the breeder that he should keep his eye on that particular puppy.

As has already been recommended, the best type of scales to use are those that react to direct pressure and register weights without having to be adjusted. In these first few weeks, reliable accurate scales are especially useful. With their aid, it is possible to follow the daily weight gains, and, at this stage, weight-gain is the surest indication that the puppies are thriving. It is an excellent sign if the birth-weight of a litter is doubled within the first week, or no later than the tenth day. Everything is in good order if the birth-weights have been trebled after two weeks.

THE SUCKLING PUPPY
What actually happens when a puppy suckles? What goes on inside the tiny mouth enveloping the teat? This is not suction such as we learn about in physics; the experts call it lick-sucking. The puppy's tongue closes around the nipple like a groove, and extracts the contents of the teat by massaging it. This behaviour has, in fact, been measured, and the result showed twenty tiny pressure movements per second. This is known as the inborn rhythm of the sucking automatism that is adapted to the flow of milk from a canine teat. It has also been ascertained that the number of lick-sucking movements changes according to the pup's degree of repletion. The replete puppy, sucking out of habit at the teat, does not produce the high number of licking movements as when it began to drink and was hungry.

The rhythmic, kneading movement of the pup's front paws working on the mammary glands (mentioned previously) and the suckling are linked together. Whenever we take the time to examine more closely some of nature's own processes, we are filled with astonishment and wonder at their technical perfection.

In the chapter on whelping, the searching movements of the pup's head have been described as it swings awkwardly from side to side until it has found its mother's teat. Nature has fitted the puppy with the best possible equipment for reaching the source of milk and emptying it in those first few vital days. The idea that the organs of perception (i.e. the eye, the ear, and the sense of smell) are decisive at this stage is quite wrong. Any breeder will soon discover that puppies are born without sight or hearing. Tests have proved that the sense of smell is only very weakly developed at the beginning. The pup's behaviour in the early stages of life is adapted to its environment owing to fixed hereditary co-ordination. If the pup encounters a key stimulus, this triggers a corresponding action.

Eberhard Trumler calls the first two weeks of a puppy's life the vegetative phase. The main tasks of the puppy in this early stage are suckling and sleeping, and it is perfectly equipped for both these actions. Trumler states: "The term vegetative for this particular phase could not be improved upon. It is, in fact, no more than the continuation of his unconscious life in his mother's womb, a time which serves only for growing and gaining weight."

However, using the biotonus test, it has been proved that significant conclusions can be drawn from the puppy's behaviour immediately after birth.

PAIN SENSITIVITY
In the first few days after birth, the puppy's sensitivity to pain is very much less pronounced than later. Small injuries bleed very little and heal quickly. Breeders make use of this period to carry out any operations that may appear necessary. The removal, for instance, of the dewclaws – that remainder of the development from the five-toed to the four-toed animal – should be done within the first three days with a pair of sharp scissors. The removal of the dewclaws lessens the danger of them getting caught and torn later in life, an episode that can turn out to be very unpleasant and can cause heavy bleeding. This applies to the dewclaws on both the front and hind legs. The fifth claw cannot be worn down naturally, since it is set much higher up the leg than the ball of the foot. There is also a danger of the claw growing into the flesh, which can cause complications.

If sharp scissors are used for this simple operation, the wound bleeds very little and is easily cleaned by the dam's tongue. As a precaution, it can, however, be dabbed with a drop of high percentage alcohol and coagulant. In a number of breeds, the tail is docked in accordance with the Breed Standard. This docking operation should also be carried out within the first three days.

INSTINCT OR SOCIAL BEHAVIOUR?
Is there any sign of social behaviour among the puppies in the vegetative phase? Puppies are generally observed lying snuggled up together, asleep. If we pick one up and put it on one side, the pup aims straight back toward the others, crawls in among them, and snuggles down. Is this not a clear indication of pronounced social behaviour?

Nevertheless, Eberhard Trumler denies any form of social behaviour in this phase. The fact that the puppies lie in close contact with one another is solely and singly a matter of instinct, an urge for warmth. When referring to the positioning of an infra-red heating lamp, it has already been mentioned that, if the lamp is correctly positioned, the puppies will lie stretched out and relaxed side by side. This observation serves to confirm that puppies lying in close contact with one another does not have its root in social behaviour.

I have come across a type of puppy-bed that has a built-in hollow in the surface, and the middle of this hollow is the warmest place in the whelping box. This is a senseless arrangement, and it can even prove dangerous if the temperature in the hollow is higher than that of the bitch. In the first weeks, the puppy gravitates instinctively towards the warmest place. The hereditary behavioural pattern tells the puppy that must be where the source of milk is. If we disturb the puppy's inborn instincts by using a heated hollow of this kind, it may well lead to serious rearing problems.

*Suckling puppies
aged two weeks.*

There is yet one more counter-proof to the theory of social contacts in the early phase. If lying in close contact were a part of the pup's natural social behaviour, a single puppy would suffer lifelong damage, especially one that was reared by hand. It has been proved that this is not the case. It is easy enough to ascertain that a hot-water bottle can act as a substitute for the rest of the litter. What we are dealing with here is a purely instinctive reaction to a source of warmth.

Sleeping, working their way to the teat, being cleaned, and sleeping again – that is the rhythm of life for our puppies in the first two weeks after birth. It is, in fact, the continuation of their unconscious life in their mother's womb. Biologists explain the behaviour of the so-called nidicolous creatures (those reared for a time in a nest) when compared with the nidifugous (those that leave the nest soon after birth) by the fact that, in the case of the nidicolous, the embryonic phase is followed by a transitional phase that makes adaptation to the new environment possible. It is extremely interesting to compare the instinctive behavioural pattern of puppies with that of a day-old calf. The calf, at that stage, is already completely integrated into the herd. It is, therefore, easier to understand why the first two weeks of a puppy's life are aptly described as the vegetative phase.

THE MOTHER'S ROLE

The breeder's task in caring for puppies during the first two weeks is limited to checking that the dam is feeding and cleaning them properly. If the bitch's maternal instincts are sound, the breeder enters the daily weight gains in the chart, and is pleased with the way his charges are thriving. Hygiene in the whelping room is the most important task, and this is something that the bitch cannot manage.

I have already described in detail how the nursing bitch should be cared for in this period. Always remember that rearing a large litter is a tremendous strain on a bitch. She needs the best attention, first-class food, and loving care. It is important to tell her frequently what a wonderful job she is doing with her puppies. Bitches who rear their puppies without problems, who nurse and wash them, are of an inestimable value to any breed of dog. Breeders should adopt measures to ensure that, in the future, in every breed of dog there are no other kind of bitches. After forty-five years of experience, I should like to congratulate every breeder who is lucky enough to own a reliable brood bitch of such sound instinct.

THE THIRD WEEK (TRANSITIONAL PHASE)

The term 'transitional phase' is an indication of the tremendous importance of this stage of the puppies' development. The pups are now at an intermediate stage in which their senses begin to awaken and unfold; this is a stage of preparation for their future social life as domestic dogs. Eberhard Trumler characterises this stage as follows: "This is a comparatively rapid transition from the purely instinctive suckling and sleeping stage to the active investigation of the immediate surroundings, and the first contacts with the siblings. The germ is sown at this stage for the diverse social behavioural patterns of the adult dog."

THE DEVELOPING SENSES

There are some signs of the awakening of the senses in the puppies' vegetative phase. Their eyes and ears open around the twelfth day, with fluctuations between the tenth and thirteenth days from breed to breed and dog to dog. The first milk teeth are cut around the eleventh day. The opening of the eyes and ears is not tantamount to seeing and hearing. It has been established that proper vision does not develop until the seventeenth day. This also applies to hearing, and the tiny nose only then begins to react to the surrounding stimuli.

Of no less importance at this stage is the mouth, armed with its tiny needle-sharp teeth. From the seventeenth day on, the puppies will be observed licking one another. The pup's mouth is busy investigating its surroundings. The puppies will be seen continually inspecting their littermates' ears, noses, or paws with their mouths.

Suckling puppies, three weeks old. The eyes are now open,
and the puppies can hear.

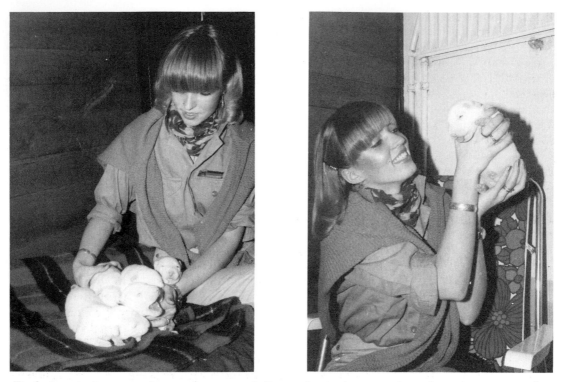

Early imprinting: puppies need scent and direct physical contact in order to accept people.

WORMING

Before turning to this intensely interesting stage when the first active social contacts begin to develop among the puppies, we must turn our attention to a task which the bitch is unable to perform – the worming of the puppies. This should be done at the beginning of the third week.

There has always been endless discussion about worming puppies. Some breeders are quite convinced that their puppies cannot possibly have worms because they have fed garlic regularly to the bitch, and this, they say, is a completely reliable remedy. Garlic is an excellent plant, wholesome both for man and animal – but it is not a worming remedy. Nevertheless, the old wives' tale continues to hold its ground, just as the old adage that distemper can be avoided without inoculations by putting a copper coin in the dog's drinking bowl. Dangerous nonsense; yet it is almost impossible to eradicate.

The puppies must be wormed. Practically every puppy is infested with worms' eggs during the embryonic period via the placenta. This is generally the case even if the bitch has been carefully wormed during her pregnancy. The experts tell us that the reason for this is the fact that worm larvae remain inactive in the bitch's body, but are reactivated by the pregnancy when they migrate and create the need to worm our puppies. The second route taken by the larvae is via the mammary glands from which they are transferred to the puppies in the milk.

Dr Raeber designates worm infestation in puppies, quite rightly, as a scourge. Puppies are usually only infested with roundworms, and sometimes with hookworms. It is essential to deal with the worms that have migrated to the puppies via the dam's bloodstream or the milk flow before they begin to lay eggs. To give some idea of the magnitude of the problem, a hookworm can lay 20,000 eggs per day, and a roundworm as many as 200,000 eggs per day. Worm infestation is injurious to the health of both puppies and adult dogs owing to the abstraction of nutrients and blood, and their excretions contain toxic substances.

When rearing puppies, afflictions of this kind must be avoided; they can otherwise lead to loss of condition and, in extreme cases, to the death of a puppy. There is also a danger of the hookworm transferring to man, and this worm infestation is especially dangerous to human beings.

There no doubt about the necessity of worming puppies, but there is always some discussion with regard to pinpointing the right moment. Many people advise early treatment – that is, between the seventh and tenth days. To me, this appears to be altogether too early. Our own puppies are never wormed until the fourteenth day, which means at the beginning of the transitional phase. Once, for very good reasons and on expert advice, we wormed a whole litter at the age of eight days. It is, of course, quite obvious that a worming remedy – of whatever kind – does contain substances that at least temporarily paralyse the worms.

We treated our eight-day-old puppies with a piperazine remedy in strict accordance with the instructions given for their weights, and for a whole day we feared for their lives. First, the pups became very restless; they cried, and when we picked them up, their tummies were seen to be badly distended. They could not be persuaded to drink from their mother. Within an hour of administering the remedy, the puppies' bodies became rigid, they were as hard as boards. We massaged them with a soft natural sponge, soaked in warm water, and, after hours of effort, we managed to ease their cramps. Those were anxious hours that I would not wish on anyone.

This experience proved to me conclusively that puppies can be endangered by too early a treatment. From the instructions issued by the pharmacological industry, it will be seen that the first treatment is recommended at the age of approximately two weeks. I fully agree with this. Some manufacturers recommend repeating the doses throughout the entire suckling period at one-week intervals. We ourselves administer the second dose at the age of four weeks and a third at six weeks, and we consider this to be quite enough.

Summing up: Worming should take place on the 14th day, and two additional treatments are called for before the puppies leave to go to their new homes.

WEANING STARTS

An important step is the first feed the puppies are given in the transitional phase. Bull Terriers are a rapidly growing breed with high weight gains during the first eight weeks, and our experience with them has shown that supplementary feeding beginning on the 12th day is advisable. According to the breed, this supplementary feeding could be postponed for from two to four days. In this respect, the daily weight gains are an all-important guide as to whether the dam's milk is still in sufficient supply for the fast-growing litter.

In the section on hand-rearing puppies, quite a few tips have already been given on this first stage of weaning. It is of the utmost importance for the first supplementary feed to be of absolutely first-class quality. In the transitional phase, we feed high-quality beef without any additional substances. The meat must be tender and completely free from fat, and the puppies will find this easy to digest. Of course, this will be the most expensive cut of meat, but you can be confident that it will agree with your puppies, and there will be no stomach upsets. Thanks to the minuteness of the quantity, always according to breed (about 10-50 grams per puppy) we should be able to afford even the most expensive of meats.

At this stage, feeding takes place entirely by hand. Each puppy is held individually in the lap. The meat is hand-warmed until it has taken on body temperature, and it is then placed in tiny portions on the puppy's tongue. This works all the better if the bitch has been separated from her pups for two hours before we begin feeding them. Sometimes, a puppy will, at first, prove a little awkward, but these early difficulties are usually overcome by the third feeding. By this time, the puppies come and sniff with interest at the meat-scented hand, and they clearly enjoy the variation from their mother's milk. When all the pups have been fed, the dam can return to her litter, and the meal is completed with a night-cap of mother's milk. The meat feed is always given at night before bedtime. The pups are then quiet throughout the night, since meat satisfies for a good deal longer than all other foods.

You may consider that it is rather early for supplementary food. Perhaps you are of the opinion that you should leave the puppies exclusively with their mother for as long as possible, that being the simplest and, at the same time, the most natural way. However, in the wild dog family that Eberhard Trumler has so vividly described in his books (especially in *The Year of the Dog*), it will be seen that on around the 18th day, the dam for the first time regurgitates her food for the puppies, thus beginning the weaning process in the middle of the transitional phase. She is generally assisted in this activity by the sire, who also regurgitates his pre-digested food for the puppies.

This food intake is a very interesting learning phase for the puppies and is a characteristic feature of this particular stage. The puppy now learns to take up this deliciously smelling stuff with its tongue, which is a great change from the previous suckling action. Feeding begins, therefore, in the wild dog family in the transitional phase.

An interesting factor is that the stimulus for the regurgitation of the food lies in the pup's begging behaviour. Instinctively, the pup butts its head against the corner of the parent's mouth, thus stimulating him or her to regurgitate. To complete the picture, this is typical canine greeting behaviour. Trumler calls it the sympathy ritual, which the dog, as a rule, extends to all the people it loves. The dog likes to greet a human being by licking him in the face, especially at the corner of his mouth, even if it means he has to jump up to do so. The dog's tongue delights in licking the human face, and this action has its roots in the sympathy ritual.

I know just what a nuisance it is when the breeder has just given his bitch a lovely dish of food and she, after devouring it, marches off to the run and regurgitates it for her pups. It is not much comfort to know that this is the correct behavioural pattern, a sign of sound instincts in your bitch, or else in your dog. These are ancient traits that no amount of training can eradicate. The best solution is to feed the bitch little and often, so that less food is regurgitated in the puppies' run. Clearly, the run must be cleaned frequently and any regurgitated food remains removed. Some breeders may feel quite pleased that there are a great many brood bitches that do not regurgitate for their pups – a loss of instinct critically observed by behaviourists, but welcomed by breeders!

THE WHELPING BOX

The dam removes the faeces and urine during the vegetative and for the first part of the transitional phase. The breeder is responsible for seeing to the grooming and cleaning of the bitch. When supplementary feeding begins, many bitches cease to remove the faeces, which by now contain certain foreign substances, and the nest can become increasingly soiled by regurgitated food. My advice is to do without bedding in the whelping box in the transitional phase as well, and to clean up the floor and the pups at frequent intervals. We make the change during the next phase.

Old, fairly thick cotton sheets have proved very useful for the transitional stage. The floor of the box is covered with a sheet, which absorbs a good deal of the urine. It goes without saying that the bedding has to be changed several times a day and there is, of course, a machine full of puppy washing at least every other day. We recommend using only this type of rather woolly sheet and no other kind of cloths or materials. The paws of the tiny pups easily become sore if the fabric is too hard. Careful observation has shown that our nest-bound pups have a very strong bond to their whelping box until the 20th day and are unwilling to leave it until that time. This behaviour changes completely after the 21st day (i.e. the first day of the fourth week – the beginning of the imprinting phase).

THE FOURTH TO SEVENTH WEEKS (IMPRINTING PHASE)

ADAPTING THE WHELPING BOX

It is an amazing fact, and one that has been scientifically established, that the behaviour of our nest-bound puppies changes spontaneously around the 21st day. The bond to the nest is loosened, and the drive to follow sets in; the pup now follows its mother like glue.

This can, of course, only come about if the breeder permits the puppies to leave the whelping box. In our case, we simply let down the side wall of our specially constructed whelping box. The front wall is replaced so that it no longer affords a way out. The slats screwed on across the slightly sloping, lowered side wall make it easy for even three-week-old pups to leave the whelping box and take off on a tour of investigation.

In the chapter on kennels and runs, I already mentioned the need at this stage onwards, for a larger run. This should be from two to six square metres (21 to 65 square feet), according to the size of the breed. This is best achieved by fixing partitions firmly to the walls of the room. An L-shape is advisable, of adjustable height so that the bitch can jump over without the puppies following her. Wire lattice with half-door is recommended so that the dam can jump out over the open top half of the door. Do not attempt to save money by using makeshift contraptions put together out of old boards. This results in a great deal more work, and it is not so effective.

Opinions about the right kind of bedding are very divided. For many years, we have used a bottom layer of dry sawdust covered with a layer of fresh hay. The sawdust serves to absorb the urine, which is considerable. The hay is soft, pliable, and sweet smelling, and the puppies love snuggling down in it. The stools can easily be picked up and disposed of in a small bin. The best type is one where the lid is opened by a foot-lever; the lid closes immediately automatically, thus minimising odour. The bin should be lined with a renewable plastic bag. We found straw less suitable than hay. It is rather hard and can injure the puppies' paws. Within a short time, it turns to chaff, the stalks break, there is a lot of dust, and the bed becomes hard and dirty. Neither have wood-shavings proved useful; it seems to generate a lot of dust, which cannot be good for the nasal membranes of the pups.

According to the size of the litter, the entire bedding (including the sawdust) must be removed every two to four days and completely replenished. You will discover that the renewal of the bedding is a real festival for the puppies; they simply love their hay! In the UK and the US many breeders now use a synthetic bedding material similar to fleece throughout the entire whelping and rearing process. The great advantage of this fabric is that any moisture soaks straight through it. If the whelping box is lined with newspaper, this absorbs the moisture, and the puppies do not get cold and wet. This synthetic fleece is machine-washable, and it is extremely durable.

DEVELOPING SOCIAL BEHAVIOUR

The freedom to move around in a large space enables the pups to attain an astonishing physical dexterity within a very few days. At the age of 21 days, the sensory abilities are already fully developed. Nose, ears, and eyes are ready for new stimuli. Behavioural changes among the pups are dramatic at this stage. The original investigation of a sibling's ears or a paw now turns into a game; hackles are raised, growling is heard, and inhibiting snapping – this is all part of the pups'

An L-shaped whelping box with safe toys.

behaviour. The surroundings, the larger playground, are thoroughly investigated. Toys dropped into the run encourage delightful new games. It is important to ensure that the toys can withstand the puppies' teeth, and that pieces cannot be chewed off and swallowed. A small, wooden dummy makes a good toy as does a large hard-rubber ball. Playing is an inherent part of a puppy's life, and there is nothing more sterile than a run in which there is nothing to play with.

Interplay among the siblings now shows the first signs of possessive behaviour, and a hierarchy begins to take shape. The salient point is the fact that within the space of a few days, our sleeping, nursing puppies have become lively, active little dogs. Watching the puppies at play can be extremely fascinating. At the beginning of this phase, it is clear that the hereditary element dominates, but as the days go by, this is overlaid by the influence of the environment. The breeder who observes his pups closely throughout this period will be in a position to advise their new owners when the time comes for the puppies to leave.

In these weeks, it becomes clear which puppy is highly dominant, which is extremely submissive – and there is a whole range of different characters between these two extremes. The insight into these inborn characteristics is of vital importance for placing each puppy in the right hands. It is not merely the new owner who has ideas about the disposition he requires in his new companion; the breeder must make a careful check of the environment and the qualifications of the puppy purchaser, so that the right dog is placed in the right hands and finds the family to which it is suited.

Eberhard Trumler in his most excellent book *The Year of the Dog* has described in great detail the rearing and conditioning in a domestic dog family living in complete freedom. It is of special interest that parents of sound instinct always respect the need of their pups to sleep. Sleeping puppies should never be woken; they must be left in peace. The naturalist warns people, quite rightly, not to be impatient, and ask too much of the puppy. This most certainly applies to the first six months of the young dog's life. The pup's need to rest should always be respected, and this applies particularly to children who are easily tempted to wake the puppy for a game whenever they themselves feel like it.

FEEDING

If you read the pet food industry's advertisements, you will be convinced that you need do no more for your pup than soak their proprietary puppy foods in water, and this will answer every need. But I should like to warn new owners never to follow this recommendation blindly.

The heading of this chapter section is "The Imprinting Phase" because this phase is characterised by the imprinting of the pups. Between the fourth and seventh weeks, the impression of the puppy's surroundings is firmly imprinted in its mind. Biologists distinguish between irreversible imprinting – a final impression that cannot be undone – and partial imprinting. Irreversible imprinting is best illustrated by the example of Konrad Lorenz and his greylag geese. If the first living creature a newly-hatched gosling encounters happens to be a human being, it will attach itself to him for life. For the gosling, the human being is its mother, father, and whole family. The gosling will show no interest at all in its own species (i.e. in other geese).

The imprinting of puppies is slightly, but only very slightly, less extreme. I shall be dealing with this point when I come to the imprinting of puppies in connection with humans and other animals. But, as regards feeding, if a puppy becomes used to commercially manufactured foods during this period, these foods will be so strongly imprinted on its mind that it will not be easy for the new owner to change the pup over to any other type of food.

Let me give you an example. We have many times imported half-grown or adult dogs from England. In the first few weeks and months, it proved almost impossible to feed these animals raw meat. They had not been given raw meat in the imprinting phase, and for them, it simply was not dog food. The same thing applies to puppies that have not been given cod-liver oil by their breeders. The new owners will find it very difficult to get their dogs to accept it. A glance at Trumler's free-living dog family can be very informative. The food regurgitated by the parents, for the most part meat from their own catch, is the food imprinted on the puppies in the imprinting phase. Puppies reared in this way will always regard meat as the right kind of food.

The example given here goes to prove that imprinted behaviour is not always irreversible. We have, with patience and persistence, always managed to get our dogs used to the food ingredients we ourselves consider to be right.

What I have stated here does not mean that I disagree, in principle, with the arguments put forward by the dog food industry. The industry tells us that a dog can be fed from the day of weaning throughout its entire life on commercially manufactured products. There are any number of first-class biologists and chemists working in the laboratories of the food industry where foods have been developed that meet all our dogs' requirements. However, there are two things that disturb me. One of these is that the quality requirements, laid down by most laws for industrially manufactured complete foods, state that there must be a guarantee that animals fed with this food over a long period will suffer from no nutritional deficiencies. I do not consider that this is enough. The second thing that I do not like is that the food is easily prepared, but the owner has to pay for this convenience throughout the dog's life. In addition to this, it has been our experience that dogs like variation, they do not have the one-sided tastes the industry would have us believe. As with everything else in life, there is a compromise in feeding. The excellent services afforded by industry should not be set aside altogether, but thought should also be given to the best way of preparing our own food for the puppies.

It is not the task of this book to deal scientifically with nutritional values for optimum puppy feeding. That would warrant an entire book on its own. On this subject though, as throughout the whole book, I should like to be able to share the experience we have gained in rearing our own puppies, in general, with very good results.

The first supplement to the dam's milk is the best cuts of lean, finely-ground beef. This is fed at the evening meal in addition to the mother's milk. As long as the scales confirm that the puppies are thriving, no extra feeding is required. In close resemblance to a family of dogs living in complete freedom, we commence supplementary feeding on the 21st day. Since, in many of our domestic dogs, the behavioural pattern of the wild canine in regurgitating semi-digested food has disappeared, and since this behaviour is not really very favourable when seen from the angle of hygiene, we always commence feeding the puppies four times a day from the fourth week onwards. It is advisable to take the bitch away from her young for approximately two hours before feeding them. If they have just had a good fill of milk, there will not be many takers for the new meal.

Our milk meal is made up of industrially produced dry food, and these are mixed with lukewarm whole cow's milk (3.5 per cent fat). If it can be obtained, sheep's or goat's milk is richer and, therefore, preferable. According to the amount needed, the milk is mixed with a few tablespoonfuls of proprietary puppy milk, one or two tablespoonfuls of honey, and the same amount of glucose. An egg can also be stirred in. We always add a grated apple (including the skin) to the milk feed, which obviates any danger of digestive troubles. A finely mashed banana is also a food that puppies adore. This mixture is allowed to stand for three to five minutes, and a teaspoonful of calcium (for larger breeds a tablespoonful) is then added. All our puppies eagerly take to this food. The consistency should be neither too liquid nor too thick. A variation, much appreciated by the pups, is a fruit yoghurt in place of the milk, and this is mixed with the puppy milk product. Care must be taken to see that this meal is always at body temperature.

The puppies quickly learn to use their tiny tongues, investigating the feeding bowl; their noses soon discover the nourishment, or else a finger can be dipped in the food and offered to individual pups for them to taste. Patience is always called for when dealing with puppies. The pups quickly learn that the bowl contains food that they love – and this is where first training steps are taken. Food uneaten after five minutes is removed; leftovers are fed either to the mother or to another of the dogs. All puppies are fed from one bowl, standing one beside the other, without a fight being allowed to begin. The best kind of puppy feeding bowl is the type where several puppies can feed at the same time, without getting in each other's way. Neither can a puppy put all four feet into the bowl at the same time. It is perfectly natural for a puppy to put its front feet into the food at this stage, and the breeder should correct this and lift the paws out. These are all things that puppies have to learn.

When feeding is over, the puppy can clean up its own paws, or one of its littermates will help. Just as often, the small muzzles wipe off food on to someone else's coat, and then there is a great deal of licking and cleaning up. If the youngsters have got in a real mess – and this happens quite frequently – they can be wiped down with a soft, moist, lukewarm cloth, after eating.

I am not a believer in giving each puppy an individual dish. Dogs are pack animals by nature, and I have never seen a bitch regurgitate a small portion for one single puppy so that each individual should have its own share. It can be clearly observed in wild dogs that the older animals

Puppy feed of the right consistency in the communal feeding bowl.

permit no quarrelling among the puppies about food. Any pup that oversteps the mark is soon set to rights. It is surely advisable to follow nature's instinctive behavioural pattern. The 'pack leader' human sees to it that everyone takes their food peacefully at feeding time. Any sign of aggressiveness is blocked at this stage, a vitally important learning process for future harmonious integration of the pup into a mixed human-dog pack.

The only meal that is not served in the common feeding bowl at the beginning of the fifth week is the beef mince (chopped beef) which, from the fourth week on, takes the place of the finely ground best beef. The best way to feed this is to divide it beforehand into equal portions and, holding the pup on your lap, to feed by hand. This prevents the greediest from gobbling up some of its littermates' share, and it also helps to bond the puppy yet closer to its human partner.

In order to provide a little variation in the diet, here are a few alternative suggestions. Puppies love good meat broth, and this can be made from marrow bones or chicken giblets. Boil up some soup vegetables with the broth, and mash them well before feeding. The broth should be thickened, either with a special proprietary puppy mixture or with finely crushed puppy meal. The mixture should be of a thickish consistency, neither too liquid nor too firm. A very important point is to feed plenty of fresh vegetables such as carrots, cauliflower, spinach, and – as mentioned earlier – a clove of garlic. When the pups are a little older, chicken, carefully stripped off the bones, can also be added to the food. The quantity of calcium additive recommended for each individual breed should never be forgotten when preparing meals of this kind.

Something of fundamental importance must be said here on the subject of calcium supplements. Many products are intended for pigs, chickens, geese and dogs. The breeder must check carefully to see whether the calcium spoils the taste of the food for the pups. Dogs have very sensitive taste buds where calcium is concerned. There are, however, special products for dogs only, which older dogs will happily eat without food. The calcium products recommended for human beings are also suited to a dog's taste, and we have used them successfully. Do not feed any vitaminised calcium products, especially those that contain vitamin D: this could lead to an overdose of vitamins. An overdose of this kind can be really injurious to puppies. I should also like to warn breeders never to feed concentrated vitamin products, since the concentrates in a preparation of this kind may prove excessive and, therefore, harmful.

For many years, our puppies have been given a supplement of cod-liver oil in capsule form. If they have been used to this from puppyhood, they will never have problems with those vital vitamins A and D. Cod-liver oil ensures healthy growth, always ensuring that it is given in the correct dosage.

Four meals a day have proved to be the right number at this stage. We give the first feed at 8 a.m.; the midday meal at 1 p.m.; meat broth with supplements at 5 p.m. and a second milk meal with various kinds of fruit; and at 10 p.m. the big meat meal. We get our puppies used to regular feeding times. This is of great importance, as the puppies have time to become really hungry between meals.

When the puppies are five weeks old, a cheaper cut of meat may be used. We like to alternate from day to day between beef muscle meat and beef heart, using paunch from time to time. Both kinds of meat must be put through the mincer (grinder). Ready ground meats of this kind are usually to be found at almost any dog food store. This meat is fed in the communal feeding bowl. The puppy that has not learned to feed quickly does not get as much, but it soon learns that its brothers and sisters are eating its share of the food. Communal feeding ensures a very good appetite.

I know that feeding paunch can offend human sensitivities, but the dogs like it that much better. It should not be forgotten that when the wild dog kills, as a rule, it goes first for the contents of the stomach. This is a clear sign of what a dog actually needs. However, canned or frozen meats are also used with excellent results. These products are obviously far more convenient and easier to feed.

From the age of five weeks, the pups can be fed outside the run, perhaps on a sheet of floor covering, or even right outside in the open. This makes it much easier to keep the inside run clean.

As regards quantities, it is better to feed too little than too much. Some puppies are greedy feeders; they stuff themselves to the brim at the feeding bowl. The puppy's stomach gets more and more distended, and the puppy looks mis-shapen. If you have feeders of this kind, it is advisable to feed them five times a day and to give them smaller portions. After the meal, the puppy should certainly have a well-filled tummy; it must be clear that it has had a good meal, but the pup should never look as though it is about to burst! If, when feeding five smaller meals, one particular puppy gets the idea of fattening itself at the expense of the littermates, the breeder should take a hand and lift it away from the feeding bowl a little earlier.

Never try to make leftover food more attractive by mixing tidbits into it. This would be a first step toward spoiling the pups: you would be training choosy eaters. Let me say once more, anything left over in the dish at the end of five minutes is firmly removed and can be given to the brood bitch as an additional treat.

One very special tidbit, and a favourite plaything for a puppy, is a large marrow bone from which scraps of meat can be torn with tiny milk teeth, without pieces of bone being bitten off. The small pack will amuse themselves with this by the hour. Small bones and large bones that splinter have no place in the pups' nursery. Many puppies have paid with their lives for swallowing small bones.

THE OUTSIDE WORLD

If the weather is good, the pups can be allowed outside from the fifth week. An ideal arrangement is a movable puppy run, which can be erected in a sheltered corner of the lawn. The puppies find a great many interesting scents in the grass; they can dig, play with an old sack, or sleep in the sun.

In the case of the short-haired breeds that have little or no undercoat, special care should be taken to see that they do not lie out on damp or cold surfaces. In dealing with kennel arrangements, it was pointed out that wooden boards can provide a very useful pallet for the puppies to lie on. Short-haired breeds should not be cosseted, that would be quite wrong; on the other hand, the undercoat has been bred out of certain breeds, and these dogs cannot tolerate cold temperatures.

A sturdy, small run saves many a rosebush in a well-cared-for garden from the teeth and paws of our little band. If the puppies' outside run is properly arranged, it makes an ideal playground. The less concern there is about the surroundings, the better the games. I consider it vital for the puppies to be outside by the sixth week at the latest. If the weather is not very good, short walks in the garden, with the mother and her young, make an excellent alternative. This can be done two or three times a day. Even if the puppies are only outside for ten minutes, it is beneficial for the pups and helps to harden them. The extra space affords an ideal opportunity for new discoveries, for testing the senses and developing physical strength. Puppies that grow up entirely in a modern, hygienic kennel are backward compared with those that have been given more freedom. They lag behind in self-assurance, in health, and in both physical and mental development.

THE LEARNING PROCESS

The expanded world affords the mother new teaching opportunities. Play-learning now begins. It may frequently be observed that the bitch invites her puppies to play. When the game becomes too wild, some breeders believe they ought to interfere. Just imagine how this particular learning stage evolves in the dog family living in the wild. There, the sire takes a hand in the play-learning activities and teaches his young good canine manners in exuberant games. If the puppy is too roughly handled by the older dog, it throws itself on its back, demonstrating submission, and learns that this has a total bite-inhibiting effect on the older dog. This is a very important learning process that will prove useful to the puppy throughout its life. Play of this kind is inbred canine behaviour; if the puppy submits, the older dog immediately suspends his attack. And the puppy? If it is of the right sort, it will march up to the older dog and show respect by nuzzling him, licking his muzzle, and holding up a paw – but the pup will show no sign of fear.

The breeder seldom has the sire on hand to participate in these puppy learning processes, and there is not often a kindly uncle available to undertake these services. The bitch must therefore take over and teach her young proper canine behaviour. The pups learn, at this stage, that any form of disobedience is countered with an energetic shake of the scruff. This is perfectly natural behaviour among dogs, teaching them obedience and respect for the older dogs, and how to stand up for themselves among their littermates. In the canine family, this is, for the most part, firmly fixed for the dog's whole life in the imprinting phase.

It is of equal importance for the pups to have people intensively imprinted on their minds during this period. Scientists have proved, without doubt, that puppies that are isolated from people in the imprinting phase are never able to develop into normal family dogs. Experiments cutting off the puppies from all human contact were carried out. These dogs remained inadequately people-imprinted for the remainder of their lives, behaving like timid, wild animals towards man. In other tests, it was proved that the more intensive the physical contact between man and puppy in the imprinting phase, the friendlier the dog behaved towards people for the whole of its life. All living creatures with which the puppy has intensive contact during the imprinting phase are accepted as its own kind. If, for instance, a Toy breed puppy is reared by a cat, false imprinting takes place, and the dog regards the cat as its own kind.

Contact at feeding time alone is not enough for imprinting. The puppy needs scent and direct physical contact in order to accept man – a very different species – as its own kind. It is interesting to compare dogs with other animal species in this respect. The well-known wild boar naturalist Heinz Maynhardt managed to gain access to a herd of wild boar by sitting in their farrowing couch in the early imprinting phase, imprinting his voice and his scent on the young. Eventually,

Maynhardt was regarded by the adult boars and sows as their own kind and, indeed, even as their equal. They expressed this by allowing him to groom them, and they in turn also groomed him.

As regards the imprinting of dogs, Eberhard Trumler emphasises the fact that daily physical contact in the imprinting stage produced especially friendly dogs. If, on the other hand, scent and physical contact are avoided, the dogs will never become friendly toward human beings; they will, at most, be a little tame. It is incorrect rearing of this kind that is at the root of the fear-induced aggression exhibited by so many dogs.

The imprinting phase is not solely decisive in regard to the relationship between man and dog; it determines to a great degree whether we rear an unintelligent dog or one whose senses are able to develop to their full potential. Trumler is of the opinion that special learning abilities are attached to specific stages. He states:

"If the puppy is unable to make use of this learning phase, there is – according to all the observations I have made up to the present – a grave danger of imbalance arising in the behavioural pattern, and of certain aspects of the learning ability failing.

"It appears to me that learning, especially in these weeks, is determined by a number of pre-programmed facets of learning ability which, though limited to certain periods, once learned, remain for the whole of the dog's life. In other words, whatever is not learned in this period can never be made good."

I feel obliged to quote the naturalist's very decided opinion here in full because I am convinced that a great many dog breeders and, sadly enough, a great many buyers of dogs are completely unaware of the significance of Trumler's research results. If this were not the case, why do we see outside kennels, some distance from human habitation, where puppies grow up almost entirely isolated from human contact? Why is the brood bitch left to rear the litter, with the breeder doing little more than feed and clean up? Although it is an excellent thing for the dam to teach her puppies good manners, intensive contact between people and the puppies is of decisive importance. Without this, they can never develop into useful, intelligent, adaptable dogs!

It is my sincere hope that the knowledge of this reciprocity will impress itself upon all breeders and upon puppy purchasers so that they avoid those breeders who rear puppies in this way. It is absolutely essential to make full use of the learning ability inherent in the imprinting phase, in order to allow the dog's positive hereditary characteristics and intelligence to develop to the full. Intensive contact of this kind costs the breeder a great deal of time, but it also gives him or her a great deal of pleasure.

Just allow me to give one concrete example. Nature has equipped all puppies with the disposition to keep their nest clean. When the nest-bound period comes to an end, it will be seen that the pups leave the whelping box to eliminate. When the bedding in the run is removed, a little of the soiled bedding or sawdust should be left in one corner of the run. The puppies, attracted to the corner by the smell, continue to make use of that spot. In this way, the foundations for a house-trained puppy are already being laid.

ACHIEVING INDEPENDENCE

The simplest, cheapest, and easiest way to feed the pups is to allow the bitch to nurse them as long as possible. I, for my part, consider it to be the breeder's task to aid her in this to the best of his or her ability. Take a look at the way four to five-week-old pups pull at the bitch! She generally stands to nurse at this stage, and the pups hang on to her for dear life. The breeder must check the puppies' claws every two or three days and cut them back whenever necessary. Nevertheless, the bitch's mammary glands show just how small claws and sharp little teeth can scratch and bite.

Puppies' lives are divided into short periods of activity, and long periods of rest.

Photos: Trumler.

When the bitch, despite her maternal instinct, tries to escape from her offspring after the first suckling, it is clearly high time for us to assist her in her task. From then on, the bitch should only be allowed in with her pups when they have had their fill at the feeding bowl. The night-cap is quite in order, but the pups, having previously fed, are not so eager.

From the fifth week on, the bitch should be separated from her pups for ever-lengthening periods. She slowly begins to return to her normal life as a family dog. Thus, it is ensured that by the time the pups leave for their new homes between the seventh and eighth weeks, she will not suffer from a retention of milk. During these latter weeks, the pups will have been fed more and more supplementary food, and the bitch's milk flow will gradually be reduced.

Unfortunately, compared with the life led by a wild dog family, we do make considerable changes. At seven weeks we are ready to separate the puppies from their mother, and from each other. I am aware that this reduces the time the bitch spends teaching her puppies. We, however, do not want to rear wild creatures but domestic dogs and, for training the mixed human-dog pack, the intensive influence exerted by man throughout the entire period is needed.

There are both negative as well as positive examples of this training of pups for a future as domestic companions. Much too frequently, I have observed breeders whose main aim is to demonstrate the aggressive characteristics of their puppies to would-be purchasers. To achieve this end, they take part actively in the puppies' games – for instance, pulling, and tearing at an old sack. The harder the pup (possessive drive) holds on, the wilder he growls, the fiercer he tears, the brighter the breeder's eyes shine, and the more the pup is praised and encouraged.

A serious fight among puppies is easily recognised by the growling tones. In the dog family, the older animals see to law and order. They intervene in the fight, pick up the offender by the scruff and give it a good shaking. Peace returns. Not so in the case of the proud breeder! In fighting, he sees the guard dog characteristic, which is his great breeding aim. I once wrote in a book about the behaviour of five Bull Terrier pups that had become so firmly clamped together, that in lifting one out, all the others were also lifted out, hanging on to one another by their jaws. Each of these mini-fighting dogs had to be prised off its littermates by hand. There was no other means of making them let go. A genuine school for fighting dogs? Since that day, we always intervened as soon as there is the slightest sign of a fight beginning, and we never had to cope with this problem again.

The breeder should make every possible effort to produce normal, friendly dogs with a low predisposition to aggression. Dogs of this kind are good to live with, easy on the nerves, and it is the responsibility of every breeder to make this a priority. If there happen to be one or two small monsters in the litter, they must be firmly called to order during the all-important imprinting phase.

Certainly pups should play; they should chase and wrestle with one another and also have their disagreements. If, however, shrill, ferocious tones are heard, clear signals of open aggression, the breeder must intervene, as would the older dogs in a dog family. The breeder must make it perfectly clear to the small rascals in the puppy pack that over-reaction of this kind will not be tolerated. Puppies learn very quickly at this stage. Believe me, thirty years of active Bull Terrier breeding make a hard school, a first-class training ground for training theories, and they do work! By intervening at the right moment, it is possible to convince a very self-confident and aggressive pup that fighting will not be tolerated. I am firmly convinced that if the breeder makes good use of the imprinting phase to eliminate aggression among the pups, this will influence the dogs' behaviour throughout their lives.

The breeder is therefore faced with two all-important tasks during the imprinting phase:

1. To enable the pups to develop their full physical potential by giving them adequate space and every good care.
2. To make such use of this, the decisive phase for the whole of the dog's life, to produce a healthy and acceptable companion.

SELLING PUPPIES (SOCIALISATION PHASE)

PLACING PUPPIES

It is not easy to breed good dogs, but it is even more difficult to place them in the right hands. After breeding some 250 puppies, I can say this from the bottom of my heart. It is, therefore, easy to understand that any painstaking breeder looks ahead with great concern to the day when he or she must part with the pups, and takes the trouble to find out in advance whether their 'children' are going to be in good hands and in the right environment.

I was once asked by a very pleasant gentleman whether he might have a puppy from us. He told me that he was a respected citizen of our town, a lawyer by profession, was married with two children, had his own house and garden and a car. He stressed all these points particularly, since he had been told it was necessary to have a certificate of good conduct from the police in order to be entrusted with an 'Allemannentrutz' puppy. I told him, without hesitation, that a certificate of good conduct was not enough, many people have those, but our requirements when placing our puppies were considerably more stringent.

This subject was dealt with in considerable detail in the chapter "The Breeder". What I should like to do here is to emphasise once more that it is a conscientious breeder's responsibility to see that puppies are placed with the right kind of people, and in an environment that will allow them to develop to their full potential. This cannot be said of a great many would-be buyers.

THE RIGHT AGE TO LEAVE HOME

When should pups go to their new homes? Some people criticise breeders who let puppies go at seven weeks, saying that they want to save money and are out for profit. In fact, many breeders are heartbroken when the time comes for them to part with their puppies. They even go so far as to postpone the fateful day, saying the puppies are still much too young! One thing is quite certain; it cannot be his dam's milk that the eight-week old pup still needs. No reasonable breeder should still be allowing a bitch to feed the pups at this stage. It is frequently argued that in order to develop its mind, the puppy needs the mother's influence and stimulating play with littermates for as long as possible. Is it, then, too early to part with a puppy at seven weeks?

The behaviourists can answer this question for us. It is an interesting fact that Eberhard Trumler, in the course of his manifold observations, discovered that in the dog family living in the wild, a fundamental change takes place on the 49th day after birth. In place of the dam, who up to that time has been at the centre of the pups' world, the sire now takes over, preparing the puppies for their future lives. The bitch, exhausted by nursing and caring for her brood, withdraws rather suddenly and leaves them pretty much to their father's care. Should anyone doubt this, I advise them to read Trumler's book *The Year of the Dog*, where it is portrayed in detail.

At the beginning of the eighth week, as a result of the changing structure within the dog family, a new phase of life begins for our pup. In this new phase, it is the sire that dominates. It is, therefore, completely logical for the human being to take over at this stage. Nature has arranged matters so that at the start of the eighth week, the beginning of the socialisation phase, the 'changing of the guard' takes place in the dog family. Therefore, what could be better than to make use of the pup's learning ability and to transfer him at this exact moment from his dam's training to that of his new owners? Seen from this viewpoint, it becomes clear that the seventh week is the best time for parting with the puppies. The new owner, who will be the cornerstone of the puppy's coming life, takes over the full responsibility, at the beginning of the socialisation phase, for the puppy's future development.

SOCIAL DEVELOPMENT

What actually takes place in the socialisation phase, between the eighth and twelfth weeks limiting this period? The sire commences systematic preparation of the pups for their future lives as members of the pack. Play-fighting among themselves, they learn not only to defend themselves but also that there is a danger of getting hurt. Attack and defence, tactical movements – all this closely resembles the games of cowboys and indians played by human children. Trumler writes that rules are developed in play activity of this kind, precluding injury to the littermates. Comparatively harmless play-fighting helps to deflect natural aggressions and teaches co-operative behaviour. The canine social order does not permit members to fight to the death. Playing in the pack is carried out under the strict dominance of the sire, and the foundations are laid for future hunting behaviour as a pack. The sire frequently takes on the role of quarry and allows his offspring to chase and, purposely also, to catch him, imprinting on them his own experience of life.

An important aspect of this early learning phase is that the father exerts a steadily increasing discipline over the pups. The dog makes it clear, for instance, that an old bone is his personal possession, and no pup is allowed to touch it. Generally, the old dog only needs to growl in warning, but if this does not have the desired effect, the puppy is properly punished; it gets a thorough shaking for opposing its father's will. The puppy learns that the only thing to do is to submit; crying, the pup throws itself upon its back, leaves the bone alone, and respects the will of the pack leader.

I should like to draw the attention of any dog owner whose dog has got out of hand to this particular scene. It is easy to perceive that it is at this exact point that the puppy must be disciplined. Let us return to the puppy that was just being punished. The pup almost instantly shows signs of affection for the adult dog, and makes it clear that it is ready to submit. From the roots of this social play activity, the relationship to the parent animals, or under different circumstances, to people, develops.

Why am I discussing this in a section on selling puppies? In the case of the domestic dog, it is not a matter of conditioning for a dog family; it is much more a question of integrating it smoothly into the human-dog pack. Cast your mind back to the beginning of the chapter, where it was shown how irreparable damage can be done by non-utilisation of the learning phases, since certain aspects of learning are limited to individual phases. In order to rear a puppy as a family dog, it should change homes at seven weeks; it adapts most easily at this stage. All the play-learning activity of the dog family now devolves to the pack leader human, who must suit the activity to the future requirements for their own dog.

In this period, it is a matter of the final socialisation within the human family of the imprinted puppy. The dog does not now learn predatory play, at least not chasing a quarry, but it learns house-training, compatibility with human children, and adaptability to the rhythm of human life. Close companionship to human beings is an inherent part of the domestic animal's life. Playing with owners, the pup learns constantly and adapts to its environment. Once again, I should like to quote Eberhard Trumler: "The brighter the play activity with the human and the more early learning is accepted as play, the greater the dog's future ability to learn. In this phase, the ability is imprinted for the dog's whole future".

Neither the breeder nor the puppy purchaser can take the responsibility for allowing the dam and littermates to condition the puppy in this phase for life in a dog pack. This could lead to lifelong difficulties in living with humans. This learning phase is so precious that it must never be allowed to pass unused!

It is for this reason that I advocate letting the puppies go to their new homes at seven weeks. A puppy may be left for one more week, but certainly not for longer. As a puppy purchaser, I should be most hesitant to take one directly from a breeder at ten weeks. Hardly any breeder is able to spend several hours every day with each single puppy; he would be heavily over-taxed. There are, of course, always exceptions, but as a general rule, puppies that change hands too late have a serious learning deficit that makes harmonious integration into the human family very difficult.

A SALES CONTRACT

Experience has shown that it is better for the breeder to enter into a sales contract with every puppy purchaser. This contract should, on the one hand, clearly set out the breeder's assurances and, on the other, the responsibilities the purchaser undertakes. For me, a contract of this kind is of supreme importance since it enables me to take back the dog if it is not well cared for, especially if it is to change hands again. The breeder's responsibility does not come to an end with the sale of the puppy!

For many years, we have parted with our puppies on the terms clearly defined in a sales contract. A modified draft form of this contract is presented in the following pages. I must admit, however, that I am not a legal expert, and I can give no assurances that a contract of this kind would conform with the law if it came to a court case. The formula that follows should, therefore, be regarded as a suggestion for a contract of your own that can, if need be, be discussed with a lawyer.

SALES CONTRACT

XY sells the (Breed)
Dog's name (kennel name), date of birth
on (Date)

This puppy has been bred by us and has been carefully and painstakingly reared. The parent animals were mated with the aim of breeding good and healthy puppies. In this respect, however, no guarantee can be given on the sale of the puppy.

XY is responsible for forwarding the kennel club pedigree within a reasonable period of time. No charge will be made for the pedigree.

The purchaser promises to keep the dog in a proper manner. It shall not be kept permanently in a kennel. If problems arise concerning keeping or training, or if the dog becomes seriously ill, the purchaser agrees to consult the breeder. If it should prove necessary for the dog to change hands, the breeder has prior purchase rights for a period limited to two weeks. Selling to a third party is only permissible after prior consultation with the breeder, whereby the main consideration is the assurance that the dog is passed to responsible owners.

The purchase price agreed to is ————————-(in words).
The puppy will be handed over at the age of seven weeks. Together with the signing of this document, a down payment of ————————-will be made. If the puppy is not taken over at the time agreed, this sum falls to the breeder. The remainder of the purchase price falls due when the puppy is taken over.

This contract is made out in duplicate; the seller and the buyer each to receive one copy.

Clear agreement when entering into a contract has served to eliminate a great deal of trouble. All breeders should come to an agreement of a similar kind with their puppy purchasers.

A beautifully reared puppy, ready to take his place in the human-dog pack.

Photo: Carol Ann Johnson.

FEEDING RECOMMENDATIONS

It has always proved extremely advantageous to provide the puppy purchaser with a feeding plan for the puppy. The feeding plan, given below, is one that has proved its usefulness to us over many years:

8a.m. One cup body-temperature unboiled milk (3.5 per cent fat) thickened with 1 tablespoonful of proprietary puppy milk. A handful of puppy meal, 1 teaspoon honey, 1 teaspoon glucose, 1/2 an apple finely grated (using a grater for baby food). Twice a week, one raw egg stirred into the food. Additive: one teaspoonful of calcium in powder form.

1p.m. One cup meat or bone broth, 1 handful compound feed, allowed to soak. Finely mashed vegetables (i.e. carrots, cauliflower, brussels sprouts, spinach, etc. Scraps of meat in the broth can also be fed (i.e. carefully boned pieces of chicken)

6p.m.   Dog biscuits for chewing, fresh fruit (pears, plums, apples, bananas, etc.). This feed should be kept small.

10p.m.   Approximately 200-250 grams raw meat, finely ground in the first few weeks, later on finely chopped. According to season, finely grated apple, grated carrot, or garlic mixed with the meat. Additive: 1 teaspoonful calcium preparation.
Either before or after the evening meal, 1 tablespoonful cod-liver oil (allow it to be taken from the spoon or feed it on a saucer, but never mix it into the feed). Cod-liver oil should be given up to the age of 14 months in summer and in winter.

Food quantities should be increased according to the dog's age. At the age of five months, we give, per meal, around one-half litre liquid measure and 500 grams of meat. The food must always be balanced: meat should never be the sole food. The calcium additive must be doubled at the commencement of teething (approximately four months), and can be given when teething is complete in tablet instead of powder form.

The above food quantities are, naturally, calculated for Bull Terrier puppies and should be increased or decreased according to the breed. My intention is to demonstrate how the new puppy owner can be informed, in a simple fashion, what his dog needs and what it has been given up to now by the breeder.

Do not forget to advise regular worming of the puppy and, when he is older, having his stools checked for parasitic infestation.

IMMUNISATION

Immunisation against the major contagious diseases is, obviously, of vital importance. The policy as to what age to start the immunisation programme varies widely. In some kennels the puppies are given an initial inoculation at six to seven weeks, as this is seen as the time when the immunity from the mother's colostrum has diminished. In order to ensure full immunisation, the purchaser must have these inoculations repeated between twelve and fourteen weeks. However, in many cases, the general policy is not to give any protection until the puppy is nine or even twelve weeks of age, when there is no chance of maternal immunity interfering with the effectiveness of the inoculation. The timing of inoculation also depends on the incidence of disease in a particular area, so, in all instances, it is best to seek the advice of your veterinarian.

I believe I have now said everything that needs to be said about parting with puppies. I should like to close by wishing you a great deal of pleasure breeding dogs!